Najib George Awad

And Freedom Became a Public-Square

Studien zur Orientalischen Kirchengeschichte

herausgegeben von

Martin Tamcke

Band 46

LIT

Najib George Awad

And Freedom Became a Public-Square

Political, Sociological and Religious Overviews on the Arab Christians and the Arabic Spring

LIT

Cover design: ICXC johnny sayigh Graphic Design (Lattakia – Syria)

Bibliographic information published by the Deutsche Nationalbibliothek
The Deutsche Nationalbibliothek lists this publication in the Deutsche Nationalbibliografie; detailed bibliographic data are available in the Internet at http://dnb.d-nb.de.

ISBN 978-3-643-90266-5

A catalogue record for this book is available from the British Library

Klosbachstr. 107
CH-8032 Zürich
Tel. +41 (0) 44-251 75 05
Fax +41 (0) 44-251 75 06
e-Mail: zuerich@lit-verlag.ch
http://www.lit-verlag.ch

LIT VERLAG Dr. W. Hopf
Berlin 2012
Fresnostr. 2
D-48159 Münster
Tel. +49 (0) 2 51-620 320
Fax +49 (0) 2 51-23 19 72
e-Mail: lit@lit-verlag.de
http://www.lit-verlag.de

Distribution:
In Germany: LIT Verlag Fresnostr. 2, D-48159 Münster
Tel. +49 (0) 2 51-620 32 22, Fax +49 (0) 2 51-922 60 99, e-mail: vertrieb@lit-verlag.de

In Austria: Medienlogistik Pichler-ÖBZ, e-mail: mlo@medien-logistik.at

In Switzerland: B + M Buch- und Medienvertrieb, e-mail: order@buch-medien.ch

In the UK: Global Book Marketing, e-mail: mo@centralbooks.com

To all the Arab and Syrian rebellions & martyrs my fellow brothers and sisters, whose sacrifice would make us free and human again

Table of Content

Preface

It is very challengingly difficult to compose a book on a phenomenon that is still well in progress. About two years ago, the Arab World was stricken by a series of radical and overwhelming revolutions that left on its context, and seems to be going to leave on the entire world, an impact that is as indelible, profound and pivotal as the impacts of the collapse of the Soviet Union, the Fall of Berlin's Wall, the Invasion of Iraq, the Palestinian-Israeli Struggle and, last but not least, September Eleven. It was not at all unexpected that revolutions that exploded in the Arab region would vehemently occupy the whole world's media, public-squares and decision-making circles with its radical and historical details, consequences and long-run outcomes.

I was personally fully engulfed and deeply personally involved with these latest historical events in the Arab world, especially the uprising in Syria, my homeland. During the past 15 months, and as the revolution was, and still is, well in progress, I decided to write this book on that radical and massively influential change in the Arab world. I wanted to focus especially on the Arab Christians as an Arab minority in this part of the Globe. I wanted to echo as much as I can the first symptoms and traces of their view of the changing situation, as well as conveying an objective depiction of their role in relation to the Arabic Spring and how they envision this role to become in the post-revolutions future. It goes without saying that I focus in my manuscript on my country's, Syria's, case. Yet, I also present points of view that are reflective of general Arabic Christian political, sociological and theological contextual interpretations of the event and their stance on it.

My text is a three-part interdisciplinary study on the very timely Arabic Spring. The first part would include chapters on the uprisings in general. The second would be chapters on the Christians in the Arab world and their view of the uprisings, with primary attention to the case of Syria. While, the third part would be a suggestion of developing Arabic contextual/intercultural religious discourse that stems out of the recent Arabic (deeply religious) world's context and changes.

Such a radically and blatantly significant and influential phase like the Arabic Spring, which has started at the beginning of 2011 and has not at all yet run its course, cannot be covered in one book or even in very few ones. Such a comprehensive coverage, as I stated earlier, is even much more difficult to be made in a book that was written soon after the first acts, at least of the Syrian revolution, started to play out. Having said that, I do not write this book to meet this demand; the demand, that is, that I hope many other Arab and international authors would fulfil in the coming future. I decided to compose this book because I do, nevertheless, realize the immense need of producing some descriptions and analysis of the events of the Arab Spring from first-hand, indigenous Arabic sociological and religious point of view, and not only from sheer political or merely secondary external one.

It is my attempt in this book to offer a very fresh, timely and literally up-to-date overview and intellectual reading of the promising ‘Spring’ in my country and in the rest of the ‘born-again’ Arab world. But, I do aim more specifically at presenting the intellectual, social, cultural and religious dynamics that drive the Arab Christians, among others, in the Arab world to develop the stances they demonstrate before the public, local and international, opinion on the revolutions, their nature and their aftermath.

It is my belief that such a book is an original, very timely and strongly needed contribution in the academic and lay-readers arena: a book to be beneficial for both those who would like to have a general idea about what happened, and is still happening, in the Arab world, as well as those who would like to get some insightful and coherent understanding of why, how and on what presumptions the Arab Christians base their appraisal of, and stances on, the Arabic Spring. No one has yet produced a publication on the Arabic uprisings from the point of view of a native Arab (a Syrian, who is supportive of his people’s fight for freedom and change and who participates by all intellectual means possible in the revolution). No one also has yet produced such a book on the uprisings from the point of view of an Arab *Christian* point of view. And, no one finally has yet produced a publication on a possible Arabic contextual theology relevant to the changing interreligious and multi-confessional scene of the post-uprisings' Arab societies. I am here putting in the readers’ hands a publication that aims at attending to this threefold task.

The book contains fresh information about the Arabic uprisings, because, as I stated above, the whole event is fresh. But it also contain historical, political, sociological and theological analyses based on recent and previous scholarship all along the study. This is why I said previously that the book would then, hopefully, talk to both scholars who are interested in that part of the world, as well as to wider society of readers who might want to have knowledge about the area and the roots and impacts of its latest changes on the Christians in the region. So, it is not just a book-length report on the situation there, but political, sociological and religious cluster of analyses of some influential and crucial broad patterns and issues that are substantially related to the situation and its ramifications on the Christians' presence in the Arabic context of the present and of the post-Arabic Spring's future.

For the production and publication of this book, I am deeply indebted to few, very special persons, who made this book's birth possible. I am deeply indebted to my friend Prof. Dr. Assaad Elias Kattan of Muenster University for reading the entire manuscript and critically assessing it. Assaad's remarks and corrections were beyond valuable and they made the content and arguments of the manuscript sharper and more thorough. Assaad also accepted kindly my invitation to write an introduction to the book. I choose Assaad, the Lebanese Antiochen Orthodox Arab fellow, to do this because I wanted a Lebanese voice to be included in my text. Though Lebanon has not faced any recent revolution on the same level of the revolutions in the other Arab countries. Yet, the Lebanese created their own 'Spring' much earlier than all of their neighbourly countries, when in 2005 they had their famous 'al-Arz Revolution'. I wanted to include a Lebanese-Christian voice in my book in order to avail to the readers a chance to hear some few remarks from it on the Arabic Spring.
I am also grateful beyond words to my friend and colleague, Prof. Dr. Dr. Martin Tamcke, of Goettingen University, who generously and supportively took on his shoulders the responsibility of bringing this text into publication. Martin has always been in deep affection on the Near East, and he has been consistently supportive to me and my ideas and writs on the region. I also would like to convey my most sincere appreciation to Prof. Tamcke's assistant, Mr. Sebastian Kramer, who kindly offered his very valuable help in preparing the manuscript for publication. Last but not least, to every man or woman, boy or girl, but also child, who strolled the streets, or offered their own lives, in the past two years, bravely demonstrating and resiliently rioting on behalf of all of us to bring freedom, democracy, progress, civil future and human dignity in the Arab world; to

these fellow citizens and brother and sisters I dedicate this book as a humble token of veneration and praise.

Najib George Awad
Hermannsburg, June, 2012

Introduction

There is no need for special emphasis that, in his attempt to reflect upon the "spring of the Arabs", Najib Awad is tackling a very timely issue. For there can be no doubt that, whatever interpretation one might give thereof, the upheavals in the Arab world we have been witnessing for more than one year would have tremendous implications on Arab societies not only politically, but also in terms of psychology and collective self-consciousness. Actually, in trying to implement their "spring", people in the Arab world are not just contesting dictatorships and totalitarian regimes, but also deconstructing those conspiracy theories that have predominated over decades and through which one sought to explain why Arab societies were allegedly retrograde and incapable of any progress whatsoever towards a genuine and sustainable democracy.

To put the accent on the radical newness of the Arab uprisings is neither identical to idealizing nor to demonizing them. This is one of the central hallmarks of Awad's book. After analyzing its motives, Awad perceives the Arab spring as an open-ended process, elaborating not only on its potential capacity to launch a brand new democratic era in the Arab world, but also on the factors that might impel us to be more cautious as to its ability to inaugurate a better future. In this regard, a special attention is devoted to political Islam. With a remarkable scholarly sense, Awad provides his readership with an interpretative clue to more thoroughly understand this multi-faceted phenomenon, and he examines the question as to how far the Arab spring might generate a societal situation in which, contrarily to the legitimate hopes and expectations of secularly oriented people like Awad himself, political Islam would eventually take over.

Yet, Awad's book can by no means be qualified as a mere analysis of the Arab spring. For its author thinks and writes not only as a political analyst, but mostly and foremost as a Christian theologian stemming from the Middle East and being profoundly moved by the recent upheavals in his country Syria and in the Arab world in general. What is really fascinating about this book is the fact that no separation whatsoever can be perceived between thought and life, scholarship and commitment. This naturally leads us to the most intriguing, and probably most creative, part of Awad's book, namely his plea for a Middle Eastern contextual theology, a plea coupled with a valuable scholarly endeavor to draw the main lines of such a theology in context. Needless to say, Awad embarks on this task without losing sight of how necessary it is to remain in dialogue with other Middle Eastern theologians who have contributed putting some stones in the huge edifice of the longed for contextual theology within the framework of the Arab World that is deeply shaped by Islam. Moreover, Awad is fully aware of the tentative character of many of his thoughts in this respect. Yet, if laying the foundations of something new is inextricably bound up with revolving within the sphere of rough drafts and unfinished ideas, it no less entails a lot of imaginative spirit and inventiveness, both very well perceivable in Awad's pages on Arab contextual theology. It is not least his credit to having reminded us of the urgency and necessity of such a theology against the background of what is today passionately moving the Arab world.

In this book, Najib Awad does not confine himself to examining the spring of the Arabs which erupted in 2011. He also explores the future ways of a craved-for spring of theology within Arab Christianity. All this makes the following pages worth reading!

Assaad E. Kattan
Münster, 14 June 2012

Part I

The Arabic Uprisings: Observations, Appraisals and Expectations

Chapter 1: From Despair and Fear into Face-to-Face Encounter

Tareq Altayyeb Muhammad Al-Bouazizi is a young Tunisian citizen who was born on March 1984 and died drastically on Januray 2011, at 27 years of age. He was born in his hometown, Sidi Bouzid, to a poor family of nine members. He could not finish his high school studies because he found himself obliged to pull his vegetable cart around the streets of his city, trying to sell vegetables and to feed his mother and younger siblings. On the 17th of December 2010, while Bouazizi was hitting the road to Sidi Bouzid's public market, a small police patrol, led by the female officer Fadia Hamdi, stood in Bouazizi's way and tried to confiscate his vegetables. To his good luck, Bouaziz's uncle saw the incident and contacted the chief of police, who coerced his patrol to return the goods and release the lad. Later that day, the female officer, Fadia Hamdi, enraged from the chief's interference and with determinative retaliation intentions, clashed with Bouaziz again in the public market, she brutally pushed his vegetables to the ground and ruthlessly slapped Bouazizi in his face, leaving him surrounded by the market's customers, soaked with his tears and deeply drowned in embarrassment and shame.

When Bouazizi went to the municipality department to appeal against the police officer the next day, his attempt was met with indifference and sarcasm, and the official authorities therein suggested for him to go home and to forget about the whole issue. With a mouth full of bitterness and indelibly disgraced dignity, Al-Bouazizi returned the next day to the municipal offices' building, and right in front of it he poured a flammable liquid all over his body and set himself alight. In less than three weeks, Al-Bouazizi's self-burning becomes, beyond every imagination, the spark that would impeccably ignite not only the public-square of Tunisia, but the streets of the other Arabic states of Egypt, Yemen, Syria, Libya, Bahren, Jordan, Saudi Arabia, Morocco and Algeria. By the 17th of March, about 33 other young Arabs, following Bouazizi's example, had set themselves on fire, also for economic and social reasons related to the corruption and tyranny in their countries. Some journalists have even started to name these cases 'the Bouazizia phenomenon'.[1] Most recently, a memorial statue of Bouazizi has been erected and installed in the French capital of Paris.[2]

Wael Said Abbas Ghonim is a young Egyptian man, born in Cairo on the 23rd of December, 1980. He earned a BA in computer science from Cairo University in 2004, followed by a Master in Business Administration from the American University of Cairo in 2007. He was involved professionally in the internet business world since 1998 when he launched the online website called 'Islam Way'. Between 2002-2005, Wael worked in the Gawab.com company before he personally formed and moderated the largest Arabic financial portal called 'Mubashar.info'. Since 2008, Ghonim has worked as the regional executive manager of Google offices for the Middle East region, which are based in Dubai. Wael's impressive scientific education and career achievements are not what cause his name to ring a loud bell in the minds of the Arabs, mostly among the youth. It is rather his reputation as the revolution's blogger and Facebook activist and campaigner against one of the hardest dictatorships in the region. The story of Wael's organized confrontation with the Mubarak regime starts in June 2010, when he established a Facebook page called 'we are all Khalid Said' from Dubai. Khalid Said is another young Egyptian, whose death was blamed on the government by his family and the human rights organizations in the country, after he was exposed to brutal and violent torture from the security forces of the city of Alexandria on the 6th of June, 2010. Wael Ghonim determinatively turned that Facebook wall into an open and free venue for everybody to express disapproval of the security forces' control of the society, and to speak openly about the corruption and tyranny of Mubarak's regime. Ghonim

---

1 See for example Ashraf Omar, "Al-Zahira Al-Bouazizia wa Suqot Al-Hall Al-Amni," (The Bouazizia Phenomenon and the Collapse of Security Option," in www.alhiwar.net 19,January. 2011.

2 For some good articles on Bouazizi's story and its ramifications, read the article on Bouazizi in www.wikipedia.org (Arabic); also in English Yasmin Rayan "The Tragic Life of a Street Vendor," in www.aljazeera.net 20, January. 2011; Brian Whithaker, "How a Man Setting Fire to Himself Sparked an Uprising in Tunisia," in www.guardian.co.uk 28, December. 2010; Rania Abouzeid, "Bouazizi: the Man who Set Himself and Tunisia on Fire," in www.time.com 21, January. 2011; and Mathieu von Rohr, "The Fruits of Mohammed: the Small Tunisian Town that Sparked the Arab Revolution," in www.spiegel.de 18, March. 2011.

himself bluntly invited the people to rise up *en masse* and demonstrate until the ruling system falls. He personally paid the price of this by being thrown in jail and kept there until well after the beginning of the revolution in Altahrir Square. Ghonim's initiative eventually led to the historical riot of the 25th of January 2011, which led to the collapse of Mubarak's rule.[3]

Muhammad Al-Bouazizi; a poor, unemployed, economically and socially oppressed Tunisian, as well as Wael Ghonim; a highly educated, successful and self-fulfilled Egyptian are two Arabs from this age, who reflect two different backgrounds and far from common personal circumstances. The former uses his body and sacrifices his life to express his anger and despair. The latter uses his intellectual skills and the words of his mouth and pen, jeopardizing his security and compromising his freedom in order to express his dissension and eagerness for change. Two different men with two different methods coincided at the same crossroad to inflame the souls of the Arab youths and energize them with a revolutionary power that, so far, succeeded in demolishing two dictatorships, and is inspiring the people in other Arab countries to add further Arab dictators to the list of the fallen. al-Bouazizi and Gohnim are just two examples of hundreds of thousands of Arab youths spread along the entire Arab countries, who dream of having a decent, secure, prosperous, just and dignified life. They represent a completely new generation, the mentality, characteristics, world-view and nature of which is yet to be perceptively pondered and perceived, and fairly and positively appraised by the Arab and the international societies alike.

The stories of these two Arab youths invite us to consider two main factors behind the uprisings that emerged out of their activities. In the case of al-Bouazizi, one can realize the central role of the economic factor in this young man's self-inflaming action and the aftermath riot of the Tunisians, but also other youths around the Arab world.

Since their independence, the Arab countries in northern Africa and the eastern Mediterranean shores suffered from various circumstances and radical political and stately changes that prevent any possible eco-

3 On Wael Ghonim and his role in Egypt's uprising, read "Wael Ghonim," in www.wikipedia.org; Mike Gigilo, "The Facebook Freedom Fighter," in www.newsweek.com 13, February. 2011; and Ian Black, "Wael Ghonim Anointed Voice of the Revolution by Tahrir Sqaure Faithful," in www.gurdian.co.uk 8, February. 2011.

nomic stability and prosperity from maintaining any reliable longevity. In her historical survey of the birth of authoritarianism in the post-independence Arab countries, Nicola Pratt points to this factor. She shows that among these countries, Egypt and Tunisia were two of the first newly established Arab republics to experience economic problems. The failure of the Egyptian state's economic plans produced a serious domestic deficit, introduced obligatory salary reductions for the public sector, it lead to the shut-down of many governmental factories and put the population under high taxes' and prices' pressure. In Tunisia, the situation was not better. The government's economic plans also caused a huge deficit, shortage of investment capital, and failure of agricultural policies.[4] Pratt described the drastic economic failures of these Arab states in the following way:

> [The state-led strategies] led to insufficiencies in production and investment allocation and neglect of the agricultural sector, and exacerbated the need for hard currency to pay for imported industrial inputs, thereby leading to fiscal problems. As domestic productivity fell, so did the state's revenue-raising abilities.[5]

As it did recently, the drastically problematic economic situation in the Arab countries like Tunisia, Egypt, but also Syria, Iraq and Algeria, did not remain within the boundaries of the economy alone. It has massive influence on the public square's overall situation, and, more problematically, it was linked to the state-building process and the regimes' authority. The failed economic strategies put the Arabic authoritarian regimes of the 60s under serious scrutiny and criticism from the population. People, especially youth and labouring segments of society, started to publicly show their discontent with their ruling regimes' failure to protect the usual standards of living in the country. This led to a number of strikes in

---

4 Nicola Pratt, *Democracy and Authoritarianism in the Arab World*, (Boulder & London: Lynne Rienner Publishers, 2007), pp. 60-68. See also Alan Richards and John Waterbury, *A Political Economy of the Middle East*, (Boulder: Westview Press, 1990), pp. 212-219, 224-249; and Eva Bellin, *Stalled Democracy: Capital, Labour and the Paradox of State-Separated Development,* (Ithaca and London: Cornell University Press, 2002), pp. 11-121.

5 Pratt, *Democracy and Authoritarianism in the Arab World*, p. 61.

Egypt, Tunisia, Algeria and Syria.[6] These strikes intensified after the famous Arab defeat against Israel in 1967, and since that time youths started to play a noticeable and significant role in their countries' political and economic development. Noticeable in this regard is the central role, which the university campuses, and student movements therein, played in the demonstrations against the Arabic defeated regimes and their failure to bring stability and prosperity to the Arabic population. Consequently, as Nicole Pratt so eloquently states,

> the widespread uprising of the students after 1967 could be considered a measure of the depth of discontent felt. One member of the post-1967 Egyptian movement told me: 'nineteen sixty seven opened our eyes and overturned our ideas. We saw the corruption of the system. My peers died in Sinai without a fight'.[7]

There is an Arabic folk saying which states 'how similar is today to yesterday'. The same governmental economic failures and corruptions that enticed the youths to riot against the Arab regimes during the 60s and after the defeat from Israel, has also today led the Arab youths of the twenty first century to the streets and empowered their call for the falling-down of the dictatorial regimes. Though many things changed in the situation and circumstances of the North African and Near Eastern Arab countries during the past five decades, the economic situation did not witness any serious improvement, and the drastic living conditions of the majority of the population therein even worsened. The studies on the conditions of employment, social policies, social sustainability and economic development in these countries have often come back with very low rates and unpromising conclusions.

In its panel discussion of March 2011, on the economic situation in the Arab world, the International Labour Organization noticed that youth unemployment in the Arab world, with its more than 23% of youth unemployment record (31.5% of which is the rate of women unemployment), illustrates an ideal example of the, "weak labour markets with too

---

6 Ibid., p.62. See also Mahmoud Hussein, Class Conflict in Egypt, 1945-1970, (New York: Monthly Review Press, 1973); Joel Beinen, Workers and Peasants in the Modern Middle East, (Cambridge: Cambridge University Press, 2001), pp. 114-141; and Rachid Tlemcani, State and Revolution in Algeria, (Boulder: Westview Press, 1987).

7 Pratt, Democracy and Authoritarianism in the Arab World, p. 69.

few and too poor employment opportunities....compounded by a poor overall investment climate and lack of growth, together with a quite limited and tightly controlled private sector."[8] This frustrating situation has exacerbated, instead of declined, in the past decade or so, as it started to inclusively influence in its negative ramifications the educated, even highly educated, youths like Wael Ghonem, side by side with its traditional law-educated, sometimes literate ones like al-Bouazizi. "The higher and lower education and income levels," the ILO's report states, "are equally affected by unemployment."[9] As an example of a similar situation in all the Arab countries, the report points at Tunisia, where the unemployment problem and the low working conditions and benefits are as drastic as in Egypt, despite the fact of the Tunisian youths' ability to get much better education than, for instance, Egypt, and Tunisia's progress in combating discrimination against women in the labour market than other Arab countries.[10] ILO's panel discussion ends up with all its participants' admittance of the urgent need for helping the Arab governments in developing strategies for substantial and clinical reduction of youth unemployment, "reinforcing democratic governance through freedom of association and collective bargaining and enhance social justice and social protection."[11]

Such a drastic economic situation and high rate of unemployment challenge made the observers of the latest uprisings conclude that the main reason behind the youths demonstrations on the streets is almost exclusively economic in nature: frustration by the rates of unemployment that prevents the youths not only to earn a living, but also impedes their marrying and settling down, let alone alienating the youths from any political and societal free chance to share in fighting the situation that was created by the corrupted and arthritic money tycoons and financial mafias of the regimes.[12] It is now believed by many analysts that these youths, after toppling the old regimes down, would now work hard to develop a new Arab world with greater productivity, economic growth and more

---

8 International Labour Organization, "Youth Unemployment in the Arab World is a Major Cause of Rebellion," in www.ilo.org 5, April. 2011.

9 ILO, "Youth Unemployment in the Arab World is a Major Cause of rebellion."

10 ILO, "Youth Unemployment in the Arab World is a Major Cause of rebellion."

11 ILO, "Youth Unemployment in the Arab World is a Major Cause of rebellion."

12 John Humphrys, "The Arab Revolution Wrong-Foots the West," in www.today.yougov.co.uk 24, March. 2011.

equal distribution of wealth. In other words, they will achieve *the* goal that made them quit their long-time silence and to challenge the status quo.[13]

Another factor about the youths who unleashed the uprisings in the Arab world, a factor, that is, we are invited to notice from the background of the Egyptian Wael Ghomaim, the educated background of the new Arab generation. The factor of education resonates with the economic, unemployment problems and corresponds with it. The Arab world is considered the region that contains the highest rate of unemployed youths in the entire world. Nevertheless, at the same time the contemporary rate of the educated young Arab in that part of the world is larger than any other time before. The youths are no more just interested in inheriting the vocational work from their fathers, which passes throughout history in the family from generation to another. They also do not want to opt for just any work whatsoever that can grant them a financial income. The youths are becoming more and more ambitious and creatively visionary. They opt for further education, whether inside their countries or abroad, so that they can eventually create their own private businesses or work on something they are interested in and believe they can create something new out of.

Faced, however, with the incompetent and corrupt economic policies in the Arab countries, these educated and highly skilled and qualified youths find themselves either killing their free time at home, doing any job that can offer them some minor income, no matter how irrelevant it is to their education or talents or passions, or seeking job vacancies and struggling to get work permits in other countries. This situation is even noticed in very rich Arabic countries like Saudi Arabia.[14] This large oil-reservoir country, like other Arab countries, is now reaping the challenging results of what it had sown in the past three decades without calculating its expenses and pre-planning for capitalizing on. A 2008 report on education in the Arab world states that the universities' numbers around the Arab world have witnessed an increase from 233 in 2003 to 385 in 2008 (with Tunisia experiencing the highest rate in universities' mushrooming). These universities, as Sami Mahroum recently noticed, turned

13 Nadia Oweidat and Cynthia P. Schneider, "A New Arab World is Coming, With or Without U.S," in www.cnn.com 28, February. 2011.

14 Deborah Amos, "Rise of Education Lifts Arab Youth's Expectations," in www.npr.org 18, March. 2011.

into the main oases for the youths to develop not only their knowledge and scientific skills, but also to exchange ideas and sentiments about their future, their countries' situations and their political and civil views.[15] This educated generation today, Mahroum continues, creates a so-called 'second society' in the Arab world and which is similar to the one we witnessed before in the communist countries in Europe.[16] This alternative society thrives via the internet, where these youths can exchange their opinions and enjoy their variety and differences away from the censoring eyes of the regimes' security forces, and free from the preconditioning rules of the like-minded, state-controlled circles of public activity.[17] It was in one of these internet, Facebook, virtual oases that Wael Ghonaim called other youths in Egypt to start the historical revolution of the 25th of January, 2011. It is also in this virtual sphere that many youths' 'second societies' are being created to demonstrate and support the streets' uprisings against other Arab regimes in Yemen, Bahrain, Saudi Arabia, Libya and, most recently and most vibrantly, Syria.

The above-mentioned two factors, economy and education, are two main elements in the latest youths' uprisings in the Arab world. Al-Bouaziz and Ghonaim's stories, backgrounds and characters invite us to take them into serious consideration and to try to understand their role in the radical change that took place in the region. However, it is my conviction that these two factors remain external and secondary. There is another more substantial and basic factor that actually lies behind the seen living conditions in the Arab world. Reducing the driving forces of the youths' uprising into mere economy and education would keep our analysis and perception of this event purely on the surface. In the following paragraphs, I would like to point at something more substantially constitutive of the nature of these youth's attitude towards the overall context of the Arab region and their feelings about the Arab world's condition in the world today. I will show that these uprisings do not just image a rage out of personal materialist concerns. It stems from a more genuine feeling

---

15 Sami Mahroum, "Arab Youths, Revolutions and the Rise of the 'Second Society'," in www.knowledge.insead.edu 14. March, 2011.

16 Mahroum, "Arab Youths, Revolutions and the Rise of the 'Second Society'."

17 Mahroum, "Arab Youths, Revolutions and the Rise of the 'Second Society'." See also on the Arab youths the report of Bobby Ghosh, "Rage, Rap and Revolution: Inside the Arab Youth Quake," in www.time.com 17, February. 2011.

of degradation and under-appreciation, which these youths' values and principles suffer from the ruling authoritarian regimes in their countries.

In October 2006, the Israeli scholar Ilan Pappe, the chair professor of History in Exeter University, England, wrote to the English-speaking readers his book *The Ethnic Cleansing of Palestine.*[18] In this book, Pappe presents a brave, authentic and microscopic historical display and analysis of what he describes as 'the ethnic cleansing that Zionism systematically exerted on the Palestinian people since the establishment of the state of Israel in the Middle East', exposing therein the 'massacres and ugly criminal activities' that were conducted by the organized troops and militia of the Hebraic state since 1947 against a whole unarmed nation. His book is an historic, valuable reference from within the sphere of the Israeli state on what Pappe deems horrendous actions against a weak, vulnerable people who radically lack any tangible support from their Arab brothers.

It is not my intention to review the book and analytically appraise its content in this chapter. The book deserves, by all means, to be translated into Arabic (the Arabic version is now in markets) and to be granted all the attention and study from the Arab intellectuals and readers of the region. What I would like to look at is what Pappe says in chapter five of his book, in the context of his exposition of the unsuccessful attempts of some of the Arab resistance at the very beginning of 1948, the year of the calamitous defeat. Pappe points to the big difference between the number of the Arab volunteers for resistance and the ones of the Israelis in these clashes, emphasizing the refusal of the Arab states to send their troops or allowing its peoples to volunteer in the resistance activities. Within the context of his speech on the numerical difference in specific, Pappe says that the Palestinians were not in shortage of those who wanted to volunteer for resistance with them. Many peoples from the surrounding Arabic countries protested against their governments' indifference to the situation. Thousands of young Arabs were ready to offer their lives for the Palestinians. Pappe maintains that although many things have been written on this overwhelmingly sentimental feeling, yet this phenomenon

---

18 Ilan Pappé, *The Ethnic Cleansing of Palestine*, (Oneworld Publications, 2007). I use here an article I published in Arabic as Najeeb G. Awad, "Men Ayna Ya'ti Rūḥ al-Fida' al-Filastīni? Yanbaghi an Nafhama 'Anfusana," (Where does the Palestinian Sacrificial Spirit Comes from? We Must Understand Ourselves), in *Assafir*, the cultural appendix, N. 11215, 06/02/2009.

remains an enigma that is hardly fair to be attributed to mere pan-Arab solidarity sentiments. Pappe concludes that the best explanation for the readiness of thousands to sacrifice their life for the Palestinians is that Palestine, like Algeria, is one of two examples of a brave and violent strife against occupation. This rejection of occupation inflamed the nationalist and patriotic zeal of the youths in the Arabic Middle Eastern countries. Yet, Pappe, again, stresses that what he suggests as an explanation is just an incomplete analysis of the will of Damascene and Iraqi youngsters to give up everything for what they considered a holy mission and not necessarily a religious one.[19]

I find in the standpoint of an Israeli historian like Ilan Pappe, with regard to the phenomenon of readiness to sacrifice one's self for the other, which he read perceptively in the Arab youths' position, a significant and essential point that should get serious attention in light of the latest Arab uprisings. It sheds light on the amount of anger and frustration that is boiling under the ashes of the devastating and catastrophic life circumstances most of these youths were born into, and which they can no longer tolerate or keep their mouths shut about. Such anger, more than any economic or materialist circumstances, invite us to see that the youths' frustration and distrust in their rulers and their pacifist and defeatist positions and attitude towards the Arab-Israeli conflict, leave alone the Arab leaders' degradation of their people's political and humanitarian intelligence, might actually be the fuelling engine of the latest public explosions. The bad economic situation and the improvement of education are just the top of a much larger and far deeper-reaching iceberg.

During the latest Israeli invasion of Gaza Strip (2008-2009), I was caught strongly by the news about the public's reaction across the entire Arab world. I paused silently before thousands of Arab youth's demanding from their countries' ruling regimes either to send their armies (that are actually intended for protecting these regimes first and foremost, if not only) to stand by the innocents of Gaza and to open their borders and arm people before allowing them to go and die with and for the Palestinians. What puzzled me was the fact that these protesters were not from traditional political parties or movements in the area, who constructed their political and ideological enmity with Israel on their first-hand involvement in the Arab-Israeli conflict over the cause of Palestine. 90 per cent of those who called for launching a mass salvific front for the sake

19 Pappé, *The Ethnic Cleansing of Palestine*, Ch. 5.

of Palestine were youths who were born many decades after 1948 and 1967.

A profound phenomenon like this caught the attention of Ilan Pappe in his historic narration of the Arab-Israeli struggle's story. Yet, it is a phenomenon that requires the Arabs' consideration before no one else's. It is a phenomenon that was waiting from the Arab regimes before others a profound, relentless pondering. Failing to perceive it, however, let alone undermining its seriousness, prevented these regimes from reconsidering their relationship with the people, and instead of starting to show some respect to this generation's values and concerns, they continued repressing the youths' frustration and denying even its existence.

One should not miss, but rather ponder seriously, the fact that those who declared their readiness to sacrifice themselves for the Palestinians are not merely simple, naïve, intellectually limited or culturally poor people, driven by pure sentiments and blind reactions. Nor are they just driven by the dogma of 'support your brother whether fairly or unfairly', or any ideologized form of strife (*Jihad*), or even any religious eagerness for the eternal, after-life paradise. I do not deny the sentimental, nationalist, religious, ethnic and tribal dimensions that control and shape the minds of many in the Arab world. I just say, instead, that there is no scientific, logical reason for always assuming the influence of these later dimensions and imposing them on all the Arabs in a premeditated and stereotypical manner. I point here at the fact that the scream in the Arabic public squares was one of the educated and intellectuals, the seculars and liberals, who do not believe at all in the ideological *Jihad* and abhor any form of extremism. It sounded to me at that time as general and more inclusive a scream than we think, or we are willing to believe, even more than what the Arabs per se are to perceive about their own youths.

What makes the modern, young Arab public ready to sacrifice everything for a cause they did not directly suffer from, though they grew up in states that consider it part of its national ideology? If the belief that what drives the Arab youths are personal economic and material needs is correct, they would not then care about a cause that does not, in the first place, influence their daily-life situation. What really makes young boys and girls in the spring of their life, at the front gate of the future, declare their willingness to give up everything and support others who live in a land they heard about yet they have never visited, and may never be able to visit? Are the Arab youths merely a 'herd of sheep' that is led by the staff and rod of their leaders, or just a human sea roaring with storms of blind sentiments, completely remote from reason, logic and depth?

This last question points to a general media stereotype about the Arabs, which used to be the most determining view in the Western world about the Arabic-speaking nation(s). One can even easily prove it to be the hidden opinion of the Arab ruling dictators on their people; let alone the fact that this image is fostered and regenerated consistently by the religious fanatics among the Arabs, who find in violence and death *the* solution for any clash, for proclaiming any standpoint or for gaining any right. Those who reject the one-sided reduction of the Arabs either to a tool in the hand of a dictatorship, a reactionist, irrational creature or to a fanatic terrorist, would undoubtedly inquire about the substance of the readiness of thousands of Arabs to redeem the Palestinians. They will especially pause at the contemporary youths who were not born in 1948 and have not lived the events and the consequences of the consecutive Arabs' defeats before Israel. Some of these youths did not even grow up within a familial and educational framework that entertains either pan-Arab slogans like 'the Arabs' countries are my homeland, from Damascus down to Baghdad' or religious concepts like 'the nation of Islam', or pride itself blindly about any tribal or nomadic origin.

The core identity of this generation, which screams loudly its readiness to go and die in Gaza, deserves a deep sociological, anthropological and cultural analysis. The Arabs are supposed to understand themselves first, before they expect the world to understand them and appraise them correctly and fairly. This is what Ilan Pappe invites for when he concedes that this redemptive, self-sacrificing phenomenon bewilders and puzzles the Arabs' antagonists and makes the rationalist and reasonable groups among them trace the components, sources and causes of this huge reservoir of self-sacrificial spirit. It seems to me, however, that throughout the past six decades of the Arab-Israeli struggle, the enemies of the Arabs spent time in analysing and deciphering the Arabs' sociological, anthropological and cultural textile (regardless of its success or failure) ten, if not a thousand times more than the Arab regimes' huge legions of intellectuals, experts and theoreticians. What usually makes these regimes pause at any scream from the public squares is fear and insecurity, not the eagerness for communication and understanding.

The Arab regimes pay attention to the reaction of the angry peoples only when this serves the purpose of the regimes' survival, and when it helps in guaranteeing the maintenance of their authoritarian power and monopoly. This alone and no other reason is what might make the Arab leaders declare in one of their, often unproductive, summits (like the one held after the Gaza invasion), for instance, an inclusive reconciliation between each other and a solidarity for the sake of the 'cause' and the service of the 'nation'. Yet, none of these regimes' rulers or their serving writers, consultants and analysts spend any shred of a time in thinking about the structure of the contemporary Arab public atmosphere, especially the question of what makes the spirit of self-sacrifice present and vivid still, and what makes it pass from generation to another despite history and time.

Ilan Pappe wrote on the ethnic cleansing against the Palestinian people not only to analyze the Arab people, but to understand in the first place his nation's state and the mindset of its founders. In his book, he launched a conversation with the Israeli and the Pro-Israeli publics alike, inviting them to ponder what Pappe deems the sociological and cultural offspring of these ethnic cleansing operations, which the Zionist troops committed against the innocent land owners. Pappe does this by simply pointing to the fact that those who stand on the opposite river bank of Israel have a serious aptitude for self-sacrifice, which can stand against any militaristic, political and ethnic domination and power.

Who within the Arab world would write today about the Arab public atmosphere, and its members' identity and character in light of this self-sacrificial attitude towards the Palestinians, and most recently in light of the latest uprisings? Who would reflect upon the contemporary generations of the Arabic states and how they deal with their problems, and the problems that hinder their brothers and sisters in the other Arabic countries? What makes the contemporary Arab who he or she is as a 'human person'? What makes the Arab intellectuals up until now empty the stage to violent and militaristic movements, and allows them to exploit this aforementioned self-sacrifice in the service of principles and resistance activities that are unlikely to serve the people, but rather enhance their weakness and losses?

I was often asked by my western friends: what makes the Syrian and Lebanese, and Arabs in general, sympathize with the Palestinians and defend their cause this seriously, vividly and zealously? Is this because you are all called 'Arabs'? Is it because the Palestinians are Muslims? Or is it because the Arab dictatorial regimes coerce people to do this? I usually respond to the first option with what Pappe says in his book: the issue is deeper than mere pan-Arab solidarity. It is for most of the Arab people a holy human cause. I then respond to the second option by saying: the Palestinians, as well as the Arabs, are not *only* Muslims. The issue lies beyond mere religion, no matter what the militaristic resistant movements (e.g. Hizbullah and Hamas), which damages the Palestinian cause radically, claim. While I respond to the third option by saying: many of those whom you witness calling on the Arabic streets for supporting and redeeming the Palestinians, may actually be of the fiercest and most radical dissenters of their countries' ruling regimes, and even wish their collapse. They might also be intellectually, deeply critical about the validity and value of the militaristic, violent and exclusivist form of resistance, which, in their opinion, does not calculate the expenses of its actions perceptively and wisely. By these answers, I aim to say to my western friends that there are thousands of the Arab youths who are ready to die for the Palestinians for a reason far deeper than the three mentioned above.

My friends used to part away more puzzled than they were before raising their questions. I also used to move ahead fully occupied with a very deep question regarding an organic phenomenon in the Arabic scene. It is a phenomenon the Arabs have not yet stopped at to study and learn anything from its analysis until this very moment. It is a phenomenon that caught the attention of Ilan Pappe and made him think and learn.

The latest uprisings in the Arab world, however, offer us, as I believe, a very valuable answer to all the above-mentioned questions, which is worth pondering. The Arab youths are angry about the overall situation in the Middle East. They are not at all happy with their leaders' approaches to the region's troubles and conflicts They are also no more part and parcel of the previous, traditional Arab public-squares, to which their parents and grandparents once belonged, and they no more follow their ancestors' action-methods or echo their convictions. The Arab youths are not just economically driven or materialistically oriented. They are rather energized with serious and radical ethical motifs and reinforced by deep and serious rejection of all the traditional imperatives, values, dogmas and webs of meaning, which the Arab world has known before. The Arab uprisings are leading to ontological and structural, and not merely circumstantial and materialistic, changes. The same fundamentally ethical, humanitarian and existential driving-forces that made the youths roam the streets, calling for supporting the Palestinians and salvaging Gaza have recently driven the youths to the streets again to withstand the totalitarian regimes' ethics, ideologies and crack downs.

Until almost the end of 2010, neither the political, ruling systems in the Arab world, nor its western supporting powers reflected any sincere intention to take the Arabic youths in the public squares seriously into consideration in the process of envisioning the future of the Near East and North Africa. Undeniable is the attention of the international research centres of political and civil studies to the conditions of human rights, democracy and freedom in the Arab world, as well as the NGOs' general call for respecting the public's rights in the Arab world and serving the purpose of its progress, let alone the typical slogans on justice, freedom, truth and prosperity, which every Arab keeps hearing from the local rulers and oppositions alike. However, none of the international sides, the Arab rulers or their opponents have taken the public's point of view seriously, listened to its real voice or took the people's ability to make the change they aspire at into serious consideration. Rather, these people's ability has often been undermined based on the presumption that the Arab public is either merely a herd of humans that is dictated by the hegemonic regimes, or merely fragmented, incompetent societal segments that desperately need the established opposition movements to unite them in one front, to mobilize their activities, and to pull them out of their miserable passivity. Until very recently, the Arabic public square's image in the mind of the international society was just a fake, insubstantial scene, a superficial 'echo' of the discourse of either the ruling regimes or their opposing foes.

The uprisings that torched the public-squares in the Arab countries drive us to ask: who exactly are those uprising youths, who in hundreds of thousands filled the streets of their countries and succeeded in eradicating the status quo, which almost nobody thought will change one day? It seems that these youths seriously and simultaneously confused the Western powers, the national, Arab oppositions and the local hegemonic regimes in the Arab world. As well, though the answer to the abovementioned question is yet to be fully, scientifically formulated, one can initially say with confidence that this rebellious Arabic public square has lately proven to the whole world that this part of the world is not a stagnant oasis, nor are its inhabitants an unreliable herd that serves the will of its providers.

The Western world witnessed with clear ambivalence and confusion[20] the young Arabic public stubbornly and straightforwardly confronting the brutal and criminal security forces of the tyrannical and corrupted Arab dictatorships with open, unarmed hands and fearless determination, and loaded only with voices and convictions that are emancipated from any affiliation to the old-fashioned and classical sectarian and dogmatic ideologies; ideologies, which these youths believe, would eventually make them bow their heads down and compromise their revolt. The Western powers observe this phenomenon with unconcealed confusion, as they see an Arabic public square that is not only new and unprecedented in terms of its members' young age, their mainly economically-driven motif and multifarious sociological identity, but also in terms of this square's non-conventional worldview, genuinely uncontrolled thought form and far from premeditated freedom. For the first time the Western world notices that the current Arabic society is made of a young generation that stands in the present historical era and belongs to a postmodernist intellectual sphere, emancipated from all forms of monolithic, absolutist and collectivist referentialism that was symptomatic of the past Arabic context. It is a postmodernist generation par excellence, shaped after the values of pluralism, relativity and heterogeneity. It does not only deem these values instruments to gain power or means of expression, but more importantly as constructive notions that are inherent to the human's being and existence. The West's caution and noticeable degree of suspicion indicates that it does not yet know how it should approach this rising generation and how it ought to deal with such a factual and influential public existence that seems to be exceeding all the preconditions and calculations that have always been taken for granted when reading the sociological and anthropological context of the region.

On the other hand, the present ruling regimes are the first victims of these uprisings in the Arabic public squares. The first lesson one wishes these rulers to learn from this situation, is the total failure and ineffectiveness of their ruling strategies and the impossibility of ignoring or

---

20 Read for example, Slavoj Žižek, "Why Fear the Arab revolutionary Spirit?" in www.guardian.co.uk 1, February. 2011; and Bernhard Zand, "What the Arab World's Past Can Tell Us about Its Future," www.spiegel.de 8, March. 2011; Thomas L. Friedman, "Pray. Hope. Prepare," in www.nytimes.com 12, April. 2011; and Barry Rubin, "Egypt's Revolution: the More they Reassure us, the More We Worry," in www.crethiplethi.com 24, February. 2011.

undermining the capabilities of peoples' anger, frustration and despair. What energizes such influence is the fact that these new Arab youths no longer abide by thc traditional culture of 'obeying the guardians' and, contrary to previous Arab generations, they are not ready to march behind any allegedly 'visionary leader', 'patriotic liberator',[21] 'freeing sect' or even to concede an idealist 'truth-possessing ideology'. Such traditional notions and slogans were once the energizing engines of the Arabic political train that brought the recent Arabic hegemonic systems into rule. These regimes can no longer rely on these imperatives to remain in power, because, like other parts of the contemporary world, the shores of the Arab world have also been washed by the high waves of postmodernity that started to crack all the foundations of the conventional forms of authoritarianism, collectivism, oneness and referentiality from within. The old-fashioned Arab regimes can no longer assume that the populations are ready to burry their criticism and rejection against all forms of political, economic and social corruption and suppression in the soil of silence. For the people in the public squares, such forms of leadership represent a fossilized, aggressive and irrelevant inheritance, their parents and grandparents once were compelled to belong to and live in, while this generation neither knows nor identifies itself with it.

Moreover, one also has to realize that even the political opponents in every Arabic country cannot overshadow the fact that the new Arabic public square attributes no representational role to the traditional national opposition and no longer really believes that this opposition either speaks on its behalf, or fits as a possible alternative to the current rotten regimes they revolt against. The youth, who lately jammed the cities and froze daily life in many Arabic countries, are not tools in the hands of their countries' known oppositions. They do not reflect in their movement, and their understanding of such movement, a form of uprising that can, by any means, be similar to the sectarian and ideological revolutions, which the Arab world experienced and which the Arabic political literature preached during the last four decades of the past century. Therefore, no

21 Sami Mahroum has perceptively notices the youths emancipation from the idea of the 'visionary leader' and 'patriotic liberator' when he describes the Arab uprisings as "a unique movement in that it does not have charismatic leaders as much as common groundswell of opinion. It is in the hands of many, rather than in the wake of one": Sami Mahroum, "Arab Youths, Revolutions and the Rise of the 'Second Society'."

conventional liberal, leftist, communist, nationalist or Islamist opposition movement in the Arab world has the right to attribute these youth's uprising to its public work, intellectual discourse or private agenda. One should rather reconsider the assumption that any overturning of the corrupt and authoritarian Arabic regimes requires a systematic and even violent opposition movement that can topple the present power and replaces it with no less able and powerful means.[22] This factually Western-made theory assumes that only the traditional, already known and existing dissentions in the Arab world are capable of such a change and no political transformation can take place except by means of their action and through their own supervision.

The youths who succeeded in tumbling the Arabic dictatorships are not at all followers of any of the traditional Arab dissentions, nor are they mobilized by them. Mistaken is the one who reads the latest events in the Arabic public squares as a political transition of the publics from the campaign of fear, obedience and subordination to the hegemonic, dictatorial regimes into the campaign of these regimes' opposing powers. For the new generation of Arabs, these traditional trends of oppositions themselves are the product of the very same outdated and equally abandoned political mentality and ideological thought, to which these postmodernist Arab youths do not belong. As the principles and premises of the tyrannical regimes are alien to them and their webs of meaning, the oppositions' understanding and implementation of the values of freedom, democracy, justice etc, leave out their antagonism with the regimes in relation to such values, which are as alien, meaningless and useless in the eyes of those who roamed the streets and called for a change of the regimes.

Be that as it may, one can validly say that the Arabic public square's movement, which started in Tunisia and Egypt and is rapidly permeating the Arab world, does not only challenge the shaky structure and liability of the Arabic tyrannical regimes. It is also undoubtedly a real challenge to the traditional image of the Arabic public square in the mind of the Western powers on one side, and to the local expectations and appraisal of this square in the eyes of the various trends of the Arab traditional oppositions, on the other.[23]

---

22 As this is correctly noticed in Khalid Haroub, "Simplistic World View Quashed by Arab Spring," in www.mideastposts.com 15. May, 2011.

23 See on this anti-tradition attitude among the Arab youth the report of Jack Shenker, Angelique Chrisafis, Tom Finn, Giles Tremlett and Martin Chulov, "Young Arabs

The Arabic public squares witness the evident birth of an unprecedented historical, constructive and unstoppable public, sociological and political transformation. We have in the region the glorious genesis of a longed for formation of a new identity for the Arabic states that exceeds the region's ruling systems and opposition trends alike. The most significant alternative that will stem out of these pivotal uprisings will not primarily be the new ruling orders that will rise up from the ashes of the previous ones, but more substantially the new active role of an Arab, broadly spread public square, emancipated from old confessional, sectarian, ideological, social, ethnic and even religious labels and divisions. A square, whose members will not go home and re-hibernate for many other decades to come, but will inhabit the streets over and over again and will unflinchingly raise their rejecting voice again whenever they believe it is necessary to do so, unhindered by fear and uninfluenced by any demand for obedience or controlling force.

Just a few months earlier, no one in the Arab or the Western world could have imagined that such a new public square can be a reality in our region. Yet, the new generations of the Arab people are shaping their own destiny today and declare to the whole world that they have not left the track of history and they will not allow anyone to derail them from it.

Chapter 2: A Possible Secularism and Civil Society? In What Form?

Until a few weeks before January 2011, when the uprisings in the Arab world kicked off, one could still notice that the dominant view on the Arab world's societal and political context departs from understanding this context in sharp contrast with the societal, political, cultural and civil components of the Western countries. Over the last century, the colonial and orientalist readings of Arab society and culture had a long-lasting influence. It has been almost common for European and American scholars to use all the scientific methods and rational arguments they know to attenuate the Arabs into mere, "slothful, preoccupied with sex, violent and incapable of self-government" people.[24] In addition, almost all the

---

Who Can't Wait to Throw Off Shackles of Tradition," in www.guardian.co.uk 14, February. 2011.

24 as it has been shown in the classical study of Edward Said, *Orientalism*, (London: Penguin Books, 1978), whose claims are also cited in Rana Qabbāni, *Europe's*

scholars of the main-stream 'West-versus-East' theory had serious doubts that the Arabs would substantially change, or that the world would one day witness the birth of civil, secular, democratic and liberal public squares in the Arab world that are similar to the civil societal settings of the Western countries. Even when such a belief in the possibility of witnessing the birth of such civil democracies and pluralist modern states in this part of the world found its way to the public intellectual scene, it hardly managed to become popular or to be seriously considered in general intellectual and political circles. Up until very recently the popular conviction remained that the notions of 'free' and 'freedom' in the political sense would never find their way to the culture and value system of the Middle Eastern people, though their literature and texts do occasionally mention these concepts.[25]

The prevalent assumption in the West maintained, instead, that an Arab civil society is far from possible, because the Arabs are illiberal and strictly conservative and tradition-oriented in their values and worldview. The Arab societies, it was believed, "have always been more about collective rights than individual ones, resulting in far less protection for the individual who has always been subsumed under the power of the tribe, or the clan or the family."[26] Thus, rather than having civil structure that would defy any threat to society's democracy and members' freedom by any form of hegemonic rule or power, the societies that represent the civil body of the Arab countries are actually used as instruments in the hands of the authoritarian rulers for exerting a collectivist control over the people and guaranteeing their own rule's survival, when this rule is threatened by any possibility for dissention. Moreover, even if such dissention rose against the ruling authorities, this opposition as such, so the presumption argues, would not bring about a truly civil, liberal, pluralist or democratic alternative state or public square. It would rather walk on the same collectivist, conservative value system path of the dictatorial predecessors. It would, more specifically, foster a, "modernization impetus

---

Myths of Orient, (Bloomington: Indiana University Press, 1986), p. 6; and Pratt, *Democracy and Authoritarianism in the Arab World*, p. 34.

25 Bernard Lewis, *What Went Wrong? the Clash between Islam and Modernity in the Middle East*, (New York: Perrenial/HarperCollins Books, 2003), p. 55.

26 thus Francesco Cavatorta and Vincent Durac, *Civil Society and Democratization in the Arab World: the Dynamics of Activism*, (London & New York: Routledge/Taylor& Francis Group, 2011), p. 21.

through religious precepts and symbolism."[27] This, eventually, means that the dominant alternative would be Islamist in nature, as this view presumes and will, "largely propose the same corporatist arrangements of the past, although underpinned by a different ideological referent, which is much easier to understand and appreciate for Arab citizens."[28]

One cannot but admit that a noticeable portion of the above-mentioned claims are not far from how the situation in the Arab world is. One of the things that back these claims' pessimism about the Arab world's civil and democratic future is the fact that up until January of 2011, all the Arab authoritarian regimes were, surprisingly, able to portray a credible image of stability and longevity, despite their dismally corrupted performance and unpopular ruling methods. "The resilience, stability, and continuity of these despotic regimes," as Laith Kubba eloquently states, "raise serious [doubting] questions about the prospects of democracy in the Arab world." It even invites a pessimistically negative response to questions like, "is democracy viable in the Arab countries? Is it compatible with the Arab political culture? Do Arabs have a preference for despotism?"[29]

This notwistanding, the view of the Arab world's situation and the pessimistic convictions about democracy and civil society in its countries started to witness retreat and to be gradually replaced with newly, post-January 2011, developed appraisals. Since that time, the optimistic belief in a possible real democratic and civil public square in that region – which argued even before the beginning of the Arab uprisings that there is much greater grounds for optimism about democracy in the Arab world, than the world is ready to admit –[30] started to gain wider ground and more serious attention. Observers around the world started, with noticeable astonishment and self-correcting attitude, to reverse the questions

---

27 Ibid., p.22; and also N. Pratt, *Democracy and Authoritarianism in the Arab World*, p. 189.

28 Cavatorta and Durac, *Civil Society and Democratization in the Arab World*, p. 22. See also R. Woltering, "The Roots of Islamist Popularity," in *Third World Quarterly*, 23, 2002, pp. 1133-1143.

29 Laith Kubba, "The Awakening of Civil Society," in *Islam and Democracy in the Middle East*, Larry Diamond, Marc F. Plattner and Daniel Brumberg (eds.), (Baltimore and London: The Johns Hopkins University Press, 2003), pp. 28-34, p. 28. For two pessimist views about a possible democracy in the Arab world, see in the same volume the arguments of Mohammad Talbi, "A Record of Failure," pp. 3-12; and Emmanuel Sivan, "Illusions of Change," pp. 13-27.

30 This is basically the argument of Kubba, "The Awakening of Civil Society," pp. 29, 33-34.

and ask, as Nicholas Kristof does in his article "Unfit for Democracy?": "is the Arab world unready for freedom?", is it really the case that if the people in the Arab world gain the control of power, the result will likely be "Somalia-style chaos, Iraq-style civil war or Iran-style oppression"? Is this the future of a Middle East ruled by the public-square? Are the Arabs politically immature to handle democracy and make a real peaceful and civil change in their countries?[31]

Nicholas Kristof argues that the Arabs who filled in the streets in the latest demonstrations prove that the Arabs nullified all the Western conventional suspicions about their readiness for democracy and freedom.[32] In his turn, Benjamin Dürr, in his article "farewell to a World of Black and White", sides with Kristof and argues that the 'black-versus-white' mentality, which was constructed after 9/11 to divide the world into 'we' and 'they'; the West and the Muslims, democracy and liberty (West), *Jihad* and oppression (Islam), has lately been unhinged and permanently silenced by the latest uprisings in the heart of the Islamic world, the Arab east.[33] Dürr, in his analysis, even goes as far as claiming that one should now reverse the old-fashioned conception of the Muslims' and the West's over-against-ness. The case now is, "Muslims stand up for freedom and democracy – and are held down by Western-backed autocrats. Muslims seem to become democrats, Europeans seem to support terror. Critics of Islam have yet to find a response to that dilemma."[34]

In an article titled "the Tension between East and West" and written almost seven years ago, Shafeeq Ghabra gives a relevant explanation to the aforementioned undermining of the Arabs and Muslims' readiness for democracy and civil society. He points at the over-simplistic, narrow and presumptive Western misunderstanding of Islam and the Arabs and the negative ramifications of such misunderstanding on the West's policies

---

31 Nicholas D. Kristof, "Unfit for Democracy?" in www.nytimes.com 26. February, 2011.

32 Kristof, "Unfit for Democracy?"

33 Benjamin Dürr, "Farewell to A World of Black and White," in www.theeuropean-magazine.com 1. March. 2011.

34 Dürr, "Farewell to A World of Black and White." Dürr invokes as an example the Dutch right-wing demagogue, Geert Wilders, who used to call Islam 'fascistic ideology' and consider Qur'ān similar to Hitler's *Mein Kampf.* Wilders, Dürr points out, "gave a crude interview in which he entangled himself in his own answers. But apart from [his usual statements] he – known as a self-appointed freedom fighter who has never lacked strong words – has remained silent."

and strategic thinking about that region. Ghabra further argues that this misunderstanding and nothing else is what actually fuels fanaticism and authoritarianism in the Arabic states and prevents any chance of political and civil democratic progresses therein.[35] This prefabricated Western view of the Arab world, Ghabra concludes, inevitably imposes a future of an unfettered conflict with this part of the world. And, I may add that it inescapably entails that the West will never be able to grasp the core elements and essential nature of any possible political, civil and societal change in the Arab world, when such a change takes place.

The latest uprisings stand victoriously against the above-mentioned premeditated views and expectations about democracy, civil-society, but even secularism, in the Arab world. For, within the context of the youth's uprisings, one can glean some remarks on the alternative political and civil systems which these youth would support to replace the known old Arabic regimes (whether the ones that collapsed, those that are about to collapse or those, which people hope to see collapsing soon).

One must admit that some of the proposals that occupied the streets were old-fashioned and outdated ideological ideas that were offered by some of the traditional opposing sides' spokesmen. Yet, these voices as such do not in fact represent the rioting youths and have not played any substantial role in their movement. So, regardless of these conventional voices, what we actually read and hear about the above-mentioned political alternative indicates that none of these young uprising masses calls for establishing a religious ruling system that does by any means accord with the traditional options (like an Islamist fanatic alternative, a fear which the non-Arabic world has already reflected on) to replace the recent dilapidated regimes. One can even go as far as saying that the youngsters' voices carried an imagination of political and statehood alternatives that are characterized with all the components of secular regimes, like human rights, democracy, pluralism, non-sectarianism, citizenship and modernity.

Nevertheless, the crucial question here is the following: which secularism can harmonize and be consistent with the cultural and sociological context of the Arab world? This question invites us to ponder for a while the notion of 'secularism' and its forms, as one can counter them in the societal settings of other people's life around the globe.

---

35 Shafeeq N. Ghabra, "The Tension between East and West," in www.commongroundnews.org 29. December. 2004.

One of the serious researchers on the phenomenon of secularism and observers of its development and various forms in the Western world's social contexts, is the Canadian philosopher Charles Taylor. In his massive and seminal book, *A Secular Age*, Taylor speaks about the history of religion-secularism relationship.[36] Rather than sticking to the popular belief in an unbridgeable rift between religion (Christianity in the case of the West) and modern, secular civilization in Europe, Taylor argues that the careful and meticulous reading of the history of the West during the past two centuries indicate that in many milieus of the modern times, "that gap has narrowed, and the tensions lost sight of."[37] This was sometimes done to an extent, Taylor maintains, that suggests, "a long-standing tendency in the West to slide towards an identification of [religious] faith and civilizational order."[38] Instead of narrowing down the modern conditions of Western secularism into mere experiences of godlessness, Taylor argues that there are other experiences of modernity that yield, for example, "citizens of a nation whose political identity is defined in religious or confessional terms...[or those] whose ability to meet the disciplines of contemporary life is bound up with [religious] conversion, so that an order-sustaining morality is felt as inseparable from faith:"[39] Be that as it may, Taylor suggests that instead of talking about secularism as an expression of 'the end of religion',[40] we ought, in the light of a coherent and far from one-sided reading of the history of Western modernity, to view secularism as an expression of the disenchantment of the Western world and the turn of religion into one factor among many equal other ones that

---

36 Charles Taylor, *A Secular Age*, (Cambridge, Mass: Harvard University Press, 2007).

37 Ibid., p.737. "Seen within the history of western civilization," Taylor adds, "the present-day welfare state can be understood as the long-term heir to the early Christian church."

38 Ibid., p.743. Taylor points at the negative consequences of such identification, as he states that "this not only makes us lose sight of the full transformation that Christians are called to, but it also makes us lose a crucial critical distance from the order which we identify as Christendom, whether it be the one at present established, or some earlier one which we are fighting to restore."

39 Ibid., pp.552-553.

40 So for example on this view A.N. Wilson, *God's Funeral: A Biography of Faith and Doubts in Western Civilization*, (New York: Ballantine Books, 1999); and Eamon Duffy, *The Stripping of the Altars: Traditional religion in England, c. 1400-c. 1580*, (New Haven and London: Yale University Press, 1992), pp. 377-503.

are pertinent to the public-square's affairs.[41] Instead of displacing and replacing religion in human life, secularism in one of its stories is, according to Taylor, a transformation process in religious life itself.[42]

Taylor's volume offers a threefold interpretation of secularism in relation to religions' role in society.[43] This interpretation is what I would like to refer to in the following lines. The first meaning of secularism that Taylor offers designates a secularism of a political nature. This political secularism is usually found in civil societies, where the ruling systems reject any reliance on religious referentiality for certifying its existence and authority, or in best-case scenarios the state makes hardly little reference to religion in its own constitution or structure. It is a secularism that prospers in the societies that completely relegate religion from the political and statehood realms upon a foundational belief in the total and strict division between religious and public affairs, relying on the civil and ethical positivist laws and constitutions, instead of any literal or direct derivation from religious imperatives or rules. In this secularist setting, not only religion does not interfere in a state's affairs, but also the government has no interest, let alone constitutional right, to meddle in the internal affairs of any religious community in society. The old history of the mutual benefit and support, which the church and state used to entertain in old theocratic contexts, is no longer valid here. One of the positive outcomes of political secularism, as W.S.F. Pickering notices, is the en-

41 Taylor calls the identification of religion and enchantment, which leads eventually to the treating of disenchantment and the end of religion as synonyms, an 'illusion' (Ibid., p.553).

42 Ibid., p.554. "We have moved," Taylor postulates, "from an era in which religious life was more 'embodied', where the presence of the sacred could be enacted in ritual, or seen, felt, touched, walked towards (in pilgrimage); into one which is more 'in the mind', where the link with God passes more through our endorsing contested interpretations –for instance, of our political identity as religiously defined, or of God as the authority and moral source underpinning our ethical life."

43 On Taylor's threefold interpretation of secularism in relation to religion, I am indebted to the perceptive presentation in Philip L. Wickeri, "The End of *Mission Dei*- Secularization, Religions and the Theology of Mission," in *Mission Revisited. between Mission Theology and Intercultural Theology*, Volker Küster (ed.), (Berlin: LIT Verlag, 2010), pp. 27-44, pp. 31-34.

hancement of religious plurality, where all religions in a society have a legislatively equal status.[44]

The second meaning of secularism, Taylor displays, is one that gives secularism a sociological dimension. It signifies a society, wherein the role of religion has attenuated not only from the political and ruling contexts, but also from the context of the daily, social and public life of the members of the society. The citizens of this society no longer resort to a religious thought form or world view, and show disregard for the religious demands and obligations in their conduct and they no longer refer to the religious books or consider them referential with regard to daily life behavior or values. The religious interest has rather lost the central place among people, and the number of the religions' affiliates has dropped down radically, as, "the personal religious faith becomes weaker or is never embraced."[45] Those who still link themselves, in one way or another, to certain religious communities or denominations no longer reflect any willingness to consistently practice religious activities or to define themselves as citizens or members of society by means of any religious feature. Such a secularism can also be described as 'personal secularization', since it reflects a personal and individual decision about casting religion away from the realm of direct contact with, or influence on, the social, ethical and practical settings of life. Though, this is not to be interpreted immediately as a resort to atheism or crude hostility towards religions. This sociological or personal secularism should rather be seen, as W.S.F. Pickering eloquently states, as, "a general attitude of indifference in seeing religion as antiquated and irrelevant to [peoples'] needs. People do not argue against it, they bypass it. Furthermore, many of those who are associated with [a religious institute] decide by themselves what doctrines and moral teachings they will accept and what they will disregard."[46]

The third meaning of secularism Taylor calls 'cultural secularism'. This secularism is seen in societies whose members moved, in their intellectual and ethical rationales, from deeming religion and belief in God a given, absolute and criterial truth that is immune from criticism or skepti-

---

44 Alister E. McGrath, (ed.), *The Blackwell Encyclopaedia of Modern Christian Thought*, (Oxford: Blackwell Publishers, 1995), "Secularization," pp. 593-598, p. 594.

45 Ibid., p.594.

46 Ibid., p.595.

cism, into merely one option among many equally personal, individual or privative other options, that are no less present, effective and valuable than the option of religiosity. In a nutshell, this secularism reflects, "the absence of religious references in cognitive propositions."[47] In such a cultural secularism setting, religion and other convictions, beliefs and values are all equal, existential and epistemological choices that exist simultaneously in the society's living sphere, and they all similarly succumb to the preconditioning factors of individual freedom, private opinion and personal conviction. In essence, the factors that are usually protected and granted to all people by law and basic human rights. Secularism in the cultural sense is one that contains within its own circle all the spectrums of religiosity, non-religiosity, atheism, agnosticism, indifference and others. It contains them all side by side and does not grant one of these positions any referential, hierarchical or authoritative role in the civil life of the state. Rather tt subjects all these trends to the critical and judgmental verification and valuation of science, to such an extent that one can call this cultural form of secularization an 'intellectual secularism' that primarily refers to, "the cognitive positions of an elite, which is seen as the intellectual leader of society –scientist, philosophers, artists, writers and so on."[48]

To go back to the Arabic uprising and the alternatives of the dilapidating regimes in the Arab world, one may ask: what form of secularism do the Arab youths imagine, and what form would they eventually opt for, if they were given the authority to decide the future of their countries? Also, which secularism is relevant to, and applicable in, the renewed Arabic societies: political, sociological or cultural secularism?

It is my conviction that answering these two questions is the most difficult and challenging task before the new uprisings' generation. I am not sure that the Arab youngsters have ready-made answers for the first question. For they unleashed their rebellion departing from down-to-earth, almost totally pragmatist concerns, and not by a theoretical, analytical or purely intellectual driving forces. In addition, the youths' voice does not carry a prefabricated ruling agenda, but rather a scream of rejection against the already present, dominant ruling order and its catastrophic ramifications on the Arabic world's situation: they did not really state what they want as an alternative; they only declared what they stand af-

47 Ibid., p.594.
48 Ibid., p.594.

firmatively against and will never tolerate any longer. In its apophetic accent, the scream of the Arab youths refers us back to alternative, yet raw and primitively elaborated wishes and values that are not yet programmed or constructed in a clear proposal.

The second question, on the other hand, is crucial and historical in extent. It cannot be attended to only by the uprisings' youths, nor can it be answered by a specific or single political party, sectarian group, dogmatic discourse, religious community or any other majority societal segment in the Arab countries. The second question is substantial and constructive par excellence, and all the people's spectra in each Arab country's public square must develop its answer via general, totally inclusive and perpetual dialogues.

One of the influential factors in relation to the possibility of secularism in the post-uprising Arab societies is the substantial difference between the Arab world's and the West's experience and perception of secularism. Carsten Wieland perceptively pays attention to such a difference when he realizes that the term 'secularism' as such must be explained and analyzed in more details in the context of the Middle East, since the Muslim Arabs and the Europeans have often various, sometimes contradictory, ideas about how one should understand this term.[49] In the West, Wieland argues, secularism is more a social development and personal experience than mere political ideology. Rather than just rejecting any religious role in the public square, secularism can also mean "the privatization of religion and the disappearance of personal faith and religious practices among population."[50] To say the least secularism emerged in the West out of the very autochthonous social, political, philosophical and public context of the Western world.

To the contrary, Wieland notices, the situation is quite different in the case of the Arab world. Ideas like stately education system, civil administration and basically the separation of religion from state were not inherent to the Arab mind. They were rather imported to the Arab region from Europe.[51] After Muhammad Ali's attempt at establishing a secular nation-

---

49 Carsten Wieland, Syria: Ballots or Bullets? Democracy, Islamism and Secularism in the Levant,(Seattle: Cune Press, 2006), pp. 87-93.

50 Ibid., p.87.

51 Ibid., p.89. Wieland argues that this happened for the first time in Egypt, when the idea of the French revolution arrived to the Egyptian shores with the naval fleet of Napoleon's expedition in 1798. This first importation was followed by an indigenous reform after secularist views in 1801 by Muhammad Ali, who, after defeating

state in Egypt in 1801, secularism played a more noticeable and tangible role in the ensuing decades, when many secular elements were incorporated into the Arabs' attempt at independence and the rise of pan-Arab nationalism. This implementation, however, as Wieland maintains, did not pave an open and welcoming way for secularism in the region, since this notion was associated in the local peoples' mind with European colonialism: secularism was deemed a suspicious colonial idea, used by the Western powers to subdue the Arab world and disparage its nationalist and religious identity. When secularism was sued in the post-colonial Arab states as an instrument in the strife between tyrant regimes to replace each other, secularism was impoverished of its intellectual and sociological components and, as Wieland states, "was thus degraded to a political instrument and an ideological façade."[52] Since every Arab state has its own political, sociological and statehood complications that vary greatly from the ones in other countries in terms of nature, history, elements, influences and implications, one cannot really say that the attitude towards secularism, and the possibility of applying secularist ideas, in each Arab state is monolithic by any means.

It is difficult to find a monolithic recipe of secularism as an answer for the multifarious, heterogeneous and complex societal contexts in the Arab countries. On one hand, the term 'secularism' has multiple meanings that are, as Charles Taylor teaches us, embedded in various political and contextual settings. One should not, thus, "assume that we are all quite clear about [it], and [that] the only possible discussion concerns whether we are for or against."[53]

On the other hand, Every Arab country's society is a multi-faceted entity, if not on the religious level (some Arab countries contain only a Muslim population) or the sectarian (some have only a Sunnite population) or the ethnic (some do not have Syriac, Kurds, Barber, Charkas or Armenian communities), then they are on the anthropological (male, female, homosexual, etc) and intercultural (a clear influence of non-Arabic cultures on society) or environmental-demographic levels (rural, urban,

---

the Mamluks and sacking them out, proclaimed himself an independent ruler of he regent of the Nile, establishing thereby, Wieland concludes, "the first modern, secular nation-state in the region." (Ibid., p.89).

52 Ibid., p.89.

53 Charles Taylor, "Forward: What is Secularism?" in *Secularism, Religion and Multicultural Citizenship*, Geoffrey Brahm Levey and Tariq Modood (eds.), (Cambridge & New York: Cambridge University Press, 2009), pp. xi-xxii, p. xi.

tribal, nomad, costal, etc). All these constitutive varieties have often been suppressed by the hegemonic and tyrannical traditional regimes in the Arab world, who either undermined its influence or tried to implement this influence in the service of these regimes' controlling ideology, using these factors as tools for creating societal, ethnic, religious and sectarian segregation, hatred and mutual intimidation, and eventually the tearing apart of the societal textile in every Arab country.

This stated, as the hegemonic and monistic regimes started to reveal signs of collapse, the question of 'which secularism?' comes at the behest of all the Arab societies' public segments in their tremendous, and rather challenging, variety. As well, until each of the Arab countries develops its own understanding and practice of secularism in its own society, one can at least hope that the three main categories of secularism can be kept in mind during this development and construction process: 1) freedom of belief or disbelief (religious liberty), 2) equality between followers of different religions and equality between religious and non-religious people, and 3) the participation of religious communities in determining the political and civil identity of society.[54]

How can such a necessary reconstruction of an answer for the question of secularism be achieved? My answer to this question is twofold; one practical and the other analytical. The practical lies, by my reckoning, in calling for open, general, foundational meetings and summits, wherein the Arab citizens from all backgrounds and orientations, hold a dialogue and figure out together which secularism expresses the newly rebuilt state. As an outcome of such interactions, one can anticipate new Arabic states, some of which are politically secular, others are sociologically secular, yet others are closer to cultural secularism than to the political or the sociological. One can also expect in the future to have Arabic countries, where the sociological secularism cannot be implemented, though the sociological structure of these countries is tolerant to cultural secularism; or other Arabic countries where the sociological secularism is not an option, though political and cultural secularisms are both acceptable; or still some Arab countries where political secularism is inapplicable, while

---

54 Ibid., p.xii. Taylor admits that these three categories can sometimes conflict. So, societies need to maintain a balance between them and focus on the good elements in each. Taylor personally adds a fourth factor, namely trying "as much as possible to maintain relations of harmony and comity between the supporters of different religions and *weltanschungen*..."

the cultural secularism is more possible. What ultimately matters is that the choice of statehood in its secular features would stem from the midst of the Arabic societies' development and context, and would be the product of the positive and constructive interaction and intermingling of its human components. The Arabs must not deal with any statehood-system as a ready-made alternative that is given to them 'from-above' or derived from any absolutist ideology that is stated in a heavenly book, or demanded by presumed jurisdictional heritage. Such resources would turn, if this was the case, into new suppressive forces that will pull the Arab world back into pre-modern ages that are far worse than the age of hegemony and tyranny.

The second analytical fold of my answer lies in carefully observing and thoroughly analyzing the political and state ramifications and developments of the uprisings in the Arab countries, as well as the impact of political Islamism on the post-revolution public squares in countries, like Tunisia, Egypt, Libya, Yemen and Syria. The latest developments and consequences of the public riots in Tunisia, Egypt, Libya, Yemen and Syria demonstrate to the observer that there is going to be a transitional period, long or short depending on each country, wherein Political Islam is going to propose itself as the most dominant and politically influential alternative in the processes of reconstructing the ruling systems in the Arab world. The Arab countries are going to witness in the near future an undeniable resurrection to the political Islamist sects and movements, and political Islam would be granted, for the first time in the post-independence history of the Fertile Crescent and North Africa, the opportunity to realize its political theories and stately agendas. This Islamism would be given such a chance not only from the Arabic public squares (including its Christian components, I believe), but also from the Western world before any other (see my argument in the ensuing chapter).

This new factor on the political and civil Arabic scene notwithstanding, the observer and analyzer of the Arabic Spring can easily spot suspicions, worries and even an extent of fear from such an option among a noticeable number of Christians, Muslims and non-religious Arabs. Such concerns are symptomatic in fact of the Muslim street before the Christian, the moderate square before the liberal, the rightist campaign before the leftist. One, initially very interesting, factor that is worth pondering in parallel to this fear, is that the latter is associated with the majority of the Arabic public's reconciliation and acceptance of the possibility of the political Islam's winning of authority via the democratic game and the electorial ballots. The majority even encourages political Islam, should it compete in ruling the state, to follow such an authority-winning process, because this would mean that democracy has found its way to the political life of the Arab world and the Arabic Spring fulfilled its mission. Despite this principal readiness to let the democratic game decide the political fate of the state, one can still detect a general apprehension and suspicion from the Islamists' winning of power in the public Arabic squares. The question here must be what could be the cause of the suspicion and concern?

One of the perennial definitions of 'political Islam' invites us to go beyond the mere reduction of this phenomenon into either just a nickname for a group of politicians who are exclusive affiliates to Islamic religion, or just an expression of a political sect or body that consists of, and is administrated by, Muslim religious figures or clerics. The public view in the Arab world usually swings between these two views. Going beyond these two rather simplistic views invites us to take into consideration one interesting and important definition of political Islam that is proposed by the Sudanese professor of Law in Emory University, Atlanta, Abdullah A. An-Na'im. According to An-Na'im, the phrase 'political Islam' stands for that attempt at mobilizing the Islamic identity in the process of achieving specific purposes that are related to the public, civil policy, whether within the framework of the internal relations between the various components of the society, or in the context of the external relations of this society with other societies around the world. 'Islamic identity' here does not merely designate the religious affiliation, but connotes more broadly a specific sociological identity that is expressive of particular cultural, behavioural, religious and doctrinal bearers.[55] In other words, essentially and primarily, political Islam is not a religious movement pursuing a political project that aims at hegemonically controlling the public by means of its religious dogma. At least, political Islam does not automatically mean this or originates it. Notionally speaking, political Islam designates the activity of a group of people, which attempts to ad-

55 Abdullah A. An-Na'im, "Political Islam in National Politics and International Relations," in *The Desecularization of the World: Resurgent Religion and World Politics*, Peter L. Berger, et. al. (ed.), (Washington, DC: Ethics and Public Policy Center/ Grand Rapids, Mich: W.B. Eerdmans Publishing Company, 1999), pp. 103-121.

dress the public and deals with public affairs, implanting this in the first place in the reconstruction and reformulation of the civil setting according to a particular preconception of the nature of human communal existence, which is ultimately supposed to image and reflect in its characteristics the sociological structure of this Islamist group. This means that political Islam is not just a political phenomenon or dogmatic power that interacts positively or negatively with other political powers in a legal democratic race for gaining the decision-making prerogatives. In its core-meaning, political Islam is a sociological and not merely political project; a civil-cultural thought form and not just a form of ruling and an ambition for state control. Olivier Roy perceptively states, conformity to specific social, ethical and communal codes, rather than necessarily faith-affiliation, is what forms the basis of society.[56] The question here would be what is disconcerting and suspicious in such a societal thought form, and why does it worry those among the contemporary pro-secularization Arabs who do not subscribe to its cause?

This question takes me to Abdullah an-Na'im's and Roy's valid call for approaching the promotional attempts of political Islam (which applies, I believe, to the case of the post-revolution Arabic countries, like Tunisia, Egypt, Yemen and Libya, and would probably also apply to Syria) as self-existing sociological, collectivist phenomena that endeavour to regenerate themselves in the different other and as the protective patrons of the society's virtues.[57] It is in the nature of these sociological movements to see its members approaching their contemporary context and living conditions from a collectivist perspective and referential vantage points. They view the public as a single entity that is monistic in social identity and follows a collectivist orientation toward societal conducts and values. Society is not seen as a gathering of particular and distinguished individuals, but a strictly unified mass, which can be seen as a lively incarnation of the chivalric slogan of 'one for all and all for one'. They also consider any challenge to their movement as a group a substan-

56 Olivier Roy, *Holy Ignorance: When Religion and Culture Part Ways*, Ros Schwartz (trans.), (London: Hurst & Company, 2010), p. 109. Elsewhere, Roy argues that this sociologization of religious ideologies is actually one of the reasons of the failure of Islam in turning itself from a religious belief of a community into a true society: Roy, *The Failure of Political Islam*, Carol Volk (trans.), (London & New York: I.B. Tauris, 2007), pp. 48-74.

57 An-Na'im, "Political Islam in National Politics and International Relations," pp. 106-111; and Roy, *Holy Ignorance*, p. 110.

tial threat against every single member in the community and jeopardy to the existence of every one of them in an even influential way; the thing that lively incarnates of the slogan 'we either drown together or survive together'. In addition, in the name of preserving the communal purity of society,[58] the followers of such a sociological collectivism treat every outsider (the one who does not affiliate to the group) with the same exclusivist and discriminative stance, stereotypically construing him or her as an enemy for the entire group, rather than a foe for few members therein. Such collectivist sociological movements, finally, rely on the strategy of mobilizing the 'many' after single, wholistic ultimatum, making the latter a melting-pot for members' particularities and differences, and turning this oneness into a protector of the community from the threatening nuances of the members' personal interests, beliefs and priorities.

Now, let us imagine such a sociological collectivist alternative system taking on the leadership stick from the collapsed and collapsing dictatorial regimes in the Arab world, what would we have in the post-revolution public squares? According to those who are suspicious and apprehensive about political Islam, this would be a replacement of political dictatorial collectivism with another no less hegemonic sociological collectivism. Those sceptical voices believe that such a possibility merits suspicion and serious concern, even if one conceded the political Islamists' full right to participate in decision-making and share in the democratic game of gaining power. Within the framework of the political Islamists' attempt at forming the society in the image of their own core values, the other constitutive elements in the society, which Olivier Roy calls 'the marginal elements, deviances and othernesses', are no longer acknowledged as part and parcel of the nature of societal life. Rather than managing them as valuable and useful components of society, these marginal elements are now considered a threat and subjected to systematic restriction, even suppression attempts.[59] In the case of today's Arab world this means that all the non-Islamists, that is the secular, liberal, non-religious, leftists, etc., are going to be looked at as challengers rather than as a source of enrichment in the society. Rather than contribution and

58 Roy, *Holy Ignorance*, p. 110.

59 Ibid., p.111. In such a situation, Roy's appraisal that "the conviction that all members of a society must explicitly share one belief system is absurd and can only result in permanent coercion" is accurate.

enrichment by means of otherness, the criterion of the citizens' belonging to the society, in this case, will be the extent of their readiness to abide by the rule of conformity and succumbing to a certain, actually coercive, zeal for forming an Islamic 'resistant identity'[60] in order to counter the incursion of a feared non-Islamic and secularist cultural and societal alternative.

On the other hand, the sceptics about political Islam in the Arab world also believe that the previously displayed collectivist sociological mentality would detain the political Islamists from accepting any positivist, secular philosophies for making the civil legislation. This would entail that international principal treaties, like the Declaration of Human Rights, would not be used or considered by the Islamists as one of the sources for the formation and reformation of the civil and state's constitution. For the Islamists, such a secular and positivist rights charta not only contradicts the Islamists' political and ideological principles. They are also inconsistent with the constituents of their existing sociological entity; the most basic among which are the values of 'conformity to the communal', 'manifestation of loyalty to the mass's values' and 'abiding with one ideological premise that makes society steep in a specific religion's (i.e. Islam's) cultural manifestations'. The Islamists cannot unreservedly buy into such a charta, because, in the first place, they do not trust the belief that, "secularization does not necessarily imply a conflict, or even a breakaway from religion," nor do they see how "a secularized society remain[s] in step with religious culture and values."[61] The Islamists, unrealistically and falsely, fear that applying such bills, like the Human Rights Charta, in society and relying on them in legislation, would alienate them (the Islamists) from their understanding of 'Muslim' society and prevent them, as believers and followers from a specific religious world-

---

60 I borrow this term from Graham Ward, *True Religion*, (Malden, USA/ Oxford, UK: Blackwell Publishers, 2003), pp. 133-138. Ward speaks about 'resistance identity' as the option the traditional religions, like Christianity and Islam, opt for in their attempt at surviving and facing, Ward, says, "a world that has become radically different from, and threatening to the existence of, the truth-claims for which they stand. In the face of cultural divergence and secular materialism, [these religions find themselves obliged to choose between either] adaptation or separatism, syncretism or purism, negotiation or war" (Ibid., pp. 134-135).

61 Roy, *Holy Ignorance*, p. 113.

view,from identifying with the surrounding, by then totally disenchanted, culture.[62]

One has here to differentiate between political Islam's stance on 'human rights' as a principle and notion, and 'Human Rights Bill' as a treaty that follows positivist preconceptions and is founded on secular philosophical premises. Political Islam would support and value the idea and the principle of 'rights', while it would find it difficult to reconcile in substance with the items of the Bill or its philosophical backbone. All the items of the Bill of Human Rights stand principally and conceptually on a philosophical presupposition of the foundation of the values of freedom, justice, equality, mercy and truth. If one asked any political Islamist body to give a value judgment on these rights, it would bluntly express its support and belief in these natural rights of the human beings, since the Qur'ān, the Sunnah and the Islamic jurisprudence alike equally propagate the values of freedom, justice, equality, mercy and truth and indelibly defend them. This notwithstanding, the case would turn into a different story when they are asked to express their view on the positivist Bill of Human Rights. Here, political Islamists would reflect a serious scepticism about the Bill and its underpinning secular philosophy. For them, the Bill is grounded in a philosophical anthropology that views the human person as individual, particular, self-dependent being, whose sheer existence is not to be preconditioned by his or her affiliation and conformation to a specific community, but to be based, instead, on her natural right to exist and to live as 'one' different and distinguished from the 'many' (see the chapter on human rights in the third part of this book).[63] The Bill calls for

---

62 Ibid., p.113-114. Roy perceptively argues that such fear from secularization of society is based on a false belief that *Sharia* can actually be fully applied as the criterion of life in society. In contrast, Roy affirms, "*sharia* is never (and never has been) fully applied…: the community of he prophet's era was a religious community and, when it later became a political society, this was part of a political process which meant that no ruler could accept the complete autonomy of *sharia*. The ruler therefore sought to curtail it in two ways: by restricting its sphere of application….or by codifying it along the lines of Western positive law, so as to include it in the field of state law."

63 For some expositions on the Islamists' reluctance to support the Human Rights Bill and its promoting organizations, see for example Benjamin Macqueen, "The reluctant Partnership between the Muslim Brotherhood and Human Rights NGOs in Egypt," in *Islam and Human Rights in Practice: perspectives Across the Ummah*, Shahram Akbarzadeh and benjamin Macqueen (eds.), (New York: Routledge, 2008), pp. 75-88; Abdulaziz Sachedina, *Islam and the Challenge of Human Rights*,

granting the human person his or her natural rights as an individual and self-existing entity, and not as a reward to the individuals' total, obedient identification with the sociological melting pot and conformity to the collective values-code.

When the sceptics about political Islam in the Arab world realize the above-mentioned situation, they imagine that any alternative Islamist regime in the post-revolution Arab societies would be exerting the following preconditioning rule on its citizens: 'you have every right as citizens to enjoy all your rights as human beings. However, and for the sake of the 'public goodwill' and the best interest of the whole society (which in this case would be decided and shaped after the presumptions and the premises of the ruling and dominating sociological majority), you must succumb to the demand of melting your intellectual, cultural, epistemological (not necessarily religious) variations in the pot of the communal unity and solid oneness, and to conform your pluralist hermeneutics of freedom, mercy, justice, equality and truth to the serves of the sociological, dominating numerical status of the cultural, authoritative, religious, ideological, or economic majority in society'.

In light of such an assumed possibility, many Arab, non-Islamist citizens find themselves driven to scepticism and serious precaution about such a collectivist sociological movement like the one of the political Islam. They do not seem to be lead into a more secure zone in relation to it by their mere knowledge that political Islam believes in the values of freedom, truth, justice, equality and mercy and promises to apply them in its ruling term.

Discovering the nature of the secularization ambition which the youths, who jammed the squares of the Arabic Spring, would strife to apply in the post-revolution Arabic societies demands, in one of its aspects, a serious observation of the above-mentioned growing concern in the Arabic public squares about the possibility of the success of political Islam in filling in the authority-gap in the forthcoming transitional phase. The near future of the Arab world would show us, as it seems, a competition between the ambition of secularization and the ambition of islamization in the Arab world. One of the most significant tasks the pro-secularization group must set before itself is to carefully ponder the so-

---

(Oxford and New York: Oxford University Press, 2009), pp. 3-40; and Katerina Dalacoura, *Islam. Liberalism and Human Rights: Implications for International Relations*, 3rd edi., (London & New York: I.B. Tauris, 2007), pp. 6-38.

ciological nature and performance of political Islam. It should take into serious consideration the core sociological nature, and not only the mere political performance, of this political phenomenon. When one perceives that political Islam is a collectivist movement and not just a political discourse based on religious premises, one would more coherently understand the root of the pro-secularization's suspicions about, and fear from, its challenging possibility: this apprehension does not stem from political Islam's religious background or political agenda. It originates, first and foremost, from the societal, cultural and anthropological ramifications and impacts, which such a current of political thought can ably leave behind.

The forthcoming future may surprise all the pro-secularization groups in the Arabic public squares with a political Islam that is much more open-minded and ready to go beyond its traditional, usually strictly preserved, boundaries. We may witness a progressive and self-reforming political Islam winning the leadership stick via fair and legal democratic, electoral competition, welcoming other politically active parties into participation in the decision-making process and revealing a serious readiness to change its collectivist world view and sociological nature. As of now, no one can affirmatively promise the non-Islamist Arab publics that political Islam is willing to admit that gaining the trust of the secularist and non-Islamist population requires turning pluralism, particularity, differentiation and the idea of 'otherness' into foundational constituents of its identity and existence, and not just mere pragmatist tools that are used for the service of facilitating the decision-making and ruling procedures.

The twofold requirement the Arab populations will face in the coming years, and the only possible passage for exploring what kind of states the rioters establish, i.e. secular or Islamist, lies practically in starting public dialogues and a national sharing of views, and it lies theoretically in carefully analyzing and studying the rapidly prevailing political Islam. The pro-secularization groups need to create a truthful and wilful openness towards understanding political Islam and perceiving it profoundly, objectively and positively, for it is an inherent element in the sociological, political and cultural textile of the Arab world. No secularization attempt can celebrate success without conversing and cooperating with political Islam.

On the other hand, the pro-Islamization population also has an equally inescapable duty to do. It must deeply perceive and appreciate the pluralist structure of the Arab world and its highly sophisticated religious, intellectual, sociological, ethnic, cultural and civil nature. Political Islam must not sweepingly simplify this sophistication and must not narrow it down, neither by means of a monistic view of human existence, nor by means of a collectivist, simplistic discourse on the relation of religion with identity and the individual self with the community. Political Islam must acknowledge the ambition of a large population among the new Arab generations to live in secularized, civil societies. It must become a co-operator, rather than a blocking wall facing the need of the Arabs to objectively, realistically and profoundly scrutinize, re-evaluate and re-modernize their own societal, ethical and civil world-view.

Would the pro-secularization groups open up and show a more trusting stance towards political Islam? Would political Islam express tolerance and positivity towards those who dream of establishing secular and civil states and societies in the future Arab world? The coming future will take care of offering the right answers to such questions.

Chapter 3: The West and the Islamist Alternative in the Arab World[64]

It has been almost a given, common view that, in its approach to the political and societal changes that may occur in the Arab world, the advanced, especially North American and Western European, states always fear any Islamist ruling system to, one day, replace the conventional authoritarian dictatorships in that part of the world. The traditional underpinning belief behind this fear is that, despite their oppressiveness, corruption and unpopularity in the eyes of their citizens, the traditional Arab dictatorships in countries like Syria, Egypt, Yemen, Jordan, Algeria, Libya and the Gulf countries, managed to maintain satisfactory and reassuring relationships with the Western powers, and to protect their best geo-strategic and economic interests and profits from the regions' rich

64 Some parts of this chapter were published in Arabic as Najeeb G. Awad, "al-Gharb wal Badīl al-Īslamawī fil-'Ālam al-'Arabī," (The West and the Islamist Alternative in the Arab World), in www.almustaqbal.com, *Nawafez*, no. 3990, 8, May. 2011, p. 9.

and versatile resources, as well as to spare the state of Israel any factual or direct threat of war. So, if any of these regimes collapsed one day, the ineluctable alternative would immediately be an Islamist power, whose fanatic political view of the Arab-Israeli conflict would make it an impending, immediate threat not only to the security of Israel, but even to the idea of its existence; whose extremist and fundamentalist view of the West as 'the Christian enemy' would energize a *salafi* ideological attitude and a *Jihādī* clashing behavior against the *Kuffārs'* (infidels) powers. In other words, terrorist Islamism would not only find safe shelter in the Arab countries and societies, but will also enjoy a massive financial, ideological and strategic support and supplication for its official states.

The above-mentioned conventional and widely spread anticipation recently witnessed noticeable invigoration, as the Arab people rose up against their states all over the Arab region, toppled one of the most important Western-allied Arab regimes in Egypt, and are about to crack-down, as it seems, another two or more long-lived and stubbornly resistant ones. Some of the conservative analysts argued that the unavoidable ruling alternative that will emerge out of these uprisings is what the west has fearfully predicted and even panicked from sheer thinking about its rising possibility.

In an article he wrote on April, 2011 on the uprisings in Syria, Philip Jenkins, for example, admits that the Arab ruling regimes, which the latest uprisings sweepingly attacked, are truly greedy despots, corrupted and authoritarian. However, Jenkins then claims that by supporting the Arab rioters unreservedly or indiscreetly, the western powers miss what Jenkins deems an overwhelming consequence, namely, "the likely *religious* [my italics] catastrophe that would follow the overthrow of the admittedly dictatorial governments."[65] Focusing on the religious minorities' situation in Syria, Jenkins alleges that any Western intervention in this country's uprisings would be supplying a death warrant for the ancient Middle Eastern Christianity. In a rhetorical accent, Jenkins states, "for anyone concerned about Christians worldwide – even if you believe firmly in democracy and human rights – it's hard to avoid this prayer: Lord, bring democracy to Syria, but not in my lifetime," before he ends his article with the following strict warning: "the religious consequences of intervention [in the Arab world's uprisings] could be horrible. Before

65 Philip Jenkins, "Death Warrants of Ancient Christianity," in www.realclearreligion.org 11, April. 2011.

planning to intervene in Syria, western nations had better start printing several million immigration visas to hand out to refugees seeking political asylum, and demanding protection from religious persecution."[66]

In an article he published in The New York Times, Thomas Friedman also follows the same islamophobic reading of the recent Arab uprisings and warns against its possible negative developments and consequences. Friedman first invokes a similarity between the recent Arab demonstrations and the democracy wave that hit Europe in 1989. Yet, he immediately parts away from comparison and begins contrasting, claiming that the Arab world's situation is exactly the opposite of Europe's. When the influence of communism was relegated in Europe, all the European countries, except Yugoslavia, were largely homogenous states with a long tradition of civil societies, which enabled them to reach stability and self-governance quickly and relatively peacefully. To the contrary, in the Arab world all the states are far from homogenous and are dominantly, "assemblages of ethnic, religious and tribal groups put together by colonial powers." This means, according to Friedman, "when you take the lid off these countries, you potentially unleash not civil society but civil war."[67] Hoping for civil societies, yet expecting civil wars as an alternative of the recent dictatorships in the Arab world, and revealing his heartily belief in the inevitability and necessity of the Arab democracy movements, yet opining that a possible birth of democracy in this region would take a very long time, Friedman, also in a rhetorical accent, concludes his article saying: "pray for Germany. Hope for South Africa. Prepare for Yugoslavia."[68]

Jenkins' and Friedman's pessimistic expectations are just a reflection of a traditional conviction in the Western world that the Arabs are not yet, if ever, ready for democracy and may actually be religiously incompatible and politically too immature to handle the demands and costs of establishing democratic systems.[69]

This having been acknowledged, one should not reduce the Western overview of the possibility of democracy in an Arab-Islamic context into the above-mentioned pessimistic and islamophobic approach. The latest

66 Jenkins, "Death Warrants of Ancient Christianity."

67 Thomas L. Friedman, "Pray. Hope. Prepare."

68 Friedman, "Pray. Hope. Prepare."

69 See an interesting brief discussion of this claim from the perspective of the recent, down-to-earth factors in the Arab world Kristof, "Unfit for Democracy."

Arab revolutions have definitely challenged many conceptions about change and development and political and societal possible alternatives in the Arab world. Yet, the change must not be restrictively attributed to the latest uprisings. There are Western scholars, who, specifically after 9/11, have actually already started revising the public appraisal of the Islamic political alternative, which some Islamist movements in the Arab world, like the Muslim Brotherhood of Egypt and Syria, represent on the ground.

There is a growing acknowledgment of an evolvement in this Islamism's political thought and a gradual construal of this evolvement an evidence of Arab Islamism's turning into a 'moderate' Islamist phenomenon in the Western intellectual and decision-making circles; working, that is, "within the [existing political] system and no longer advocating the violent overthrow of the government, a reality that has in fact led them gradually to alter their political theories and perspectives..."[70] What the analysts, like Aşef Bayat, for example, conclude from the Muslim Brotherhood's new tendency to follow democracy and non-Islamist statehood slogan is that "Islamism, it appeared, ceased to be primarily a political project and became simply an 'Islamic phenomenon', a struggle against secular values in order to elevate personal piety, morality, Islamic identity and ethos."[71] In his turn, Graham Fuller concurs with Bayat's view and emphasizes the Islamists' shift in orientation towards moderation and democracy in the following way.

> The majority of Islamist movements have long since reached the conclusion that democratization is the best overall vehicle by which to present their agenda to the public and to gain political influence...Islamists are becoming prime advocates of concepts of democracy and human rights, precisely because they are the primary victims of its absence.[72]

---

70 Valerie J. Hoffman, "Islam, Human Rights and Interfaith Relations: Some Contemporary Egyptian Perspectives," in *Political Theology*, 5(11), 2010, pp. 691-716, p. 698.

71 Aşef Bayat, *Making Islam Democratic: Social Movements in the Post-Islamist Turn*, (Stanford: Stanford University Press, 2007), p. 145.

72 Graham F. Fuller, *The Future of Political Islam*, (New York: Palgrave Macmillan, 2003), p. 29. See also a similar view with even more optimistic tune in Raymond Baker, *Islam without Fear: Egypt and the New Islamists*, (Cambridge, MA: Harvard University Press, 2003).

In light of the above-mentioned shift in the Western view of Islamism's relation to democracy and civil statehood, one can now ask: Would it be possible to see in the coming future the Western world supporting Islamist regimes replacing the falling conventional dictatorships in the Arab world, or should we rather expect an escalation in the West's fear and offensiveness toward the possible rising and prevalence of such an Islamist option in the region? In the ensuing paragraphs, I will argue that what we should expect is a Western support and facilitation, rather than fear and discouragement, of an Islamist alternative in the Arab world.

Yes, the Western world would not stand against the establishment of Islamist ruling systems in the Arab world anymore. I am aware that this claim would cause many to accuse me of political nearsightedness and intellectual eccentricity. The Arabs watching the decision-making politicians in the West expressing their preference of maintaining the status quo in the Arab world and to hear their readiness to flatter the tyrannical and corrupted regimes therein (all this under the slogan of the concern about protecting the stability of the Arab countries, guaranteeing the security and fair treatment of its minorities and fostering the region's ethnic, religious and cultural plurality). This seems to be reaching its end so soon, as one can see from the Americans' and the Europeans' very recent willingness to build bridges with Islamist alternatives in Tunisia, Egypt, Libya and even Syria. One can also find a support for the realistic possibility of such a paradigm shift in the historical friendly relationships between the Western powers and the Arabic Gulf's, clearly and crudely *salafi*, ruling systems. Finally, one can also glean valid verification of such a possible change in views from the growing alliance and cooperation between America and Turkey.

In light of these political and geostrategic relations and alliances between the so-called 'secular Western states' and the clearly 'religious and Islamist states', the above-mentioned, long-standing, conventionally claimed phobia of an Islamist ruling system in the Arab World of the Near East are no longer the most accurate lenses one should use to read the recent Western powers' views and visions about what the situation would mount to in the Arab world in light of the latest uprisings. These lenses, in specific, would not offer us, in my judgment, the most authentic image of the West's assumptions about the nature of the alternative statehood and ruling systems, which these uprisings should actually be encouraged, if not even implicitly pushed, to produce.

It is my conviction that the western powers' support of Islamist alternatives in the Arab world is neither practically impossible, nor theoretically implausible to the western strategic and geopolitical calculations. There are features and traces of new political and strategic proposals that began to impress the thought of the West's politicians and intellectuals about the Near East and the relationship of Islam with the world. This new political paradigm shift originates from the overall western phobia of the Islam of the immigrants in Europe and America, in general, and its serious concern regarding the influence of political Islam in the western world's societies as such, in specific.

During the past two decades, some western authors began to reflect in a voice louder than ever before highly sceptical, and sometimes bluntly offensive, views about the political Islamic trends of thought of the Muslims who live in the West. Strongly intrigued and totally puzzled by the rapid and fierce resurgence of Political Islam all over the world, the Iranian Revolution of 1979 and, after September 11, the international attacks of Islamist terrorism, authors like Oriana Fallaci, for example, bluntly state their belief that there is a huge gap between Islam and western culture. Islam, as Fallaci argues, cannot be part of the western sphere because the former illustrates in its presence violence, fanaticism and extremism, and reveals a conspicuous attempt at demolishing the Western culture and heritage.[73] For the followers of this conviction, as Abdullah Saeed shows, "Muslims are engaged in a struggle for global dominance, control and subjugation of the religious 'Other'." This view goes as far as arguing that Muslims in the West, Saeed continues, "are a serious threat to Western societies and that they should be countered by various decisive actions." The main reason for this belief is that "Muslims cannot be loyal citizens of a western nation-state, because their loyalty is to Islam."[74]

Fallaci's and others' negative appraisal of Islam aims at playing the role of an alarming bell for the West. It endeavours to say to the non-Islamic world the following: we cannot at all deny the existence of *politi-*

---

73 Orian Fallaci, *The Rage and the Pride*, (New York: Rizzoli, 2002). Fallaci's view is also cited in Abdullah Saeed, "Muslims in the West and Their Attitudes to Full Participation in Western Societies: Some Reflections," in *Secularism, Religion and Multicultural Citizenship*, pp. 200-215.

74 Saeed, "Muslims in the West and Their Attitudes to Full Participation in Western Societies: Some Reflections," p. 200.

cal Islam by solely concentrating on *religious* Islam, as if such a concentration can emancipate Islam from its political nature and this nature's influential impact on the world's fate and conditions. To the contrary, this approach further argues, the more dominantly present and lived Islam among the Muslim immigrants is actually the politically and sociologically, rather than necessarily the religiously or spiritually, shaped and driven one. Philip Jenkins, for example, notes that the dominant type of Muslims one can actually meet in the West must be described as 'cultural Muslims', who represent, as Jenkins opines, "a large population [Muslims] who identify little with religion in any form, who are anything but religious in an approved or institutional sense."[75] Others concur with Jenkins' view and conjecture that any popular impression of mass Muslim devotion and strict commitment to practicing religious rites and spiritual duties is just an optical illusion; a false, unrealistic and delusional stereotype.[76] The story is different, according to this view, when considering the Muslim immigrants' commitments to certain socio-political views and agendas that are fostered by Muslim clerics and intellectuals and used for mobilizing the Muslims' in a unified activist movement in the West.

Regardless of its offensive and highly sceptical tune, the above displayed call for paying more serious attention to political Islam's influential impact on the life of the Muslim immigrants in the West is valid and reliable from a socio-political perspective. Every resident in today's Europe and United States can realize that political Islam is a real and present factor that is actually far more rampant than Islam's religious discourse in the Western world. Moreover, this political discourse is proving day after day its ability to intimidate and threaten many societies and countries around the world, even in the places where Islam as a religious discourse is not dominant or popular, and where Muslims (until now at least) do not represent more than a marginal or a quiescent minor-

75 Philip Jenkins, *God's continent: Christianity, Islam and Europe's Religious Crisis*, (Oxford & New York: Oxford University Press, 2007), p. 122. Jenkins continues saying that "in France presently, just 5 percent of Muslims reported praying every day, figures that suggest almost Anglican detachment from formal religious commitment."

76 Jørgen Nielsen; Brigitte Maréchal and Stefano Dassetto (eds.), *Muslims in the Enlarged Europe: Religion and Society*, (Leiden: Brill Publishers, 2003), and Olivier Roy, *Globalized Islam: the Search for a New Ummah*, (New York; Columbia University Press, 2004), pp. 148-231.

ity. Permeating almost all the globe's corners, political Islam plays an undeniable, direct or indirect, international role in shaping the fate and the future of the advanced countries.[77] This role is won by the Islamic political discourse due to economic, cultural and security factors, like the impact of the huge financial and oil deposits of the Gulf countries and its influence on the world's economies, the escalating need for 'dialogue of cultures' to replace the the 'clash of civilizations' to deal with the immigrant Muslim communities in the heart of Western societies, and last but not least, the inescapable need of pulling the Islamic world into an alliance against Islamist terrorism, instead of facing the hard consequences of its possible sympathy with the terrorists because of their religious affiliations.

The bottom line of the above displayed negative appraisal of the Muslims' presence in the Western societies is the realization that the Muslim communities have started to interfere in the political, civil and jurisdictional activities and discussions in America and almost all the European countries. One of the most interesting aspects of this growing influence lies in the fact that the call for the Muslims' integration in the societies of their expatriation lands is no more just a demand or an expectation exerted, or even sometimes forced, upon the Muslim immigrants from the hosting non-Muslim and secularist societies and states. It has recently become an invitation that is addressed to these communities from Muslim-western intellectuals, who enjoy a representative role and status among the Muslim immigrants in the West.

One of these representative, integration-fostering voices is Tareq Ramadan. In his book on the Muslims in the West, Ramadan explicitly and affirmatively calls his Muslim immigrant fellows not only to integrate but also to participate in contributing practically, proactively and positively to their hosting societies. Ramadan's eloquent invitation is worth quoting in length here:

---

77 On the influence of Islam politically, economically, jurisdictionally, sociologically, educationally, etc. around the world, see, for instance, Werner Ende and Udo Steinback (eds.), *Islam in the Word Today: A Handbook of Politics, Religion, Culture and Society*, (Ithaca and London: Cornell University Press, 2010), Prt. II, Sec. 1,2, 4 in relation to this chapter; and Theodore Karasik and Cheryl Benard, "Muslim Diasporas and Networks," in *The Muslim World after 9/11*, Angel M. Rabasa; Cheryl Benard; Peter Chalk; C. Christine Fair; Theodore Karasik; Rollie Lal; Ian Lesser and David Thaler, (Arlington, VA: RAND Corporation, 2004), pp. 433-478.

> the universality of the message of Islam and the principle of integration that is at its heart invites us to integrate everything that is positive, to move forward selectively, and to act from within, as full members in our society, in order to promote what is good, to work against injustices and discrimination, and to develop alternatives that do not restrict *fiqh* in the west to thinking of itself as on the defensive, moving in a protective fashion, giving the name of 'exemptions' (*rukhas*) to what in the long term could take on the colour of surrender. The intellectual revolution we are referring to here...compels us, from within, as free citizens in societies under the rule of law, to strengthen our faith and to use our intelligence to find solutions and alternatives to the problems of our societies- to move from integration to contribution, from, adaptation to reform and transformation.[78]

Ramadan's call in the cited statement evinces actually two dimensions: one sociological and the other political. On the sociological level, his call is useful for the Western host societies, since it invites the Muslims to appreciate their new environment, to openly involve in their societies' life and to willingly carry their responsibilities and fulfil their duties as citizens like any others, instead of just complaining about their undermined or unfairly granted rights and needs. It is a positive call for belonging and affiliating with the societal and cultural sphere of the West, which defies in fact the overgeneralizing, negative and suspicious views of people like Oriana Fallaci about the Muslims presence in the West.

On the other hand, Ramadan's words carry challenging and intriguing political connotations that make the West seriously worry and pause at the role that Ramadan invites his Muslim compatriots to play. If the Muslims in the West are expected to contribute to the political and state situation of the Western societies by means of calling for transformation and reformation that resonates with their Islamic religious message, as Ramadan states, this, then, means that what the Muslim immigrants – especially those among them who escaped from their homeland due to political reasons – failed to achieve in the Arab and Islamic world because of the persecution and oppression they experienced due to their political-religious convictions, they are now called to work hard for and to relentlessly practice and fight for in their expatriation lands. If they did not do

78 Tariq Ramadan, *Western Muslims and the Future of Islam*, (Oxford and New York: Oxford University Press, 2004), p. 55.

this, they will not be adherent or loyal to the 'universal message of Islam'.

Such an implication of a Ramadan-like call from within for proactive, rather than protective participation in societal and stately reform is not at all unseen or unperceived by the Western publication. This is why the politicians and decision-makers in these immigration countries, in return, have started to realize that the whole sociological, cultural, civil and jurisdictional principles and structures in the West are now exposed to an opposite ideological, political and dogmatic deconstruction attempt that is orchestrated by political Islam's discourses and energized by Islamist calls for transformation and reformation. Some of the politically oriented Islamic organizations and movements in Europe went even further than Ramadan by requesting legal permission for establishing an Islamic *Shura* council to supervise and superintend the affairs of the Islamic minorities, acting as almost a parallel shadow-state within the state.[79] Some other Islamic political movements announced Europe and America as '*Jihad* land' for spreading Islamic faith,[80] justifying this move by the rapid numerical increase of the Muslim population; the thing that will make them in the coming few decades the demographically dominant community and grant them, by sheer democratic and human rights' virtue, the right to foster a state that is Islamist, or at least religious, in character and mentality.

The aforementioned situation is now the real and most noticeable stance the West expresses in its approach to political Islam. The traditional fear from political Islam's role in the Middle East, its challenge of the powerful countries' economic interests in that strategic part of the world, or its threat to Israel are no more the core cause or the primary decisive concern in the relation with Islam. The main source of fear and

79 On the Muslims in Europe and the influence of their political and societal demands on European societies past and present, see for example Jørgen S. Nielsen, *Muslims in Western Europe*, 3rd ed. (Edinburgh: Edinburgh University Press, 2004); Gilles Kepel, *Allah in the West: Islamic Movements in America and Europe*, Susan Millner (trans.), (Oxford: Polity Press, 2004); and Peter G. Riddell and Peter Cotterell, *Islam in Context: Past, Present and Future*, (Grand Rapids, Mich: Baker Academic, 2003).

80 On the growth of Jihadi Islam in Europe, see for instance Alison Pargeter, *The New Frontiers of Jihad: Radical Islam in Europe*, (London: I.B. Tauris, 2008); and Lorenzo Vidino, *Al Qaeda in Europe: the New Battleground of International Jihad*, (New York: Prometheus Books, 2006).

concern about the Islamic political ambition is today the influence of political Islam on the sociological, political, civil and security foundations of the Western countries before any other.[81]

In light of this new challenge, it is not implausible to expect of the western strategists' and decision-makers' a re-reading of the world's geopolitical map and their reimaging of the Middle East's region in accordance with what they deem necessary to deal with it. One of the ways to deal with political Islam's threat is to say: if we cannot confront political Islam and curb its impulsiveness anymore, why do we not sit with it at a negotiating table and purport to offer helping it achieve its alternative political agenda, and why do not we help this Islam fulfil its ruling and ambitions to gain power in a way that can enable us to cast away this ambition from our own societies and primary realms of existence as far as possible? Why do not we grant it the chance to fulfil its ruling political dream in its homeland, the Arab world?

If the West did this, it will not be the first time the Western powers resort to such a strategy in modern history. A similar logic drove Europe, under the leadership of England, to encourage the Zionists to establish their hoped-for state in Palestine.[82] The main and most central purpose

---

81 Such a concern about the internal situation of the western societies in relation to the influence of political Islam, rather than any real concern about this Islam's influence on the situation of the non-western world, is what I personally detect in the views of various European and American scholars who are interested in probing political Islam in the west. See for example Michelle Pace, "The EU, US and Political Islam: An Introduction to Strategies for Engagement," and Oz Hassan, "America's Freedom Dilemma for the Middle East: Interest or Democracy?" both in Michelle Pace (ed.), *Europe, the USA and Political Islam; Strategies for Engagement*, (New York: Palgrave Macmillan, 2011); pp. 1-10, 161-191 consecutively; see also Bruce Bawer, *While Europe Slept: How radical Islam is Destroying the West from Within*, (New York: Broadway Books, 2006); and Brigitte Gabriel, *The Must Be Stopped: Why We Must Defeat Radical Islam and How We Can Do it?* (New York: St. Martin's Press, 2008).

82 For some historical expositions on the fulfilment of the Zionist dream and the role of England in specific and Europe in general in fulfilling this dream in the 19th century, see for example, Mitri Raheb, "Displacement Theopolitics: A Century of Interplay between Theology and Politics in Palestine," in *The Invention of History: A Century of Interplay between Theology and Politics in Palestine*, Mitri Raheb (ed.), (Bethlehem: Diyar Publisher, 2011), pp. 9-32; Michael Polowetzky, *Jerusalem Recovered: Victorian Intellectuals and the Birth of Modern Zionism*, (Westport, CT: Greenwood Publishing Group, 1995); David N. Meyers, *Re-inventing the Jewish Past: European Jewish Intellectuals and the Zionist Return to History*, (New York

back then was casting away the Jewish community and emancipating the European economic and cultural context from its impressive and admirable influence and dominating successfulness. Upon a similar logic, the strategic equation about the Muslims in the West becomes: encouraging, even aiding, political Islam to direct its attention towards the Arabic homeland and to aim at proposing its state as an alternative to the conventional Arabic regimes. Within this expected pragmatist framework, it goes without saying that this is not done out of sincere alliance or mutual trust, but out of a pragmatist concern about redirecting the demolishing Islamic train into a different rail track.

The latest historical uprisings in the Arab world demonstrate that the option of the political Islam's replacement of the old regimes as a new ruling system is not far from reality. It might actually even be the most likely alternative in the forthcoming transitional period. The Arabic Islamist political movement managed, despite all the pressure and persecution, to preserve links with the Arab countries' local public. It also succeeded throughout the years of underground operation in developing its organizational structure, recruiting a noticeably countable amount of followers, enhancing its financial resources and extending significant cooperative relations with other Islamist movements around the world.[83] Careful observers can realize that the zealous spirit of the non-religious, secularist and civil-minded youths, who are the true agents of the latest change in the Arab world, are not yet capable of presenting themselves as a solidly defined and reliable political and ruling alternative; at least not in the near, foreseeable future. More importantly still, the West will not truly support this young public-square and would not deem it an alternative. It will rather shake hands with the Islamist option and no other. This would be in harmony with Europe's and America's growing feeling that the only way to eradicate the Islamist challenge from the heart of the Western world might be nothing else than paving the way for it to turn its

---

& Oxford: Oxford University Press, 1995); and Jonathan Frankel and Steven J. Zipperstein (eds.), *Assimilation and Community: the Jews in the Nineteenth-Century Europe*, (Cambridge and New York: Cambridge University Press, 2004).

83 On the role of political Islam in Arabic societies, see for example Michael Gilsenan, *Recognizing Islam: Religion and Society in the Modern Arab World*, (New York: Pantheon Books, 1983); Najib Ghadban, *Democratization and the Islamist Challenge in the Arab World*, (Boulder, Col: Westview Press, 1997); and Kemal H. Karpat (ed.), *Political and Social Thought in the Contemporary Middle East*, (Westport, USA/London, UK: Praeger Publishers, 1982).

face away from the West and focus on the promising possibility of becoming the political solution for the post-uprising Arab world.

The question would now be: which version of political Islam would the West back up and welcome in the Arab world? I can comfortably say that, if they were given the final word and had the upper hand in this, the Western powers would definitely reject any *salafi* or *jihadi* or violent and confrontational Islam. The closest, already available, Islamic political alternatives, one can assume that the West may favour, are the examples of the Turkish and the Gulfi regimes. The Turkish Islamist version proved its reliability as an ally in relation to maintaining the West's interests in the region and positively protecting the strategic geopolitical balance the West wants the region to follow in the face of the threat of the Iranian growing influence.[84] The Turkish Islamist regime has become in the past years one of the most resorted to by ambassadors and mediators between the region's clashing sides (like between Syria and Israel, or between Iran and the Gulf states, or even between Hamas and Fatḥ in the Palestinian camp and between the political antagonists in Lebanon).

On the other hand, the Gulfi Islamist example has also proven its openness towards the West and its deep concern about maintaining a long-lasting friendship and a relationship with the Western world based on mutual interests. Some of the Gulfi regimes, like Qatar and Oman, even gave up the offensive language against Israel and started to tail semi-diplomatic connections with it.[85] Such political Islam, like the Turkish and the Gulfi, does not intimidate the West's strategic agenda. This Islam also, and despite its support to the Palestinians and their right in establishing their own strong and autonomous state, does not proclaim virulence towards Israel and it does not wish to wipe it off the map. Add

---

84 On Islam in Turkey and the ramifications of Turkey's Islamist identity on its relations with the west and its revived ambitions in relation to the Arab world, see Gareth Jenkins, *Political Islam in Turkey: Running West, Heading East?* (New York: Palgrave Macmillan, 2008), pp. 141-212. And on the dynamics of relationship and mutual interest between Turkey and the west, see Philip H. Gordon and Omer Taspinar, *Winning Turkey: How America, Europe and Turkey Can Revive a Fading Partnership*, (Washington: the Brookings Institution, 2008), pp. 49-84.

85 For recent studies on the Gulfi countries in relation to the latest uprisings in the Arab world, see Bruce O. Riedel, "Saudi Arabia: The Elephant in the Living Rooms," and Suzanne Maloney, "Kuwait, Qatar, Oman and the UAE: the Nervous Bystanders," both in *The Arab Awakening: America and the Transformation of the Middle East*, Kenneth M. Pollack, et al., (Washington: the Brookings Institution, 2011), pp. 159-167, 176-187 consecutively.

to this, and due to its Sunnite confessional identity, such an Islamist alternative is no less antagonist and foe to Iran than America, Europe and Israel. It can be thought of, in this case, as a defensive first front against it. The Iranian factor may actually be a strong motif behind the West's willingness to welcome a non-violent Islamist alternative in Egypt, but also in Syria, if this meant that Syria would join the 'moderate Arabs' campaign again and would tame the militaristic and confrontational secret role of the Islamist campaign against Israel, but mainly in the West itself. If one would follow the logical process of this displayed proposal to its final conclusions, one then should not be surprised if the Muslims Brotherhood organization in Egypt and Syrian and its counterparts in Tunisia, Algeria and Libya was given the green-card from the West, but also from Israel, to start working for its longed-for dream.

The remaining conventional Arabic dictatorships might be seriously mistaken, if they think that the West is still consistently and statically adopting their hypothetical alarming from the catastrophic consequences of the rise of an Islamist ruling alternative in Israel's neighbourhood. These dictatorships might seriously be deluding themselves, if they still think that the West would back them up against their essentially Islamic societies, and help them renew their ruling license. The Arabic region is transforming in such a rapid and radical manner that exceeds in the speedy pace of its surprises and eventual developments all the readily proliferated analysis, anticipations and conclusions. Nevertheless, what one cannot ignore or undermine anymore is the accent shift in the Western political and decision-making circles' appraisals and assessments of the role of political Islam in the Arabic public square.

What, on the other hand, the non-Muslim, non-religious and secularist Arabs cannot postpone dealing with and relating to anymore, is the fact that the Arab world is an Islamic world, whether one likes it or not. The time, when we all, as children of that part of the world, witness the falling down of the nationalist, liberalist, leftist, and pan-Arabist discourses in our societies, is now over. The non-Muslim, secularist, liberal and even non-Islamist Muslim groups must ready themselves intellectually and socially to the possible establishment of Islamist alternatives in the Arab world with the permission and the support of no one else but the Western powers, and on the basis of the West's own best interests and self-rescuing concern. How can the minorities prepare themselves for this?

This question takes us directly to the second part of this study's tripod. In the following part, I will be offering a collection of chapters on how the Christians lived and survived and how they view their presence in the Arab world as a religious minority living and coexisting with a majority Muslim one.

****

Yet, before delving into the second part of this study let me now shed light on some further relevant aspects related to the Syrian revolution. Of the pivotal incidents that took place in relation to the Arabic Spring and the uprising in Syria, two very significant and implicative events that are pertinent to the discussion on the Islamist alternative in the Arab world and the western stance on it, which I discussed in the first part of this chapter, need to be paused at and discussed here.[86] One is related to the revolution in Syria; while the other is linked to the characterizing aftermath of the post-revolution's political developments in Tunisia and Egypt. The first event is the assault on Cairo, which the supporters of the Syrian opposition that is represented by the National Transitional Council committed against the supporters of the Syrian opposition that is represented by the National Coordination Committee. Such an assault marks deep rifts and serious discrepancies between the various Syrian dissenters' stances on the revolution's nature, goals and process; the disconcerting gap, that is, that all of us must probe carefully. The second event is the American Secretary of Foreign Affairs Hillary Clinton's declaration, and for the first time in such an explicit manner, that the United States do not mind constructing common interest relationships with the Islamists who are expected to replace the dictatorial regimes in Tunisia and Egypt, if not the Arab world in general.

In the first part of this chapter I argued that, contrary to its traditional stance, the West today is more reconciled with the possible existence of political Islamist alternatives in the Arab world, even in the Arab countries who are neighbours to Israel. The West would, furthermore, be the primary supporter and ultimate benefactor of aiding political Islam in its authoritarian ambitions in the region. The West, as I argued, would opt

86 The ensuing paragraphs of this section are derived from my Article in Arabic, Najeeb G. Awad, "Ma ʿAlaqat al-Thawra fi Suriyya bel-Mauqif minal Islām As-sīyyasī," (what is the relation of the revolution in Syria with the stance on Political Islam) in *Nawafiz, al-Mustaqbal Newspaper*, 20, November. 2011, N. 4179, p. 9.

for this on the basis of its belief that such a support would tame and belittle the threats of the sociological, cultural and civil ambitions of political Islam in the Western societies by shifting its primary track. The Western powers hope that by supporting the fulfilment of political Islam's ambitions in the Arab world they will be able to reorient the spears of the latter towards its homeland and ultimately drive it to give up its recent focus on the Western world. Today with secretary Clinton's direct expression of America's readiness to ally with any Islamist alternative in the Arab world, the Western powers declare that they stand behind such an option and they reflect their readiness not only to deal with its inevitable reality, but also to frankly bargain and cut strategic deals with it, conceding all the requirements such an alliance deal demands: committing to the give-and-take requirement and the 'embrace-winning-and-accept-losing' rule.

From the perspective of 'give-and-take' deals-cutting, the alphabet of the expected alliance and mutual interest friendship would be as follows: the West would wait for the Islamists to establish pluralist systems that follow the democratic rules of political activity. By committing themselves to this precondition, the Islamists would help the decision making centres in the West in their attempt at re-polishing the image of political Islam and justifying their (the Western powers') alliance with it in front of the secularist and liberal public square and civil society organizations in the Western countries. By the help of the political Islam's commitment to the democratic ruling-game, the Western decision-making centres would promise to give a deaf ear to the critical appraisals of the national and international civil society institutions, human rights activists and the organizations that defend democracy, plurality and civil society values when these latter raise their voices against these growing Islamist regimes' expected ambitions at sociologically, culturally and legislatively islamizing the Arab societies.

In return to the above-mentioned Western lenience towards the social, cultural and legislative islamization of Arab societies, these newly born Islamist regimes are expected to pledge their commitment to the West following a threefold agenda: first, they must promise that they will not threaten the existence and the security of the state of Israel, but rather cooperate in finding a solution to the Arab-Israeli struggle by succumbing to the international endeavour of reducing it into mere Palestinian-Israeli disagreement and by pushing the Palestinians into the table of negotiation, persuading them to compromise their demands and pushing them into accepting a peace-agreement which is patronized by the West and tailored by Israel. Secondly, these Islamist regimes should pledge to clearly and strictly ally with the Western campaign in its clash with the Iranian strategic ambitions, under the name of the Sunnite Arab world's abhorrence of the Iranians' Shi'ism and its ideological and dogmatic attempt at shi'izing the Near East. Thirdly, these newly born Islamist regimes must guarantee the continuous supply of energy to the West, and would maintain the Arab countries' status as the first weapons' buyers in the world; this would help the West in its strife for financial and economic stabilization in the midst of the recent European and American drastic economic recession, massive national debts and unprecedentedly high rate of unemployment crisis. What we should expect to witness, in other words, is an attempt at cutting geostrategic deals with the new Islamist regimes that are very much similar in nature and content to the deals the Americans already have with Turkey and the Gulf countries. The core principle of these alliances is: practice sociological, cultural and legislative islamization in your countries as you like, but stay away from the islamization of the internal political situation of the stately system and also elide from any Islamist approach to the regional geopolitical calculations.

Now with regard to the relation of this equation to the revolution in Syria and the deep rift between the opposition's spectrums, we have to read the Syrian revolution within the framework of the above-mentioned new development in the West's geo-political calculations and options. I do believe that it is necessary to read the Syrian internal and external opposition branches' continuous strategic and tactical mistakes and contradictions – especially the ones that are related to the matters of timing, performance, planning and political interactivity – as strongly demonstrating that all the branches of the Syrian oppositions have lost their chance to play the role of the primary and most influential player in the Syrian scene, let alone the chance to have an impact on the final destination of the revolution. The implosion of the Syrian regime, though inevitable and impending, is no longer in the hands of the National Transitional Council or the National Coordination Committee, and it might even no longer be in the hands of the people on the streets either.

I am not suggesting that the regime would survive and that it will win. The opposite is actually the truth. During the past months, the Syrian regime proved to everybody its conspicuous collapse and its tangible lack of any further control over the daily life and process of the Syrian society, despite the unflinching existence and brutality of its artillery and security forces machine and its cordoning off of the people's affairs in the streets. The head of the regime has totally failed in convincing the world about his ability to deal with the recent crisis on the basis of any political prudence and discretion or the expected wisdom and stances of the statesman. The discourse of reformation, which the president introduced himself to the Syrian public and to the world as its godfather in Syria, has radically failed and proved its falsehood, as it has been immediately replaced by demagogy, violence and coercion. By this, the regime lost the control over its fate and survival, and its destiny has now become conditioned by the general strategic calculations of the presently detectable deal between the West and political Islam in the Arab world, including Syria. Throughout the past ten years, the West has witnessed and verified the Syrian regime's inability to be the West's partner in achieving its threefold strategic agenda in the region; the agenda, that is, which the regime would have granted a place for itself in the new equation had it succumbed to it. To the contrary, the Islamist alternative seems to be willing to show readiness to commit itself to this preconditioning strategic tripod and to cut a deal on it with the West. Therefore, the Ba'thist regime has undoubtedly lost the reasons of its existence on the futural map of the region.

To come back to the Syrian opposition's role, it can no more, in my view, aspire to occupy the role of the main player in the Syrian revolution's scene. It will not be at all the main cause of the regime's collapse. The National Transitional Council has failed in presenting itself as the real, let alone the only, power that is capable of toppling the regime and its rulers by means of either sheer public force, political vision, or any future-oriented strategic view, which the Syrian public can rely on in the post-Ba'th era. On the other hand, the National Coordination Committee, from the very beginning, did not gain broad and influential public support inside Syria, and it did not gain any serious or reliable attention from the West, although its members and followers are the most prominent nationalist, historical dissenting figures inside Syria during the past four decades. In addition to this, there is a deep intellectual and strategic difference between the discourses of these two opposing movements, which fragments their approaches and views and confuses the political performance inside the circles of each; the thing that we started to perpetually witness during the past months, which reached its drastic climax in the embarrassing and shameful assault of the National Council's supporters against the members of the National Coordination Committee that took place in Cairo.

From a realist and pragmatist political point of view, it is easy to expect that the opposition, most probably the National Transitional Council, would be pushed to replace the inevitably falling regime. It is also foreseeable that the creators of this Council and its supporters (the Turks, French and Americans, in specific) would press towards introducing this Council as the expected, and maybe unfortunately the 'only', political alternative in the new Syria, whether this Council gained the support of the majority of the Syrian population or it drastically did not. Yet, this should not blindfold and prevent us from realizing that the regime's implosion and the success of the public riot were not primarily in the hands of either the opposition or the Syrian public-square. If the Syrians found themselves before the inescapable requirement of dealing with the National Transitional Council as the conjectured alternative of the falling regime, there would be a noticeable suspicion among them that the new ruling system should be called the 'winner', for the complexities of the Syrian scene reveal that this winner can be any side except the Syrian official opposing bodies.

What I want to suggest from the previous argument is that we have to read the scandal of the deep rift (and its ensuing aggressiveness) between the opposition segments in Syria, and the implications of these serious differences, within a broader geopolitical framework that is related to the latest Western stance on the rising of political Islam in the region and the West's readiness to cut a new deal based on mutual interest with this alternative. If the regime in Syria was to be demolished, its fall would be the outcome of this new deal, not the result of the oppositions' or the street's role (though the heroic Syrian public-square is the main factor and cause behind the beginning of the end of the regime). On the other hand, if a miracle beyond the boundaries of the analytical logic and available data would happen to take place, namely if the president remained in rule for a transitional period, this also would not be a sign of the regime's victory over the rioting street and the opposition. Both the regime and its fate, on one side, and the oppositions and the fate of the street's protests, on the other, have become part and parcel of a bigger and more complicated game; just one milestone in a longer and more curvy map-track.

The increase of the oppositions' differences and clashes was not but an outcome of a stance-change in their sponsors', Western and local, regional and international, substantial and constructive approach to political Islam and the attempt of the influential powers in the region to re-order the pawns of the Middle Eastern chess board.

Part II
The Christians of the Arab World and the Region's Transformation

Chapter 1: The Christians in the Arab World

When foreigners visit the Near East, aiming at getting acquainted with the region's situation and observing the Christians' condition in context of the Muslim majority in the Arab world, they tend to view the religious life in general, and the one of the Christians' in specific, rather sentimentally, if not euphorically as well. They would immediately admire the daily intermingling of the Christians and the Muslims (and the Jews, as in Jerusalem). As excited tourists, they would also express, as David Kerr once articulated in his description of Jerusalem, fascination with, "the stunning array of architecture," of the various churches in the area

> Syriac churches that witness the earliest development of Christianity in the region; Armenian churches in the style of the earliest Christian pilgrims to Jerusalem; churches in the orthodox style of the Byzantine Greeks who built so much of the original Christian architecture of the holy city [Jerusalem]; the Coptic and Ethiopian churches representing the ancient pilgrimage tradition of African Christianity; the Latin architectural styles of medieval Catholic Crusaders and of the Franciscan mission in the *Terra Sancta* and the western-style churches of the Anglican, Lutheran and Reformed traditions…[87]

This religious mosaic, which is actually inherent to the Near Eastern context ever since it existed in history,[88] is, no doubt, fascinating and unde-

87 David A. Kerr, "A Western Christian Appreciation of the Eastern Christianity," in *Who Are the Christians in the Middle East?* Betty Jane Bailey & J. Martin Bailey, (Grand Rapids, USA/Cambridge, UK: W.B. Eerdmans Publishing Company, 2003), pp. 3-11, pp. 3-4.

88 In an article on the recent Arab uprisings, Thomas Friedman points perceptively to this background in the whole Arab world when he states, comparing this region with Europe, "let us start with the structure of the Arab state. Think about the 1989 democracy wave in Europe. In Europe, virtually every state was like Germany, a

niably impressive. The Near Easterners have always prided themselves about it in front of the whole world.

However, when it comes to perceiving the real situation of the Christians in the Arab world and constructing a realistic picture about their life therein, this stunning array of churchly architecture and external intermingling in daily life, let alone the multi-denominational and multicultural life it depicts, can sometimes be a serious concealment, rather than disclosure, of the real situation. The external rich history of plurality that is portrayed via the architectural versatility hides underneath it an internal, parallel history of suffering, uncertainty, fear, pressure, difficulties, death and perpetual strife for survival as a minority in a non-Christian majority world. The Christians also recognize this parallel history as no less, if no more, stunning, still progressing process of existence in the region. It is the other, grim side of their historical existence's story in the area, which, as David Kerr also acknowledges,[89] overburdened the Christians and their diversity alike with theological disagreements between the churches, the *dhimmi* statues the Muslims imposed on the non-Muslim citizens of the Caliphate, the drastic ramifications of the crusaders' invasion of the region in the name of Christ and many other rules and situations that perpetuated, rather than demolished, the Christians difficult conditions.

In the Christian churches of the Near East or the Arab world, one not only audits the echoes of the abovementioned past history of survival through difficulties. One also encounters the features of the Arab Christians' difficulties in today's world as well. The Christians of the Arab world are no longer treated as *dhimmis* today, and the Muslims do no longer consider themselves remnants of, or allies of, those Templar, who came from Europe to 'repossess the Holy City, Jerusalem' with a crucifix ornamenting their shields and military jumpers. However, the Christians of the Near East do still live under critical and difficult situations related to their number and influence.

In today's scholarship, the researchers of World Christianity and its intercultural, global relationships tend to point in an emphatic accent to the fact of the transformation of Christianity in modernity from a dominantly

---

homogenous nation, except Yugoslavia. The Arab world is exactly the opposite. There, virtually every state is like Yugoslavia – except Egypt, Tunisia and Morocco": Friedman, "Pray. Hope. Prepare."

89 Kerr, "A Western Christian Appreciation of the Eastern Christianity," p. 5.

European and North American, religious phenomenon (and these powers' colonizing tool sometimes) into a worldwide, genuine and cultural, ethnically and geographically versatile community.[90] They even go further in affirming that this transformation reveals a crucial geographical shift of Christianity's graphite centre from Europe and the north-western half of the globe into its south-eastern half, as well as to the rapidly escalating spread of Christian belief through Africa, Latin America, Middle-Asia and the Far East. In his book of 2007, Philip Jenkins eloquently describes this inexorable move of Christianity southward, when he says that

> over the last century, however, the centre of gravity in the Christian world has shifted inexorably southward, to Africa and Latin America. Today, the larger Christian communities on the planet are to be found in those regions. If we want to visualize a 'typical' contemporary Christian, we should think of a woman living in a village in Nigeria, or in a Brazilian *favela*. In parts of Asia too, churches are growing rapidly, in numbers and self-confidence. As Kenyan scholar John Mbiti has observed, 'the centres of the church's universality [are] no longer in Geneva, Rome, Athens, Paris, London, New York, but Kinshasa, Buenos Aires, Addis Ababa and Manila.' Whatever Europeans or North Americans may believe, Christianity is doing very well indeed in the global south – not just surviving but expanding.[91]

Yet, in their stress on Christianity's worldwide growth on these continents, these scholars hardly talk about a similar Christian demographic growth or religious development in the Near-East or the Arab world. Contrary to Africa, Asia and Latin America, one can hardly notice a radical, evident growth of the Christian community in the Muslim majority area, like the Arab world. Despite the renewal and revival movements

---

90 Noel Davies and Martin Conway, *World Christianity in the Twentieth Century*, (London: SCM Press, 2008), p. 12: "overall, however, there can be no doubt that by the end of the twentieth century the Christianity that was at the beginning so definitely identified with the colonizing powers of Europe and North America has been widened and recast into a genuinely worldwide community. No doubt with a huge complexity of distinct sub-units and internal differences, even quarrels."

91 Philip Jenkins, *The Next Christendom: the Coming of Global Christianity*, rev. ed., (Oxford & New York: Oxford University Press, 2007), pp. 1-2. See also Kwame Bediako, *Christianity in Africa*, (Edinburgh: Edinburgh University Press/Orbis Books, 1995), p. 154.

one can witness in the autochthonous Near Eastern churches, like the Coptic Church in Egypt. Despite also the evangelising activities of the Arabic-speaking, fundamental and charismatic Protestant churches, like the ones of Syria, Lebanon, Jordan and Palestine, the Christians' numbers in this part of the world have drastically decreased during the twentieth century due to the high immigration rate of the region's Christians. The scale of the Christians' decline is on the demographic, sociological and cultural scales indelibly high, as a fast look at the radical drop-down of the Christians' percentage in the region's countries during the past forty years clearly shows. In his chapter on the Christians in the Arab world, the ex-General Secretary of the Middle East Council of Churches, Riad Jarjour, states some examples about the Christians' declination in the Arab World:

> Forty years ago Christians in Iraq made up 6 percent of the population; today they are only 3 percent. Before the civil war in Lebanon began in 1975, Christians constituted half of the population; today they are about 40 percent. In 1948 Christians composed 50 percent of Jerusalem's residents; today they are not more than 1o percent and a significant number of these are expatriates.[92]

The suffering and persecution the Christians have experienced in some of the Arab countries (like Egypt and most recently Iraq), and the general political, economic and social suppression and difficulties in other Arab countries (like Syria, Lebanon and Palestine), all exerted on the Christians unbearable pressures and compelled a large number of them to immigrate into other lands, searching for better and more secure contexts, opportunities and future. One can validly say that while the world still speaks about eastern Christianity and its historical presence in the Arab world, most of the eastern Christians, who represent this heritage and carry it in their narratives, memories, convictions, values and even genes, live outside the eastern Christianity's homeland. To borrow Pierre Nora's eloquent words, while the churches, graveyards and other material elements of eastern Christendom's history still play the role of *'lieux de memoire'* or the places of memory in the region, the '*milieux de Memoire'* or "the familiar landscapes of living memory," namely the living

92 Riad Jarjour, "The Future of Christians in the Arab World," in *Who Are the Christians in the Middle East?*, pp. 12-21, pp. 13-14.

beings and successive generations of Christians, have either almost disappeared or conspicuously became very few.[93]

Those foreigners who visit the Middle East driven be religious interests do not just come over to converge with the Christians on the ground of the birthplace of Christianity, where Jesus Christ was born, lived, had his ministry and crucifixion. They also, if not primarily, come to conduct first-hand observation and experience primary contact with those Christians who still exist in the midst of the Muslim world. One of the main particularities that demarcates the Christians of the East from other Christian communities in the Western, if not the entire, world is the story of their survival and consistent presence in the world of Islam, of how they preserved their religious identity and faith in this context and of what sort of integration and adaptation methods they followed to make the Muslims consider them part and parcel of the Arabic-Islamic culture.

In his study of the beginning of the eastern Christians' gain of an endured, peaceful and sustainable presence in the world of Islam, Sidney Griffith perceptively states that

> the Christians who lived in the word of Islam shaped their enduring ecclesial identities, both culturally and intellectually, within the context of several local determining circumstances: their encounter with the Muslims, their adoption of the Arabic language, and their isolation from other Christian communities outside of the Islamic world.[94]

The new situation, which the eastern Christians found themselves required to survive in, not only expresses the beginning of these Christians' Arabization in terms of culture and theology. It also represents the first

---

93 Pierre Nora, *Zwischen Geschichte und Gedächtnis*, (Frankfurt am Main: Fischer, 1998), p. 11. Also cited in Ania Peleikis, "The Making and Unmaking of Memories: the Case of a Multi-Confessional Village in Lebanon," in *Memory and Violence in the Middle East and North Africa*, Ussama Makdisi and Paul A. Silverstein (eds.), (Bloomington and Indianapolis: Indiana University Press, 2006), pp. 133-150, p. 140.

94 Sidney H. Griffith, *The Church in the Shadow of the Mosque: Christians and Muslims in the World of Islam*, (Princeton: Princeton University Press, 2008), p. 130. Griffith believes that this isolation from other Christians applies even to the Melkite Church, who professed the faith of the Byzantine imperial orthodoxy.

chapter in the narrative of these churches' historical alienation from their Latin western brethren, ecclesially and politically.

When the westerners or non-easterners visit the homeland of eastern Christianity chasing after the historical marks and fingerprints of this history, they express their fascination with the Christian mosaic in the region and, puzzled, they wonder how these various Christian denominations could make it through that history without compromising this impressive variety. The same impressiveness was in fact symptomatic of the attitude of the Muslims of the Arab peninsula when they invaded the land of Syria for the first time and encountered its local inhabitants. The Muslim observers and thinkers, who paused at these various Christians churches' existence in the midst of the Muslim caliphate, did not content themselves with the first impression of fascination. They rather endeavoured seriously to go beyond it, as Griffith notices, towards making their best efforts to "describe and understand the difference between the Melkites, Jacobites, Nestorians and their associated ecclesial communities."[95] In their studies of the Christians, the Muslims noticed mere theological differences that, despite their seriousness, fail in concealing these churches' agreement on almost every element in Christian faith, as the Muslims believed. Griffith goes even as far as saying that this Islamic scholarly initiative drove the Christians themselves to highlight their commonalities more deliberately than before in replacement of their traditional focus on discrepancies, opting eventually for developing an ecumenical presentation of Christianity to withstand the Muslims' critiques and challenges to Christian faith. Griffith's eloquent description of this worth citation in length:

---

95 Ibid., pp.140-141. Griffith names in particular Muslim authors like Abū 'Īsā al-Warrāq (d. ca. 860), the Mu'tazilite 'Abd al-Jabbār al-Hamadhānī (d. 1025), and the Andalūsī scholar Ibn Ḥazm (994-1064). See on them David Thomas, *Anti-Christian Polemics in Early Islam: Abū 'Īsā al-Warrāq's 'Against the Trinity'*, (Cambridge: Cambridge University Press, 1992), no. 45; D. Thomas, *Early Muslim Polemics Against Christianity: Abū 'Īsā al-Warrāq's 'Against the Incaranation'*, (Cambridge: Cambridge University Press, 2002), no. 59; S. Stern, "'Abd al-Jabbār's Account of How Christ's Religion Was Falsified by the Adoption of Roman Customs," in *Journal of Theological Studies*, 19, 1968, pp. 128-185; Gabriel Said Reynolds, *A Muslim Theologian in the Sectarian Milieu: 'Abd al-Jabbār and the Critique of Christian Origins,* (Leiden: Brill, 2004), Islamic History and Civilization Studies and Texts, Vol. 56; and Theodore Pulcini, *Exegesis as Polemical Discourse: Ibn Ḥazm on Jewish and Christian Scriptures*, (Atlanta: Scholars Press, 1998).

> there were also some ecumenists among the Christians writers who thought that in the face of the multiple challenges from Islam it would behove the Christians to look beyond their mutual differences for the sake of presenting a united defence of Christianity's claim to be the true religion.[96]

This ecumenical strategy, in addition to the adoption of Arabic language, not only served in uniting the Christian fronts before the Muslims' polemics. They also, as Griffith maintains, opened a public communication channel with the Muslims about religion and culture.[97] These interactions venues, in turn, made the Christians opt for rewriting their theology in new key terms, other than the conventional Greek and Syriac ones. Yet, and more significantly still, interactions with Islam drove these Christians into developing a new identity and societal, let alone religious, character as 'Arab Christians'. This arabization process may actually be the main cause of the Muslim scholars' realization in the legacy of Islam, especially during the earliest phase of the process of Islam's self-definition, of the Christian elements that, "provided both the template and the foil for so much of what would become the characteristically Islamic exegetical and liturgical idiom."[98]

This early phase of the relation between the eastern Christians and their Arabic Muslim context never remained the title of the beginning of their story together. It showed, instead, its face in the ensuing centuries of the region's history. Even after the Christian communities declined into demographic insignificance, and despite these communities' primary occupation with survival by means of establishing support links with the Christians outside the Islamic world, the Christians did not quit aspiring to playing an influential role in the region's destiny by means of purporting to present themselves before their Muslim compatriots as an ecumenically unified and solidly consistent, social and religious body.

This strategy became the more necessary centuries later; when, the Christians found themselves struggling to survive under the hegemonic

---

96 Griffith, *The Church in the Shadow of the Mosque*, p. 141.

97 Ibid., p.156.

98 Ibid., p.159. See also on the Christian impact John wansbrough, The Sectarian Milieu. Content and Composition of Islamic Salvation History, (Oxford: Oxford University Press, 1978). There is also a similar Jewish impact on the Islamic legacy pointed at, for example, in Uri Rubin, *Between Bible and Qur'ān: the Children of Israel and the Islamic Self-Image*, (Princeton: Princeton University Press, 1999).

rule of the Ottoman Empire. Under the Turks' rule, the Christians had to present as much a monolithic identity as their denominational variety allows in a society, where the individual's legal status, as Bruce Masters notices, is, "vested in one's religious identity as much as it was in one's gender," and, "the question of who constituted the majority and the minority," was transparently influential.[99] In the midst of this context, the Christians faced another integration and adaptation expectation, as they found themselves surviving the minority status's pressurizing consequences by revising and modelling their contacts to European merchants and missionaries according to the evolvement of the sultanate's diplomatic and political calculations and alliances,[100] and also verifying their endogenous, national identities and affiliations to the region in accordance with the public ideological fluctuations and trends.[101] Living in such a monistic, collectivist and homogenized social, political and religious setting, the Christians almost habituated the Muslim majority's undermining of and indifferences to their denominational particularities and ecclesial distinctions and to treating them, instead, "as constituting one 'nation' (*millet*) even while recognizing what were to them the undoubtedly irrelevant, and most probably capricious, divisions upon which the Christians had insisted."[102]

In conclusion, underneath the external facade of variety, colourful interaction and interreligious co-existence, which fascinates the foreign tourists and visitors in the Arab Near East, lurks another more sophisticated, and less ideal and bright, history, wherein the Christians purported

---

99 Bruce Masters, *Christians and Jews in the Ottoman Arab World: the Roots of Secularism*, (Cambridge: Cambridge University Press, 2001), pp. 5-6.

100 Bernard Lewis points to trade and diplomacy as two factors of the relation between the Turks and the west: Lewis, *What Went Wrong?*, pp. 3-34. Lewis argues that even when the Turks were victorious in their military advancing through south-eastern Europe, they would still rely in getting their needed supplies and equipments on the European merchants, experts and banks (Ibid., p.13). On the other hand, the Ottomans learned, according to Lewis, the art of diplomacy also from the Europeans and used it to modify or reduce the military outcomes. For them, diplomacy was all about "how to negotiate the best terms they could after a military defeat" (Ibid., p.19). In both cases, I believe, the Turks used the eastern Christians (and Jews) as mediators between them and the European merchants, business men and politicians and they expected the relations between the Christian churches in the Middle East and their western brethren to serve the sultanate's best interests.

101 Masters, *Christians and Jews in the Ottoman Arab World*, p. 13.

102 Ibid., p.64.

to survive and maintain their rich, variable particularities despite the Muslim's reduction of them into single monolithic, homogenous *millet*, and notwithstanding the Muslims' identification of the Christians with the often distrusted and hated European powers, because they both share the same religious faith.[103] Unless one apprehends in depth these challenges and their role in the formation of the eastern Christians' story in the Arab world, it is hardly possible to see in the external image of the Christian-Muslim coexistence in the region an entrance to the internal maze of this coexistence's details in the past, but more significantly in the present. I will be speaking in further detail about the Christians' relationship to their living conditions among an Arab-Muslim majority in the following chapter.

Chapter 2: The Christians' Drainage and the 'Persecution' Threat

The causes of the Christians' displacement from the Arab world vary according to the context and circumstances of each of the countries, where the Christians are part of the population.

In Lebanon, where they were they provided almost 50 percent of the population until recently, the Christians were first torn apart and fragmented and later forced out of the country because of the 15 year-long civil strife. The civil war that began in 1975 and apparently ended in 1989 has cost the country, "two hundred thousands of dead, hundreds of thousands more wounded both physically and psychologically, and a country in ruins." This war's ramifications, as Saree Maqdisī eloquently states, still linger on in [the Lebanese'] discordant time',[104] jeopardizing the country's unity and putting it perpetually at the brink of renewed division. The war between the sects, whether the ones of Lebanon or those who fought each other *on* its land, not only displaced the Christians from conventional Lebanese villages that used to be oases of coexistence and trans-confessional interaction.[105] It more drastically coerced the Christians to flee in large numbers from the Near East and the drastically un-

103 Ibid., p.194.

104 Saree Makdisi, "Beirut, a City without History?" in *Memory and Violence in the Middle East and North Africa*, pp. 201-214, p. 201.

105 Peilikis, "The Making and Unmaking of Memories: the Case of a Multi-confessional Village in Lebanon," pp. 133-138.

stable and insecure conditions of Lebanon, as the latter remains until this very moment part of the battlefield zone of the Arab-Israeli and Iranian-American clashes. There is no doubt that Lebanon's fragile situation drives all the Lebanese, Christians and Muslims alike, to opt for emigration. Yet, in light of the Muslim majority framework of the Arab social fabric, the decline of the number of Lebanese Christians' would proportionally lay its negative impacts on the overall Christian existence in the region, turning the Christians in the Arab world, and not only in Lebanon, into a much smaller minority than it already is. Though the Christians in Lebanon are still principally and jurisdictionally considered as a constitutive and inherent element in the Lebanese state and nation by their Muslim compatriots from all denominations, the question of religious and sectarian coexistence and what form of partnership should be applied in the country remains a verily open question.[106]

In Iraq, the Christians have still another story to tell.[107] Up until the last days of the Ba'thi regime of Saddam Hussein, the Christians, despite Saddam's ruthless and brutal rule, enjoyed a relatively peaceful and secure existence. This situation radically changed after Gulf-War I and rapidly became much worse since the US-led invasion of the country in 2003. Yet, the history of the Christians in the country indicates that they had times of difficulties during the past centuries, two not very old examples of which would be the Ottoman Turks' massacre of the Assyrians in the second half of the nineteenth century and the native Iraqis massacre of the Christians in the country in 1933, right after the independence.[108] The massive rate of losses of such and other massacres, led after 1947 to the Christians' emigration from Iraq mainly to America.

During the Ba'thi regime's rule in Iraq, the Christians were granted freedom of worship just like other religious sects in the country, though the secular ideology of the regime, like in the case in Syria, and despite its recognition of Islam as the state's religion, used to strictly limit the role of religions and to compel a common Arab identity as the base of

---

106 See the brief, yet valuable, collection of views and opinions on the issue of coexistence in Theodore Hanf, *E Pluribus Unum? Lebanese Opinions & Attitudes on Coexistence*, (Byblos: International Centre for Human Sciences/ Friedrich-Ebert-Stiftung, 2007).

107 On Christianity in Iraq in the modern time, read Anthony O'Mahony, "Christianity in Modern Iraq," in *International Journal for the Study of the Christian Church*, 2(4), 2004, pp. 121-142.

108 Bailey & Bailey, *Who Are the Christians in the Middle East?*, p. 162-165.

belonging to, and living in, the republic.[109] On the economic, educational and civil service levels, the Christians also used to enjoy equal treatment and privileges, except for some occasions.[110] When, however, some of the socioeconomic difficulties would strangle the general condition of the country, the Christians would experience some violent reactions from religious extremists, without this, till that time, lead to any systematic, fanatic and brutal persecution from the Muslims towards their Christian fellow citizens. On the other hand, receiving good treatment from Saddam's regime (some of the Christians were even in prominent governmental positions) did not save the Christians from death and did not spare their churches from destruction when, for instance, Saddam's special-forces attacked the Kurdish areas.[111]

The Iraqi Christians' situation got drastically worse after the invasion of 2003 and the collapse of Saddam's regime, and they have abandoned the country in masses ever since. According to the Chaldian Catholic Bishop of Baghdad, Andraeos Abouna, of the 1.2 million Christians of the country hardly 600,000 have remained in the country after the invasion, and 75 per cent of Baghdad's Christians have deserted the city for good.[112] This means that the three to five percent of the population, which the Christians used to make up in Iraq, is not going to be retrieved in any seen future. The Christians found themselves trapped helplessly and hopelessly in-between the fiercely and violently clashing Muslim sects in post-Saddam Iraq. Their houses, shops and churches experience vandalism and loathing on an almost daily basis, and they personally were defined by Al-Qaida's Iraqi affiliates as the 'infidels' and 'collaborators', who use their dirty religious places (churches) as bases for the enemies of Islam. Such fanatic and offensive views led, for example, in October 2010 to the terrible hostage takeover and the ensuing brutal and bloody massacre of the parishioners and the priests of the Church of Our Lady of Salvation in Baghdad.[113] The operators of this single crime left behind 58 casualties, 75 injured. The two priests celebrating the mass that day were

109 See on this O'Mahony, "Christianity in Modern Iraq," pp. 128-133.

110 Bailey & Bailey, *Who Are the Christians in the Middle East?*, pp. 164-165.

111 Davies & Conway, *World Christianity in the 20th Century*, p. 97.

112 A report titled "Christians Flee Sectarian Violence in Iraq," in America, August 28-September 4, 2006, p. 6.

113 Rosie Malek-Yonan and Soner Önder, "The Baghdad Assyrian Church Massacre: Waiting for Godot!," in *Assyrian International News Agency*, http://www.aina.org/releases/20101124002721.htm , 11,24, 2010.

also dead, one of which was heartlessly and mercilessly beheaded. Such crimes not only terrified the Iraqi Christians and forced them more rapidly outside the country. They also influence the other Arab Christians in the region and make them always look toward the West for refuge and escape.

If the pressurizing situation in Iraq is relatively recent in the life of the Christians, it is not so in the life of the Christians of Palestine; they not only face the challenge of coexisting with a rapidly growing Islamic extremism, but also a strongly influential and no less fanatic Jewish extremism as well. Within the Israeli state's territories, the Christians represent about two percent of the total population. Though they hold Israeli passports and they are jurisdictionally considered 'legal citizens', they are known, with the other Palestinians (Muslims and Druzes), who refused to abandon their possessions and depart, by the discriminative name 'the Arab Israeli'. Within the Palestinian expected-to-be state's territories, the Christians are estimated to be three percent of the whole population. There too, the Christians' life is not secure, as the life of all the Palestinians in general can hardly be described as such. But, since they are a minority, the drastic economic and humanitarian consequences of the bleak and suffocating political situation lays heavily on the Christians and coerces them to seek more fulfilling circumstances for themselves and their families abroad. No wonder that due to this desperate and hopeless situation there are hundreds of thousands of Palestinian Christians who live in the diaspora, and which represent more than 60 percent of all the Palestinian Christians.[114]

There is no argument that the Palestinian Christians are privileged with a geographical prerogative, which other Arab Christians do not have. They belong to, and live in, what is considered by all the Christians around the world as the 'Holy Land' and the 'Birthplace' of Christianity's founders (Jesus of Nazareth, first, and the Apostles, second). Yet, despite this location's uniqueness, and while other Arab Christians are a single

---

114 Bailey & Bailey, *Who Are the Christians in the Middle East?*, p. 156. According the Palestinina Lutheran priest and theologian, Rev. Dr. Mitri Rahib, there are around 120,000 Palestinian Christian in Israel and 60,000 in the West Bank and Gaza Strip, while in the diaspora there are around 300,000 Palestinian Christians. over all, the Palestinian Christians are 500,000 in number, which makes them 7-10% of the total Palestinian population: Mitri Raheb, "Sailing Through Troubled Waters: Palestinian Christians in the Holy Land," in *Dialog: A Journal of Theology*, 2(41), 2002, pp. 97-102, p. 98.

minority in their Muslim-majority countries, the Christian Palestinians are "a 'double minority' existing with varying degrees of discomfort alongside two much larger religious communities," namely the Muslims and the Jews.[115] Another unique feature in the Palestinian Christians' life is related to their ecclesial institutions. Although the Israeli State and the Palestinian territories are segregated from each other with all kinds of security checkpoints and separation walls, the ecclesiastical structures of the different Christian denominations are strongly unified and work as a single entity among the two states, the fact that gives the churches a useful and practically fruitful prerogative in fostering peace and mediating between the communities of the clashing sides, should the Palestinians and the Israelis allowed them to and supported them in doing so.[116]

In 2005 the patriarchs and the heads of churches in Jerusalem, many of whom are Palestinian Christians, issued an Easter message, wherein they told all the inhabitants of the holy land:

> we [the Christians] are sent to our society to fill it with the power of love that builds and gives back life to what has demolished...we are called to raise the *olive branch of forgiveness*...with the power of forgiveness, we persevere in claiming our rights, our freedom, our Land and our dignity, together with security for all, as we also persevere in affirming the possibility for the two peoples {Palestinians and Israelis] to live together in peace.[117]

115 Bailey & Bailey, *Who Are the Christians in the Middle East?*, p. 150.

116 One of the perspectives of such a role is the social, nonviolent, proactive and inclusive work to be conducted by the Christians churches, not only for their own communities but also as a symbol of mediatorial reconciliation and tolerance means between the Jews and the Arabs in general. Read on this potential Saliba Sarsar, "Palestinian Christians: Religion, Conflict and the Struggle for Just Peace," in *Holy Land Studies*, 2(4), 2005, pp. 27-50. Another perspective is developing a Palestinian Liberation theology that mediate between the western Christians and the eastern Muslims, convincing both of the relevance of a Christian theology of justification for a political solution to the Israeli-Palestinian struggle. See on this option Laura C. Robson, "Palestinian Liberation Theology, Muslim-Christian Relations and the Arab-Israeli Conflict," in *Islam and Christian-Muslim Relations*, 1(21), 2010, pp. 39-50.

117 www.wfn.org 3, April. 2005 and also in Saliba Sarsar, "Palestinian Christians: Religion, Conflict and the Struggle for Just Peace," p. 51.

In his presentation of the alternative that the Palestinian Christians present to mediate between the two conflicting sides in reaction to the violent attitude each maintains towards the other, Saliba Sarsar shows that the mediatorial role of the Christians lies in their belief in the steadfastness against the Israeli occupation of the Palestinian territories, yet also their conviction and insistence on a non-violent strategy for achieving this purpose.[118] The Palestinian Christians closely identify with Palestinian nationalism and raise their voices in advocating it. Yet, they also respect the Israelis' nationalism and insist on inviting both sides to free their concern about nationalism from any violent, confrontational or denying method.[119] One of the most prominent Palestinian Christians, who in his approach represents a mediatorial standpoint in the conflict and the Palestinain-Israeli relations, is patriarch Michael Sabbah. Patriarch Sabbah builds his reconciliatory approach to the conflict on the following four pillars: truth, justice, love and freedom, which implies in relation to the hoped-for peace acknowledgment of rights and duties, respect of other's rights and to act responsibly in the world, feeling solidarity towards the other's needs and finally opting for choices that accord with natural reason.[120] In this mediatorial, violence countering approach to the

118 Sarsar, "Palestinian Christians: Religion, Conflict and the Struggle for Just Peace," p. 39. For some variables on this principle, see for example Jonathan Kuttab and Mubarak Awad, "Non-Violent Resistance in Palestine: Pursuing Alternative Strategies," in www.palestinecenter.org 29, March. 2002; and Edward W. Said, *The Politics of dispossession: the Struggle for Palestinian Self-Determination*, (New York: Pantheon, 1994); Sami al-Deeb, "From Dhimma Regime to One Democratic State in Palestine/Israel" in www.lpj.org ; and al-Deeb, "For a Single Democratic and Secular State," in www.lpj.org 2003; and 'Azmi Bshara, "Arab Citizens of Palestine: Little to Celebrate," in *Tikkun Magazine* 13(4), www.tikkun.org July/August. 1998.

119 Sarsar, "Palestinian Christians: Religion, Conflict and the Struggle for Just Peace," p. 40. See also Michael Dumper, "The Christian Churches of Jerusalem in the Post-Oslo Period,." in *Journal of Palestine Studies*, 31(2), 2002, pp. 51-65.

120 Michel Sabbah, "Sunday Homily to *Pax Christi* International in New Jersey, USA," in www.storage.paxchristi.net 23, May. 2004. Other church Palestinian leaders have also similar mediatorial approach to the conflict. See, for example Rafiq Khoury, *Identity Cards of a Son of the Country*, (Cambridge, MA: Harvard University Press, 2003); Bernard Sabella, "Of Pilots, Suicide Bombings and Leadership," at *Theological Reflections* in www.cmep.org 10, October. 2003; Ross Dunn, "Arab Christians Urge Israeli Compatriots to Mend Divisions," in *Ecumenical News International* at www.orthodoxnews.netfirms.com 15, May. 2003; Na'im S. 'Atīq, "There is Another Way: the Way of Nonviolence, the Way of fidelity," in

conflict like the above displayed one, the Palestinian Christians offer, in Sarsar's words, "an inclusive vision for Palestinians and Israelis." Yet, this mediatorial approach is not fully appreciated or allowed noticeable impact on the conflict, for the Palestinian Christians are accused by the Israelis and the American Christians of nationalism and by the extremist Arabs of lack of patriotism.[121]

In general, one can say that the Palestinian Christians, though a minority like other Christians in the Arab world, are not a marginalized or a self-centred group, but rather a socially, ecclesiastically and educationally engaged and contributive community, especially in the West Bank. They insist on this role in society, because they share the same fears and hopes with their neighbours, the Muslims and the Jews, and they stand on the same front of the call for having a peaceful, secure and prosperous future for the Arabs and the Jews alike.[122] Be that as it may, when it comes to persecution, Mitri Raheb maintains that if "persecution means systematic policy of discrimination because of beliefs,... Neither in Israel nor in Palestine are Christians persecuted for [their] faith in Christ." Yet, Rev. Raheb continues, in both contexts the Christians face serious difficulties and pressures. In the Palestinian territories, the Christians, like the Muslims, suffer from the Israeli occupation and its impossible preconditions and rules, and they feel that the Muslims and Christians stand in total solidarity when it comes to this paralyzing condition.[123] While, in Israel the Palestinian Christians are treated, as Raheb maintains, discrimina-

---

Corner Stone, 28, 2003, pp. 1-3; Jerry Levin, "Historic Gatherings in Birmingham: Hear Naim Ateek Make Case for 'Justice with Mercy' for Palestine," in www.adventbirmingham.org. 2001; Jean Zaru, "A Christian Palestinian Life – Faith and Struggle," in www.globalministries.org 30, October. 2003; Riah Abu el-Assal, *Caught in Between: the Extraordinary Story of an Arab Palestinian Christian Israeli*, (London: SPCK, 1999); Munib A. Younan, *Witnessing for Peace in Jerusalem and the World*, Fred Strickert (ed.,), (Minneapolis: Fortress Press, 2003); and Elias Chacour et. al, Mary E. Jensen, *We Belong to the Land*, (San Francisco: HarperCollines Publishers, 1992).

121 Sarsar, "Palestinian Christians: Religion, Conflict and the Struggle for Just Peace," p. 43. See on this double-accusation attitude Mitri Raheb, *I Am A Palestinian Christian*, Ruth C.L. Gritsch (trans.), (Minneapolis: Fortress Press, 1995), p. 102.

122 Raheb, "Sailing Through Troubled Waters: Palestinian Christians in the Holy Land," p. 99.

123 For a good article on such solidarity between the Christian and the Muslim Palestinians read Glenn Bowman, "A Death revisited: Solidarity and Dissonance in a Muslim-Christian Palestinian Community," in *Memory and Violence in the Middle East and North Africa*, pp. 27-49.

tively as second-class citizens because they are looked at primarily as Arabs, that is 'non-Jews'.[124] Such a difficult circumstance, as Raheb concludes, makes "the symbol of the church as a ship sailing through troubled waters…an apt description of the Palestinian Christian community…it takes great efforts for a small community like the Palestinian Christian community to resist all the different groups who try to pirate this ship and to lead it to their own ends."[125]

In Egypt, where we have the largest Christian group in the Arab world, in terms of its members' number and not in terms of its percentage in the population, the causes of emigration are different from the ones of Lebanon or any other Arab country.[126] The Egyptian Christians introduce themselves as the descendents of the ancient race of the Pharaohs, who inhibited the land since the dawn of earliest civilization in Egypt. They also claim to have embraced Christianity via the apostolic work of the apostle Mark in 64 CE. The word 'Copt' itself is derived from the Greek word *Aiguptos*, which itself might be a philological variation from the ancient pharaonitic city '*Hwt-ka-Ptah'* , also known by the name 'Memphis'.[127] In the year 641 AD, Egypt was invaded by the Muslim troops of the Arab of the peninsula. During the time of the invasion, the Christians

---

124 Raheb, "Sailing Through Troubled Waters: Palestinian Christians in the Holy Land," p. 100. In his description of the Israeli State's religious nature, Geoffrey Levey points out that "the ethno-religious character of the Jews for whom the state was created, the 'status-quo' concessions to the religious parties at the state's founding, the absence of any civil alternative to prescribed religious jurisdictions such as marriage and divorce – which sees many non-observant Israelis opting to marry abroad – and an electoral system that magnifies the influence of minor sectarian parties all combine seriously to entangle religion and politics": Geoffrey Brahm Levey, "Secularism and Religion in a Multicultural Age," in *Secularism, Religion and Multicultural Citizenship*, pp. 1-24, p. 12.

125 Raheb, "Sailing Through Troubled Waters: Palestinian Christians in the Holy Land," p. 101.

126 For a general survey of the Copts' life situation and its development in the present Egypt, see the inclusive presentation in Christine Chaillot, "The Life and Situation of the Coptic Orthodox Church Today," in *Studies in World Christianity*, 3(15), 2009, pp. 199-216.

127 Randall P. Henderson, "The Egyptian Coptic Christians: the Conflict between Identity and Equality." in *Islam and Christian-Muslim Relations*, 16(2), 2005, pp. 155-166, pp. 155-157. See also J. Kamil, *Christianity in the Land of the Pharaohs*, (London & New York: Routledge, 2002).

made up 80 per cent of the whole population of the land,[128] and the relations between the Copts and the new Muslim comers witnessed positive and peaceful cooperation and coexistence, contrasting the formers' negative and unfriendly attitude toward the Byzantine previous rulers, despite the Byzantines' Christian belief.[129] In the following centuries, from the fourteenth century onwards, the Muslims' treatment of the Copts was influenced by the intellectual and ideological trends that permeated the Egyptian society, like secularism, nationalism, pan-Arabism and pan-Islamism. This sometimes brought with it bad consequences, yet some other times it brought good ones. The Copts, nevertheless, opted for sharing an Arab identity with their Muslim neighbours, such a choice that made the Copts experience with their Muslim compatriots the same threats to their one identity by various other foreign powers that invaded Egypt throughout the centuries.[130]

It is of evident difficulty, as Randall Henderson correctly notices, to formulate one objective and factual understanding of the relation of the Copts and the Muslims in Egypt, given the complicated and multifaceted interactions between these two communities throughout the thirteen centuries of coexistence in Egypt.[131] This difficulty notwithstanding, one can still concur with Henderson's belief that, "one challenge left for Coptic Christian leadership is providing Egyptian Christians with an identity that is associated not only with the cross of martyrdom and persecution, but with emancipation and the motivation to take what is theirs."[132] One of the postulates of this belief is the division that some scholars spot within

128 N.A. Malek, "The Copts: from An Ethnic Majority to a Religious Minority," in *Acts of the Fifth International Congress of Coptic Studies*, D.W. Johnson (ed.), (Rome: International Association of Coptic Studies, 1993), pp. 299-312, pp. 299-300.

129 Henderson, "The Egyptian Coptic Christians: the Conflict between Identity and Equality." p. 156. See also A.H. Siddiqi, *Non-Muslims under Muslim Rule and Muslims under Non-Muslim Rule*, (Karachi: Jamiyatul Falah Publication, 1969), pp. 57-59.

130 Henderson, "The Egyptian Coptic Christians: the Conflict between Identity and Equality." pp. 157-158. See also Muhammad El-Hadi Afifi, *The Arabs and the United Nations*, (London: Longmans, Green & Co., 1964); and S.S. Hasan, *Christians Versus Muslims in Modern Egypt: the Century-Long Struggle for Coptic Equality*, (Oxford: Oxford University Press, 2003).

131 Henderson, "The Egyptian Coptic Christians: the Conflict between Identity and Equality." p. 159.

132 Ibid., p.165.

the Coptic community, the approach of which should be followed by the Christians in Egypt in their relationship with their Muslim society.

In his study of the Copts' relations to the Muslims in modern Egypt, Paul Sedra touches upon this issue in a useful, detailed manner, suggesting an existence of two strands of thought among the Copts on their status in Egyptian society.[133] He calls the first 'the national unity' approach and the second 'the persecution discourse', referring in his display to various Copt intellectuals who are divided between them. On the national unity discourse, Sedra states its followers' insistence that "the Copts – as integral part of Egypt – have all the characteristics of the Egyptians" and they do not represent a minority, but are rather "so harmoniously integrated into Egyptian society as to be distinguishable from Muslims."[134] In their validation of this approach, this group, as Sedra notices, invests heavily into invoking powerful stories from the history of the country's interreligious co-existence. They recall, for example, the famous national victory of 1973's war against Israel, reminiscing how the Christian soldiers in the Egyptian army observed Ramadan's fasting in solidarity with their Muslim comrades, and how, in return, the Muslim army officers would quote verses from the Qur'ān and the Bible alike in their speeches.[135] Others from this group would praise the fact that the father of the Grand Mufti of Egypt, Muḥammad Said Ṭanṭāwī, had a Copt neighbour, with whom he farmed the land and whose wife was a friend of the Mufti's mother and whose children played together.[136] When they are asked about the foundations of their position, the national unity's supporters point at what they deem "the distinctiveness of Egyptian identity." This distinction, they

133 Paul Sedra, "Class Cleavages and Ethnic Conflict: Coptic Christian Communities in Modern Egyptian Politics," in *Islam and Christians-Muslim Relations*, 10(2), 1999, pp. 219-235.

134 Ibid., p.221. See also Milad Ḥanna, *The Seven Pillars of Egyptian Identity*, 2nd ed., A.Z. el-Sherif (trans.), (Cairo: General Egyptian Book Organization, 1994).

135 Sedra, "Class Cleavages and Ethnic Conflict: Coptic Christian Communities in Modern Egyptian Politics," p. 221; and William S. Kelada, "Christian-Muslim Relations in Egypt," in *The Vatican, Islam and the Middle East*, Kail C. Ellis (ed.), (Syracuse: Syracuse University Press, 1987), pp. 243-262.

136 Sedra, "Class Cleavages and Ethnic Conflict: Coptic Christian Communities in Modern Egyptian Politics," p. 221; and Ḥanna, *The Seven Pillars of Egyptian Identity*, p. 59. See also for other stories M. Fawzi, *al-Bābā Kirollos wa 'Abd al-Nāṣir* (The Pope Kiryllous and Abd al-Nāṣir), (Cairo: al-Waṭan Press, 1993); and Iris H. al-Maṣri, *The Story of the Copts; the True Story of Christianity in Egypt*, (Cairo: St. Anthony Coptic Orthodox Monastery, 1982).

emphasize, incarnates in a strong "sense of belonging to the land of Egypt," instead of belonging to a religious affiliation, and it plays the role of "a unifying bond that guarantees the continuation of a unique Egyptian world view."[137] They even go as far as considering the boundaries between religious obligations "permeable," for in Egypt, they claim, there is a unique Islam, "with Sunni face, Shi'ite blood, Coptic heart and Pharaonic bones."[138]

On the other end of the spectrum lies a totally contrasting approach to the Copts' status in Egypt, called 'the persecution discourse'. The advocates of this view starkly oppose the Copts to the Muslims, not only religiously, Sedra notices, but also historically, culturally and even racially.[139] The followers of the persecution discourse refuse any diplomatic or sentimental historical, nostalgic appraisal. They opt instead for what they construe a more realistic and graphically wide and unbridgeable gulf between the Copts and the Muslims in Egypt. In their opinion, this gulf cannot be covered, as long as the direct descendents of the ancient Egyptians (Copts) are treated by their Arab invaders (Muslims) as strangers on their land up until today.[140] Such an estrangement appears today, they continue, in the Muslim's oppression of the Copts, which influences, "religious belief and practice, civil service appointments, political representation, personal status law, education, the media and security."[141]

---

137 Sedra, "Class Cleavages and Ethnic Conflict: Coptic Christian Communities in Modern Egyptian Politics," p. 222; and Kelada, "Christian-Muslim Relations in Egypt," p. 248.

138 Sedra, "Class Cleavages and Ethnic Conflict: Coptic Christian Communities in Modern Egyptian Politics," p. 222; and Ḥanna, *The Seven Pillars of Egyptian Identity*, p. 13.

139 Sedra, "Class Cleavages and Ethnic Conflict: Coptic Christian Communities in Modern Egyptian Politics," p. 221. Sedra cites from an Egyptian exponent of discourse his saying "when two Egyptians or more meet, the first thing they learn about each other is who is a Christian and who is a Muslim. Their future interactions and relationships will be founded on this knowledge." See Shawqy F. Karas, *The Copts Since the Arab Invasion: Strangers in Their Land*, (Jersey City: American Coptic Association, 1985), pp. 97-98.

140 Sedra, "Class Cleavages and Ethnic Conflict: Coptic Christian Communities in Modern Egyptian Politics," p. 222.

141 Ibid., p.222. See also John Eibner (ed.), *Christians in Egypt: Church Under Siege*, (Zurich: Institute for Religious Minorities in the Islamic World, 1993); K. al-Gawhary, "Copts in the Egyptian Fabric," in *Middle East Report*, Sumer, 1996, pp. 21-22; and S. Shafiq, *al-Aqbāṭ bayn al-Ḥirmān al-Kanasi wal-Waṭani* (The Copts between Churchly and National Excommunication), (Cairo: Dār al-Amin, 1996).

Moreover, the persecution discourse's followers also argue that the Muslim religious institutions are not exempted from propagating offensive and inimical attitude towards the Copts. For, the Shaykhs of the mosques often insert fierce anti-Christian rhetoric into their preaching. On the other hand, they do not even spare the government in their polemic, affirming that instead of protecting the Copts from such dangerous aggressiveness, the government scandalously fails in offering sufficient security to the Christians and their churches since the 80s' sectarian violence surged up in the country.[142]

These two approaches to the Christians' status in Muslim-dominated Egypt gain almost equal ground, and attract almost even numbers of followers within the Coptic population, inside and outside the country. Their points of view permeate and lay their impact on all the internal and external issues that the Copts deem part and parcel of their existence and role in the country, especially the Copts' relationships with foreign intruders into the Egyptian arena. Paul Sedra notices that, with regard to this issue in specific, the national unity and persecution discourses differ noticeably in their understanding of how the Copts should interact with the outside world. The former praises the historical fact of the Christians' and Muslims' formation of a united front against any external encroachment into the land. The slogan that lingers on the horizon in support of this unity is the Copts and Muslims' simultaneous claim that, "Egypt for the Egyptians."[143] To the contrary, the latter discourse considers the Arab Muslims per se the foreigners and strangers on the Egyptian soil. They also appraise the Copt's history in the shadow of these new comers, "a lengthy tale of persecution, massacres, coerced conversions, of devastated and burned churches."[144]

---

142 Sedra, "Class Cleavages and Ethnic Conflict: Coptic Christian Communities in Modern Egyptian Politics," p. 222; and Eibner, *Christians in Egypt: Church Under Siege*, p. 20.

143 Sedra, "Class Cleavages and Ethnic Conflict: Coptic Christian Communities in Modern Egyptian Politics," p. 223; and Ḥanna, *The Seven Pillars of Egyptian Identity*, p. 126.

144 Sedra, "Class Cleavages and Ethnic Conflict: Coptic Christian Communities in Modern Egyptian Politics," p. 223. Popular in this view is the reminiscing of the age of the caliph al-Ḥakam's rule and the one of the Mamlukees dynasty. See, for example, Y. Masriya, "A Christian Minority: the Copts in Egypt," in *Case Studies in Human Rights and Fundamental Freedoms: a World Survey*, W.A. Veenhoven (ed.), (The Hague: Martinus Nijhoff, 1976), Vol. 4, pp. 77-92.

Sedra concludes from the overall discrepancies between national unity and persecution discourses that one cannot narrow down the Copts view of their presence and role in Egypt into one, monolithic strand of thought. He, nevertheless, spots a growing prevalence of the persecution discourse in Egypt since the middle of 1980s, especially after the establishment of the Egyptian Organization for Human Rights, EOHR. Joining EOHR enabled the Copts who follow this discourse to campaign and lobby the public square against the Islamist "extermination efforts" and unveiling and simultaneously charging Mubarak regime's shortcomings in protecting the Christians from such efforts.[145]

During the ruling decades of Mubarak's regime, Egypt has been internally stable. It had no sectarian clashes among Muslim communities (the country is dominantly Sunnite, with a Shi'ite minority much smaller than the Christian one) and it did not witness civil war between religious groups or ethnicities like the one in Lebanon. The Christians in Egypt do not, therefore, suffer from a sectarian or political oppression. They rather experience what one can plausibly describe as a 'sociological persecution' with religious foundation. One has to realize here that this sociological persecution is not merely contemporary and it ought not to be narrowly ascribed to the rise of Islamist fanaticism and *salafi* movements that started to permeate the Egyptian political, social and cultural scene after Abd al-Naṣir's death in 1970 and its aftermath political and cultural trends that made Islam the basis of all aspects of society and politics.[146] This sociological persecution goes back many centuries ago in the history of this African land, as I mentioned above.[147] This sociological persecution has, nonetheless, been intensified during the twentieth century, especiallyin the last four decades of Mubarak's rule, due to the escalation of the political Islamist role and influence in Egyptian society. Though the

145 Sedra, "Class Cleavages and Ethnic Conflict: Coptic Christian Communities in Modern Egyptian Politics," pp. 131-232. See also W. Cofsky, "Copts Bear the Brunt of Islamic Extremism," in *Christianity Today*, 8, March, 1993; and V. Sherry, "The Predicament of Egypt's Christian Minority," in *The Christian Century*, 14, July, 1993.

146 See on the emergence of Islamism in Egypt V. Hoffman, "Islam, Human Rights and Interfaith Relations: Some Contemporary Egyptian Perspectives," pp. 693ff.

147 On the multifaceted, complex historical process of the Muslim-Copts relationship in Egypt see David Zeidan, "The Copts-Equal, Protected or Persecuted? The Impact of Islamization on Muslim-Christian Relations in Modern Egypt," in *Islam and Christian-Muslim Relations*, 1(10), 1999, pp. 53-67.

Coptic clerical authorities, led by the late Anba Shenodah III, were always careful in maintaining good diplomatic relations and widely open communicative ways with Mubarak's regime, some of their intellectuals could not but notice with bitterness, and express with clear disappointment, that this regime was not much better in protecting the Copts from social persecution than previous regimes. Shawqy Karas, for example expresses this frustration when he transpires that

> President Mubarak has been continuing the same policy of religious oppression and discrimination against Egypt's Christians without physical attacks. Psychological and economic warfare have been intensified by the Egyptian government and mass media against them, keeping any violence at a minimum to avoid any reaction by the Copts in Egypt or abroad.[148]

As the Copts unceasingly witnessed restrictions exerted on their religious freedom and practices, disproportionate representation of their elite members in the civil service and the national decision-making circles, let alone the torching of their churches, and the killing and vandalizing of their brothers and sisters by Muslim extremists, they determinatively seek refuge from this sociological pressure in any other foreign society ready to grant them residence.[149]

In their usual diplomatic and flattering interaction with both the authorities and the society, the Coptic Church's prelates tried to detain the inhibition of the above-mentioned frustration's influence on the Coptic community and its role in society. Yet, as Paul Sedra notices, the Pope Shenodah III and his clerical assistants perceive quite clearly the difficulty of reversing the political mobilization ability of such frustration and feeling of social injustice among the Copt's middle class (but also the youths).[150] While Sedra is correct in his observation of the rising of the Copt's interference in the internal public and political affairs of Egypt, his fear of a 'Coptic' resistance versus an 'Islamist' one, and a possible

---

148 Karas, *The Copts Since the Arab Invasion*, p. 207; and Henderson, "The Egyptian Coptic Christians: the Conflict between Identity and Equality," p. 164.

149 See on Egypt's Copts the brief yet fair presentations of B. Bailey & J. Bailey, *Who Are the Christians in the Middle East?* , pp. 144-149; and N. Davies & M. Conway, *World Christianity in the 20th Century*, pp. 96-97.

150 Sedra, "Class Cleavages and Ethnic Conflict: Coptic Christian Communities in Modern Egyptian Politics," p. 233.

sectarian divide appeared to be far from reality in the light of the latest events. The latest uprising that struck the country and turned its situation upside down put Sedra's fear on hold, for on al-Taḥrir Square both the Copts and the Muslim youths alike were united and far from really divided in their rebellion and call for freedom in the face of Mubarak's regime. Does this mean that the followers of the persecution discourse were proven wrong? Not necessarily. This is still a very open question. It just means that the Copts now actually have to strive more seriously with the question of which discourse they should opt for, the national unity or the persecution one, in their expected role and relations with their wider Muslim society.

The Christian youths of Egypt participated in the riots that led to the downfall of Mubarak's regime. The Coptic ecclesial leadership had often good relationships with the previous regime, though the latter did not protect the church and the Copt community from the Muslims' violent attacks and church-torching during the past ten years. The young Copts' anger has noticeably escalated after the last terrorist bombing of The Church of the Two Saints in Alexandria, shortly before the uprising of the 25th of January took place. This is why the Coptic youths did not obey the church prelates' forbiddance of participation in the revolution and they did not express support to the church's official announcement on national television that, "the things that are happening…are against God's will" and were not content with the appearance of some of the Coptic Orthodox representatives in the pro-Mubarak rallies. This is why, eventually, thousands of young Copts, as Paul-Gordon Chandler correctly notices, "disregarded their pope's comments and joined the protests with their Muslim brothers and sisters."[151] This support of the uprising was welcomed and positively appreciated by the Muslims in the country, and al-Tahrir square started to witness a mutual tutelage from each one of the groups to the other during prayer times, as well as the country's Muslim sheikhs started also to address Muslims and Copts as the two arms of the Egyptian nation's body. It is too early to say whether this communal and tolerant spirit towards the Christians would prevail and characterize the future Egypt. Yet, one may optimistically extract with Paul-Gordon Chandler

151 Paul-Gordon Chandler, "Muslims and Copts Together," in *Christians Century*, March. 22, 2011, pp. 10-11, p. 11.

from the pluralistic dimension of these last events in the country signs of, "the new interfaith worldview," of the young, rioting Egyptians.[152]

When it comes to Syria, my homeland, I can talk extensively on the Christians situation and the history of their role in the country. However, I would like to briefly pay a short visit to the Christians' situation in this country. I would make a brief display at this section because I will speak at great length about the Syrian Christians' relation to their Muslim context and their position towards the recent uprising in Syria in the subsequent section. In brief, the situation of the Christians in Syria is also a story of its own and is especially different from the stories of Christians in the abovementioned countries. The Syrian Christians are different from the Lebanese Christians with regard to the role they play in the power-game and power-division in the state. While the Lebanese Christians are fully involved in the political life of the country and its shares by means of the Maronite community's occupation of one of the three highest authority positions (presidency) in the Cider Land, the Syrian Christians do not have political ambitions and they restrain themselves consciously and strictly from any involvement in the power-sharing game. The Syrian Christians differ from Palestinian Christians in being a single, rather than a double minority, as well as in the fact that the pressure and difficult conditions they may experience are exerted upon them from the ruling regime and not from either an external occupying force, or an internal demographic majority (like the Jews). When these difficulties appear on the surface, all the society's citizens, Muslims or Christians, who are disloyal to the ruling regime, would suffer from it equally. On the other hand, the Syrian Christians are different from the Egyptian and Iraqi Christian communities in the fact that the former are not subjected to a sociological or religious persecution from the Muslim majority. The Syrian Christian community certainly suffers from all the aftereffects of any external instability and insecurity, or internal oppression and tyranny that can hit the country's overall population. Yet, this would not be because of this community's religious, specifically, non-Islamic identity, like it is in Egypt and Iraq.

The Christians in Syria make up around 8 to 10 percent of the population, which is a little than 2 million citizens. They always keep in mind that, besides its very old and autochthonous Christian history, Syria is equally deeply rooted in the history of Islam, especially during the

152 Ibid., p.11.

Umayyads' era of the 8th and 9th centuries AD, when Damascus was the capital of the Caliphate and the centre of Islamic civilization. This strong Islamic legacy is fully acknowledged and realistically perceived by the Christians in the country, who always live with the deep awareness of the substantial and indelible Islamic features of the Syrian society. Despite the lack of serious dialogue with the Muslims over political and civil society issues due to the ruling regime's strict prohibitions of public discussion of politics and religion, the Christians, nevertheless, tend to maintain an open, friendly and embracing relationship with their wider Islamic environment and they strongly preserve the best relations of coexistence and interaction with their Muslim neighbours, almost considering the Islamic heritage and history of the country to be from the same womb they also culturally came from.

During the last four decades Syria has been under the hegemonic rule of the al- Ba'th party. Like its brother-party in Saddam's Iraq, the Syrian Ba'th presents itself as secular in ideology. Moreover, though the country's constitution states that the head of state must be Muslim, the Christians are granted freedom to practice their religion and to build churches and own ecclesial properties, and the government provides the churches and the mosques alike with free the utilities (like electricity and water).[153] From his first-hand observation of Syrian society, Carsten Wieland, for example, notices that

> Christian churches can develop freely in Syria and are often very well endowed financially. The government subsidizes them by building asphalt roads to remote monasteries and other projects. Like mosques, churches are exempt from taxes on their purchases. Many Christians are traders, craftsmen, and merchants and have achieved a relative degree of prosperity. They are in a similar social and economic position as the class of Sunni traders.[154]

These privileges, however, do not mean that the Christians in Syria are not declining in number like other Christians in the Arab world. Like their brothers in the neighbouring countries, being a minority compels the Christians to look for another more economically secure and socially tolerant context in the expatriation lands when they no longer find it in

153 Bailey & Bailey, Who Are the Christians in the Middle East? p. 193.
154 C. Wieland, Syria: Ballots or Bullets? p. 33.

the homeland. The Christians' emigration rate witnessed a noticeable increase since the early eighties of the last century, when the Ba'thi regime clashed with the Muslim brotherhood and started a systematic imposition of the emergency law over all of the population. Then, many Christians, but also Muslims, from all denominations fled the country and never returned. Recently, the very drastic conditions of corruption, economic atrophy and recession, and the high rate of unemployment and poverty during the 'second Assadi' rule have also forced thousands of Syrian youths, mostly Christian, to seek better life opportunities and a real future abroad. One can say that the reputation of Syria as the safest land for the Christians in the Arab world does not seem to make the country more successful than other Arab countries in keeping the Christians in the perpetually troubled region.

Chapter 3: The Christians and the 'Islamist Threat' Theory: Reflections on Syria (1)

In the ensuing three chapters, I will make reflections on the Christians' situation in Syria and how they view the recent uprisings and what kind of a role they envision themselves to be playing in them. I will start the first chapter with the question of the general political situation of Syria before the latest uprising in the country. More specifically, I will tackle the question of the Islamist threat on the country and whether such a threat has evident roots in the Syrian societal soil, or whether it is rather ill-founded. In the following chapters, I will talk more directly about the general image of Syria in the eyes of its Christian children. I do present these reflections as a Christian Syrian citizen, who was born in, has grown up in, and is still in close touch with today's Syrian society, despite his presence in the immigration land. What I jot down in these three chapters is what I personally hold to be reflective of the situation of the Christians in this Arab land, as well as what I can confidentially claim as the common view of many Syrian Christians I personally know, I conversed with, I read about or I heard of over the past years.

One of the main concerns of the Christians in Syria is the role of political Islam in the country's public square. As I will be pointing out in the subsequent chapter, quite a few number of Syrians, Christians mainly but also Muslims, share a general fear of any political alternative with a religionist, specifically Islamist, agenda to take over rule from the recent Ba'thist regime, and to turn the country into a backward, *salafi* caliphate overnight, and imposes Shari'a as the state's constitution and the sole legislative source, with all the nightmares of *dhimmitude*, persecution and discrimination the Christians can imagine to be exposed to if this happens. I will not at all be divulging a secret in what I just stated. The international society around the world knows about these fears, and innumerable Westerners have heard Christians, and also Muslims, reflecting before them their serious bewilderment, if such an Islamist alternative ruled the Arab world. Being a resident and worker in the Western world for almost ten years, I can even say that sometimes I hear the Westerners speaking about this Islamist alternative as a real and immanent danger in an accent more troublesome and urgent than when Christian Arabs talk about it.

Recently, and in light of the latest uprisings that inflamed the public squares along almost all the countries in the Arab world, the question of the danger of the Islamist alternative popped up on the surface again. Many people around the globe, who observe with awe and puzzlement the drastic and rapid changes in that part of the world at the moment, now raise the question: what kind of states and regimes will generate from the latest uprisings? Is it possible that the alternative of the falling dictatorships, which were after all reassuring to the developed world in its apparent secularism and tolerance, is inevitably an Islamist one? In Syria, this question is also urgent and it seems to be shaping the international society's position toward the uprisings in the country. Though the American and European media broadcasts, as much as they can, selected news about the events in Syria and clearly show the regimes' brutality and violence. And, notwithstanding, the growing general condemnation of al-Assad's regimes' methods of dealing with the people's protests, one can still hear Western people reflecting a common belief that their countries must probably still support the remaining of al-Assad's regime in rule because it, allegedly, protects the Christians and grants them religious freedom and security and prevents any persecution exerted by the Muslim Sunnites against them. These people mostly support this view upon the belief that their words are a mere echo of what the Syrian Christians themselves perpetually repeat when they speak about their homeland, Syria.

It is not far from truth that many Syrian Christians, especially in the immigration lands, believe that the al-Assad regime is the sole and core-tutelage against the country's Sunnite majority. They always tend to wish that no other regime would take over in Syria, because any other alternative would be Islamist and fanatic, and would work against the Christians of the country, as well as the Christian societies of the West.

Having said the above, is this discourse of the Christians immigrants always identical with and expressive of the realistic and first-hand experience of the Christians inside Syria? And, is the threat of an Islamist political ruling alternative really suppressed by virtue of the Ba'thi regime's rule? Is there a version to the story of the relation between al-Assad regime and the role of political Islam in Syria, other than the scenario which the West knows? In the ensuing paragraphs, I will offer another version of the story, wherein I convey another internal view of the role of the regime in the presence or absence of Islamic fanaticism in the country. I would argue that it is the regime and nothing else, whose nature and relationship with the Syrian people that actually makes this threat impending and real in Syria. The regime is not the protector of the Christians or any other minority in the country. It is rather a pragmatist ruling power that is ready to foster any situation, no matter how risky it may be, in the service of its survival and best interest.

One of the factors the Western world does not seem to be aware of is that there are Christians, at least in Syria, who do not echo the above-mentioned fear of an Islamist political alternative to the Ba'thi regime. Though the voice of these people is minor within the Syrian Christian minority, its presence in the Syrian public square is recognized and its political oppositional position against the regime and its Islamist-phobia theory is known among the intellectuals and activist in the country.

Besides the writer of this study, I can mention here a more Christian renowned, influential and active figure in the history of liberal, intellectual and political dissention in Syria, namely the journalist, thinker and civil activist, Michel Kilo. Kilo's name is known in some of the decision-making circles of the West, and some international human rights' activists and organizations have in the past years issued petitions for releasing Michel Kilo and other civil active dissenters, when these people were detained in prison, to both al-Assad junior's and al-Assad senior's regimes. But, Kilo's intellectual contribution to the fostering of civil-society and liberal, free and democratic state in Syria is still understudied and, unfortunately, hardly viewed as a Christian point of view that diverges far away from the conventional, passive and loyalist discourse of the clerical and lay spokesmen of the Christian community in the country. In the following, I would like to shed light at Michel Kilo's view of political Islam in Syria, specifically the the Muslim Brotherhood. I would like to offer an example of a unique Christian voice which I and other Christians, though a minority, support and find validity in. It is a voice from within Syria about whether or not the theory that the political Islamist alternative of the recent dictatorial regime would definitely be a threat to the non-Muslim minorities in the country.

Let me first start with some biographical words about the person himself. Michel Kilo was born in Lattakia, Syria in 1940, to a lower-class family. He spent his childhood and finished his basic education in his hometown. From those days, he used to reminisce about his father always saying 'how can one be *only* Christian in a [Arabic, Islamic] historical atmosphere, which offered you your culture, language, civilization and a central part of your identity?' His father's view influenced his childhood and shaped his identity and orientation toward Syrian society in his adulthood. After finishing his graduate and postgraduate studies in Philosophy (Münster, Germany), and practicing Journalism in Damascus and France, Kilo spent most of his life in Syria working as a journalist, political analyst and translator, and has ever since been a political and civil activist, calling for liberty, democracy, civil-society and freedom of thinking and political conviction. His political and intellectual stances, which express his belief in a pluralist, free, civil and democratic Syria, made him inescapably one of the most strenuous dissenters against al-Assad father's and son's rule and made the latters' regime consider him one of the most threatening and challenging free voices before the regime's hegemony and domination. This threatening status was intensified as Kilo played a pioneering and leading role in the oppositions' revivalism at the beginning of 'al-Assad the Son's rule'. Kilo's name was then strongly associated with what is known as 'the Spring of Damascus', which erupted and died down between 2000 and 2001. In his observation of the Damascus Spring phenomenon in Syria, and the leading role which the frontline activist Michel Kilo played in writing its petitions and related articles, Carsten Wieland describes Kilo and points to the philosophy behind his civil-society activism in the following words:

> A Christian, Kilo studied several years in the northern German town of Münster and speaks fluent German. His philosophy of a grass-roots democracy stems from that time, and he prefers a plethora of small initiatives to a large party, which makes persecution by the state machinery more difficult. The former communist describes himself as a humanist. 'The regime has to accept that freedom is the greatest principle in life', he says. 'In a modern society you can no longer separate state and society because the free human being is the central principle'. Kilo is convinced that every ideological party in power will enter a period of crisis because real life is much more complicated than any *Weltanschauung*.[155]

The above-mentioned views caused Kilo much damage and suppression by the regime, and exposed him to almost consistent, strict censorship and interrogations from the Assadis' security forces. Due to his political opposition, it was expected for Kilo to be arrested and jailed twice during Hafiz and Bashar al-Assad's terms. The first happened during the 1970s, after which he left the country and went to France, where he stayed until the end of the 1980s. The second arrest was during the 'Spring of Damascus'' events, 2000-2001.[156] During that brief bright break in Syria's long oppression under the recent regime, Michel Kilo, like many other open-minded Syrian intellectuals, systematically and publicly called for fostering civil society and democracy, the lifting of the state of emergency and the launching of a national reconciliation in the country.[157] Kilo was

155 C. Wieland, Syria: Ballots or Bullets? p.115.

156 The writer of these lines was one of those who were interrogated by the security forces during that period because of an article titled "al-Īṣlaḥ wa Tawryth al-Khaouf," (Reformation and the Inheritance of Fear). The security forces bullied my father to force me coming to Syria from England, where I was then pursuing my doctoral studies, and voluntarily surrender myself to the security forces; the thing I did after few months, when I visited Syria and was exposed to the interrogation. In the following years, 2004 and 2009, I would be interrogated again for other articles I wrote and for my relations with dissenters, like Michel Kilo, by two other different security forces departments. The article that led to my first encounter with the security forces has never been published later on.

157 On this period, read the reflections of Radwan Ziadeh, Radwan Ziadeh, *Power and Policy in Syria: the Intelligence Services, Foreign Relations and Democracy in the Modern Middle East*, (London & New York: I.B. Tauris, 2011, pp. 48-54, 66-69; Fred A. Reed, *Shattered Images: the Rise of Militant Iconoclasm in Syria*, (Vancouver: Talonbooks, 2003), pp. 79-96; Flynt Leverett, *Inheriting Syria: Bashar's*

summoned, interrogated and bullied by the regime's security forces. Yet, after co-signing the 'Beirut-Damascus'' declaration in March 2006, Kilo was arrested and accused of 'weakening the nationalist sentiments' of the people, 'underrating the state's prestige' and 'arousing sectarian hatred'.[158] After having been tried in civil and then military courts, Kilo was jailed for three years and eventually released from prison in 19, May 2009.

In 2004, when Bashar al-Assad regime's tension with the Muslim Brotherhood was on a noticeable escalation-tide again, Michel Kilo (by that time in-between arrests) wrote an article in which he presented a brave and unique Christian appraisal of the Muslim Brotherhood in Syria. Kilo starts his argument with a suspicion about the Western belief that if the Ba'th regime fell down, the alternative in Syria would be a fanatic, fundamentalist Islam. Rejecting the association of political Islam in Syria with fundamentalism, Kilo takes his readers back to the history of political Islam in contemporary Syria. He focuses on the Muslim Brotherhood's historical, far from aggressive or violent records. The Brotherhood, he maintains, used to be a purely political party like any other. It participated in the parliamentary elections, nominated candidates with clear political programs. Its opinions about the countries general affairs were always stated publicly. It owned many headquarters in Syrian cities. It had normal, complex alliance or competition relations with other political parties, and it worked for achieving its agenda via a public, legislative, religious and political discourse. In other words, throughout its history, the Muslim Brotherhood was in its discourse and performance demonstrative of a political party *par excellence*.[159] Despite the religious underpinning elements of the Muslim Brotherhood's discourse, its ideological literatures, Kilo notices, do not call for resorting to violence, do not consider armed actions as instruments of change, and they do not virtually state that this party is not civil in orientation and methods. On

---

Trial by Fire, (Washington: Brookings Institutions Press, 2005), pp. 57-98; Eyal Zisser, *Commanding Syria: BasherAl-Asad and the First Years in Power*, (London New York: I.B. Tauris, 2007), pp. 77-89; and Carsten Wieland, *Syria: Ballots or Bullets?* pp. 45-47, 114-137.

158 Michel Kilo personally wrote from the prison an article about the circumstances that led to his arrest. see: Michel Kilo, "Qssat ''Teqali wa-'Ttihāmi," (The Story of my Arrest and Accusation), in www.shril-sy.info 11 December. 2006.

159 Kilo, "Mata Kāna al-Īslām fī Sūriyya Oṣūliyyan?" (When Was Islam in Syria Fundamentalist?) in www.all4syria.info 25, May. 2004.

the other hand, and notwithstanding the supporting or dissenting stances it makes on religiously-founded values, the Syrian Muslim Brotherhood had never in their history called for islamizing the state by coercion or via illegal non-constitutional means, and it had not been led by fanatic figures, who anathematize others or call on their followers to break with the real situation of the Syrian society.[160] From this historical and analytical visit, Kilo gleans that Muslim Brotherhood was a moderate and not extremist force.[161]

Kilo, nevertheless, perceives that the end of 1950s, beginning of 1960s witnessed internal interaction inside the Muslim Brotherhood party, which inseminated a tendency towards extremism and fundamentalism. The questions the party then substantially struggled with were: what must we do, if the political discourse and interaction failed in bringing into reality the hoped-for change, especially when the margins of political activity shrank down due to the military regime's control of the mosques, suppression of religion, and strict censorship of political, parliamentary and media work? Should we dismantle the party and convert its human resources into a military organization, since the ruling party controls the state's army and police forces and uses them to suppress other parties? The outcome of this conceptual and theoretical struggle in the party, Kilo continues, was the unfortunate growth of the fanatic and confrontational voice, which played the central role in the aftermath of the vicious and brutal war with al-Assad senior's regime in the early 1980s, which ended with creating the drastically deep rift in Syrian society, as well as causing the Muslim Brotherhood's loss of its political and parliamentary, let alone legal, presence and work in the country.[162]

In his reflection on these unforgettably difficult events of the 1980s Syria, Kilo personally invokes a conversation he had in one of the security forces' interrogation departments with another political detainee from the Muslim Brotherhood called Qasem Musa. Musa told Kilo that in the beginning, the followers of the violent, confrontational front in the Brotherhood were very few, while the moderate and reasonable were the ma-

160 Kilo, "Mata Kāna al-Īslām fī Sūriyya Oṣūliyyan?"

161 Kilo, "Mata Kāna al-Īslām fī Sūriyya Oṣūliyyan?" They remained so, Kilo maintains, when other parties in the country, like the nationalists', started to consider force the only way for dealing with the hegemony of the then arising role of the army-officers and their enhancing involvement in politics, which brought eventually figures like Ḥafez al-Assad into rule.

162 Kilo, "Mata Kāna al-Īslām fī Sūriyya Oṣūliyyan?"

jority. Yet, the situation was reversed afterwards, as the Ba'thi regime's tyrannical feast started to hit other political parties more aggressively, and as the then Muslim Brotherhood's most influential voices made numerous political miscalculations and indiscreetly gave up the party's historical moderation and tolerance.[163] Admitting the indelibly destructive consequences of this political and ideological trap, which the Muslim Brotherhood dropped itself into, and paid the unbearably high price for, Kilo, nonetheless, opines that such opting for violent withstanding instead of political action is always an open possibility for every other party, and not only the Islamists, in a state the ruling power of which avails in its performance, hegemony and one-sidedness all the causes and motivations for. The possibility of violence is not the natural outcome of the presence of political Islam in the society. This danger would originate in Syria anyhow, Kilo affirms, from the regime's sweeping aggressive treatment of society in general, and from the opposition in specific, and its absolutist deeming of any different political or societal point of view an imperialist, Zionist conspiracy against the whole country.[164]

When his analysis arrives at the present Syria, Michel Kilo notices that the Syrian ruling regime succeeded in sawing in the public's mind the inaccurate idea that Muslim Brotherhood is by nature a fanatic, aggressive movement, and that it has been so ever since its genesis in Syria's political scene. The regime's public relations machine worked resiliently to erase any other view about the Brotherhood from the national records, or even the public memory, emphatically alleging that the country would be patriotically and socially drained and impoverished if political Islam retrieved its presence in the public square, or if the authorities permitted people to contact or dialogue with its followers.[165] Kilo stands against this conspiracy theory and terrifying policy, believing that it does not heal the deep national, confessionalist and societal wound in the body of the nation. It rather slams shut all the doors that are supposed to remain open between the different Syrian citizens and the various political parties alike, and instead blocks any possible hope for a national reconciliation, mutual forgiveness, corresponsive admittance of, and apology for, the past mistakes, and a comprehensive, unified public abhorrence of violence, intolerance and fanaticism. The deep, lethal wound in the Syrian

163 Kilo, "Mata Kāna al-Īslām fī Sūriyya Oṣūliyyan?"
164 Kilo, "Mata Kāna al-Īslām fī Sūriyya Oṣūliyyan?"
165 Kilo, "Mata Kāna al-Īslām fī Sūriyya Oṣūliyyan?"

body is still open and infectious, Kilo states. Syria, he insists, needs all its children, the Islamists included, in order to reach the end of the dark tunnel, which Syria as authority, society, state, parties and citizens is stuck into. Only such reconciliation would transform Syria, Kilo concludes, from a 'police-state' into a political state of free citizens.[166]

Driven by the above-mentioned belief in reconciliation, Michel Kilo wrote two articles during the past couple of months of the Syrian revolution age, wherein he called the Christians, their church prelates before any one else, to reflect such a reconciliatory and partnership spirit toward their Muslim compatriots. He bravely invited them to play a patriotic role by declaring their support to the Syrian population's call for freedom, democracy, justice and change, and at least condemning ethically and humanly the systematic reliance of the regime on violence and military persecution.[167] In his article, Kilo points to the deep rift that divides the segments of the Syrian society because of the recent events. He specifically points to the Christian Syrians' stance of the revolution, criticizing in specific those among them, who irresponsibly and publicly support the regime regardless of its brutality and in a scandalous disregard to the feelings of those families who lost children, parents and relatives at the hand of the regime's killing machine. Kilo argues that these Christians, who blindly support the regime, and despite their small number, convey the wrong message to the Muslims of the country about the Christians' affiliation to the population's right demands, and they try to fudge and cast to the margin the other Syrian Christians' rather sympathy with and support of the people's revolution.

---

166 Kilo, "Mata Kāna al-Īslām fī Sūriyya Oṣūliyyan?" In a more recent article he wrote after his release from prison, Michel Kilo wrote another reflection on Islam and fundamentalism, wherein he shows how the fanatic branch of political Islam takes the Muslims apart from the real tolerance and openness of Islam towards the different other. See: M. Kilo, "Kalīmat 'An al-Īslām wal-Oṣūlīyyah," (Words on Islam and Fundamentalism) in www.ahewar.org 23, August. 2010. This article aroused various reactions. See for example al-Ṭāher Ībrahem, "al-'Khwān al-Mūslimon fī Sūrriyyah…'An Qurb Marra Thaniya," (The Muslim Brotherhood in Syria..on a Close Distance, Again) in www.hem.bredband.net . Some of the reactions were offensively negative and went as far as accusing Kilo, the Christian, of planning to convert to Islam. See Nedhal N'ayseh, "Hall Yoshher Michel Kilo Īslāmaho?" (Would Michel Kilo Declare His Islam?) in www.aherwar.org 28, August. 2010.

167 M. Kilo, "Daʿwat al-Massīḥiyyah īla al-ʿaql," (Inviting Christianity to Reasoning), in www.assafir.com , N. 11962, 13, Aug. 2011, p. 19.

Kilo places his criticism within the wider framework of the Christians' historical role and contribution to the life of the Muslim-Arabic region. He reminds his readers of the Christians' evident affiliation to the cultural and societal context of their Muslim-majority environment and their affirmed belonging to the destiny and fate of the people of the region, regardless of any religious differences. Kilo then asks the Syrian Christians, who support the regime, if they have given up this history and turned from an inherent element of the Arabs historical community into one of the contingent components of a circumstantial and falling authoritarian system. Kilo then end his article by asking the Christian churches to rationalize and moralize their stance on the Syrian revolution, to choose the side of the people and to play a more prophetic role in the drastic situation; a role that alone makes the church the true church of the 'Son of Man'. The war of the Christians in the region, Kilo wisely maintained, is not against the Muslims, but against every enemy of the human's rights of freedom, justice and integral life.[168]

The presentation of a local Christian voice, as shown above, calling for reviewing the political Islam in Syria from a different, more realistic perspective invites us to reconsider the traditional questions we usually ask about Syria and its future and about the situation of Islam in it. It invites us, instead, to start asking other questions. One of the main questions I propose we should start asking is: why would the Syrian regime foster the above-mentioned negative view about the Muslim Brotherhood, instead of opting for Michel Kilo's invitation for reconciliation and bridging the sectarian, political and societal rift? To answer this question, we actually need to look at the history of the Regime's strategic relationship with the influential powers in the Middle East and its role within the power-share and profit-distribution games therein.

Since the beginning of the 1980s, the Syrian Ba'thist regime presented itself to the world as a non-religious, crudely secular system. It worked hard to prove to the major international powers that its existence in rule in an axial and strategic country like Syria in the Arab world is a safety valve in the face of the rise and spread of Islamic extremism and terrorism. And the regime implemented this thesis intensively at the aftermath

---

168 These ideas were also the core of Michel Kilo's latest response to the Maronite Patriarch's, Mar Bchara Butrous al-Raʿī, comments on the Syrian revolution in his pastoral trip to France. See on this: M. Kilo, "Ḥadīth maʿ Gibṭaṭih," (A Conversation with His Immanence), in www.assafir.com , N. 11989, 17, Sept. 2011, p. 19.

of the Muslim Brotherhood uprising at the early 1980s. This theory was the regime's justification-means of its violent and brutal crackdown and eradication not only of the Muslim Brotherhood's existence, but also of any form of political Islam, if not political non-Ba'thist activity in general, in the country's public squares.[169] The regime further managed in the subsequent years to build alliances with the influential forces in the Near East's geopolitical context and to occupy the position of the first and most ferocious fighter against the *Islamist jihadi* movements and religious fanatic terrorism in the region.

From that point onward, the regime would relentlessly rear this image and feed it up, especially during the last two decades of the twentieth century, when Al-Assad succeeded in cracking down his younger brother's attempted coup. As al-Assad managed to renew the relationships with the Western supporters of his younger brother's failed attempt, he turned his face towards the country's internal setting, building various mutual interest alliances with the influential members and sides in the Sunnite community inside the country (especially the merchants). This guaranteed the Ba'thi regime political, religious, economic and public security for the coming years, at least up until the tenth year of Hafiz al-Assad son-heir's rule. The foundation of this success was Hafiz al-Assad's witty and persuasive ability to present himself to the non-Sunnite and non-Muslim segments of the Syrian population as the first protector of their rights and the guardian of their existence against the threat of the religious fanatic group that anathematizes every 'other'. By means of the excuse of the 'Islamist threat', the regime gradually introduced new restriction and controlling measures that led to the harsh, sometimes vio-

---

169 According to Radwan Ziadeh, the military crackdown of the Muslim Brotherhood's uprising resulted in the death of between 5000 and 15000 civilians, most of whom died beneath the debris of the city of Hama, which al-Assad's army forces almost demolished completely. This crackdown, Ziadeh continues, was followed by a campaign of arrests of more than 100,000 of activists, opponents and even advocates of the regime: Radwan Ziadeh, *Power and Policy in Syria: the Intelligence Services, Foreign Relations and Democracy in the Modern Middle East*, (London & New York: I.B. Tauris, 2011), p. 29. See also on these events and their aftermath Thomas Friedman, *From Beirut to Jerusalem*, (New York: Farrar, Straus & Giroux, 1989), pp. 76-105; Raymound A. Hinnebusch, *Authoritarian Power and State Formation in Ba'thist Syria: Army, Party and Peasant*, (Boulder: Westview Press, 1998), pp. 291-300; and Nikolaos van Dam, *The Struggle for Power in Syria: Politics and Society under Assad and the Ba'th Party*, (London: I.B. Tauris, 1996), pp. 165-172.

lent, restrain of civil-society's general activity, the thing that was often justified by means of scaring the public from the islamist violence that can jeopardize the society's stability by sneaking into it from any unintentional public lenience.[170] Al-Assad, the father and the son alike, have persistently shown readiness to pay all the costs of maintaining this image that was as cunning and eager in extent, as his need to gain the rewards of such an image and to benefit from it strategically and existentially.

As the regime perceptively anticipated the collapse of the rapidly weakening communist campaign and the, just as rapidly growing, hegemony of the American-Western campaign across the Middle East, it started to search for other cards to bring to the negotiation table, eventually persuading its Western negotiators of the regime's need for the West's interests in the area. Al-Assad deeply apprehended the need of Israel and the West to the existence of, at least seemingly, secular, pluralist and moderate regime to control and monitor the growing religious-political activities in Israel's neighbouring countries. This new equation became evident during the beginning of the 1990s and the first war against Iraq. Then, it seemed that the regime bought a new survival license from America; a license that offered the regime some rest and release from the economic pressure, which Syria suffered from, because of its anti-Western alliances in the previous years. Even the Americans, who blamed Al-Assad and bullied him because of his alliance with Iran's al-Khumayni and his earlier allegiance with the Soviet Union's communist cause, was then fully ready to reward the regime for its support of, and participation in, the first Iraq-war. This rewarding attitude meant turning one blind eye, firstly, to the regime's domestic brutality and persecution of all the non-Ba'thist political activists, and from all ideologies and sides, by means of an alleged attempt at securing the country from any Islamist or other kinds of extremism; and secondly turning another blind eye to the regime's atrocious and fully hegemonic control of, and interference in, Lebanon's internal affairs. The West granted al-Assad full-scale authority in Lebanon based on the conviction that the one who managed to demolish terrorism in his country, is capable of controlling and taming the Islamist resistance and its political role in Lebanon, eventually sparing Israel its threat. This Western compromise was done according to a specific, prefabricated strategy of balance, the violation of which was sometimes willingly opted for by either the regime or the

---

170 Pratt, Democracy and Authoritarianism in the Arab World, p. 101.

Lebanese Islamist resistance, at one time, or by Israel and the West, at another.

Since the invasion of Iraq in 2003 and the collapse of Saddam Hussein's Ba'thi regime there, many Arab political analysts perpetually maintain that the previous strategic equation that granted the Syrian regime survival and validity has recently lost its previous success' merits and circumstances. Some of them go as far as saying that the West uses, publically and behind the closed doors, this equation before anything else to mobilize the international opinion against the Syrian regime. Since September 11 and the second Iraq-War, these analysts observe, the Americans explicitly accused Bashar al-Assad's regime of backing the Iraqi Islamist (specifically Sunnite) resistance against the Americans and the Palestinian Islamist resistance (also Sunnite) against Israel, let alone America's serious resentment and irritation from Syria's support of its Iranian ally's strong and evident interference in the region.

The above-mentioned historical-political narrative shows that one should seriously question the genuineness and truthfulness of the thesis that the Syrian Ba'thi regime represents a first line of defence against Islamist or any other religious fanatic and extremist political project in the Near East, just because this ruling sect was founded on an originally secular ideology, or just because the strongest ruling personnel in this regime, when considering sects, belong to a non-Sunnite minority group (the Alawites). Before saying that 'al-Assad the Son's regime', and al-Assad the father's before it, is a guarantee of the non-Sunnite and non-Muslim minorities' secure, peaceful and prosperous presence in the country, one must keep in mind the complex political and geostrategic alliances and links between the fighting-powers and the rules of the power-sharing game in the region. This game indicates that it is quite plausible and verifiable a proposal, which suggests that the Syrian regime itself is the creator and the primal beneficiary of the 'Islamist threat against the minorities and the Western interests' theory.

Be that as it may, the issue of the Syrian regime's relation to, and the extent of its involvement in, a secret common interests alliance with some religiously ideologized, confrontational movements is very serious, and one should not undermine the significance of the reflection on its possible impending consequences on the country. If it is the case that the regime in Syria has truly decided to embrace the Islamist violent movements, as the distal and the proximal accuses him of, there is a real danger that this alliance and nothing else is what allowed such extremism to enter the country, to live underground during the last ten years and, one would then say, to uncover its presence and attempt at entering into a street war with the regime in the recent uprisings. If this is the case, then the question must not only be 'what is the regime's position from Political Islam?', but more radically 'which Islam threatens the Syrian regime in reality and which Islam this regime feels that it serves its own interests at the moment?'

It seems to me that the latest uprising in Syria and the regime's public declaration of another war against Islamist fanaticism, which, as the regime claims, attempts at turning Syria into an Islamist caliphate, invites us to say that the answer to the above-mentioned question is: it is the fanatic and extremist political Islam that serves the regime's purpose and resonates with its strife for survival. I would even go as far as arguing that this answer can also be gleaned from the regime's position against the Syrian Muslim Brotherhood's discourse in the past ten years.

Noteworthy in the past few years are the declarations that were issued by the Syrian Muslim Brotherhood to state this groups' political and ideological discourse in the light of the changes in the regional scene. One of the most important declarations was issued by the Muslim Brotherhood in 2001 under the title 'the National Honour Charter'.[171] In this charter, one realizes a moderate political tone, accompanied with admittance that the eighties' uprising was a mistake and a categorical renounce and rejection of violence as a method for achieving political goals. Noticeable also is the brothers' support of political, societal and ethnic plurality in Syria and their belief that the only future for the country lies in a civil-contract ruling system. Moreover, one can also point at various official invitations, the General Observer of the group sent to the regime in Syria for fulfill-

171 In 2001, the Muslim Brotherhood issued a declaration called 'National Honour Charter', wherein the group declared a break-away from its past ideological confrontational heritage and emphasized its belief in plurality and civil society. This charter was welcomed, appraised and discussed by the Syrian intellectuals, yet totally ignored by the regime. For some articles on this charter, see Firas Qaṣṣaṣ, "Qera'a Mukhtalifah le-Methaq al-Sharaf al-Waṭanī le-Jama'at al-'Īkhwān al-Muslimīn fī Suriyya," (A Different Reading of the National Honour Charter of the Muslim Brotherhood in Syria), in www.ahewar.org no. 229, 24, August. 2002; and Subḥi Ḥadīdī, "Wajeb Mulaqāt al-'Īkhwān al-Muslimīn fī Ḥiwār al-Methaq al-Waṭanī," (The Duty of Meeting with the Muslim Brotherhood around the National Charter) in www.aherwar.org no. 230, 26, August. 2002.

ing reconciliation and beginning a new positive relationship between the two bitter foes. However, as Radwan Ziadeh recently points out, "none of the negotiations between al-Bayānūnī [the ex-general super-intender of the brotherhood] and the Syrian security forces managed to solve the problem either of the Muslim Brotherhood's roles as a political party or of the return of its leaders [from exile]."[172] Be that as it may, those who monitored these attempts and their ramifications cannot but maintain that the regime did not take them positively and did not change its suspicion toward and rejection of any political Islam inside Syria.

Consequently, one cannot but assume that the regime's rejection means that such a reconciliatory, moderate and non-violent political Islam does not serve the regime's best interest and strategic agenda. It rather threatens the authority's complex interest structure and probably unveils before the minorities the superficiality of the regime's 'Islamism threat' theory. If the political Islam was given the chance to prove to the Syrian public square that it is determined to abide by moderation and tolerance towards plurality, it is ready to pay the price of compromising the exclusionary tendencies of its closed religious ideology for such moderation and plurality, and that it is willing to completely part ways with such ideology in political and realistic practices, then the regime will not be able to deny that it is faced with a serious challenge to its core-existence. In light of the latest revolution in Syria, one can even go as far as saying that the regime realizes day after day that it can no longer be able to turn a deaf ear to the real possibility of the birth of a moderate political Islam (and not only a moderate religious Islamic discourse, as the one we already hear in the Syrian mosques) right inside Syria, in the midst of its public square and in front of the eyes of its security forces and army. During the revolutions' past months, the regime's media has completely failed in blindfolding the public about the emergence of a public Islamist phenomenon inside the very territories of Syria itself, whose followers clearly and publicly declare that they accept pluralism and concede the secularisation and civility of the state, willingly ready to put their hands in the hands of every other secularist and leftist political trend in the country and are ready to show respect, acceptance of and protection for the minorities' rights. Yet, up until these last couple of weeks, the regime in Syria stubbornly clings to its old violent and far from politically and stately reliable methods. It does not demonstrate any

172 Ziadeh, *Power and Policy in Syria*, p. 149.

willingness to open a serious reconciliation channel with this political Islam or to accept its existence and revolution as a fact that substantially and irretrievably changed the country forever. The regime rather insists on using its old 'Islamism danger' theory to justify its bloody and brutal reaction to the people's call for freedom and reformation to such an extent which strongly indicates that the regime wager only and strictly on this 'war against terrorism' scenario in its strife for survival.

Which Syrian political Islam threatens al-Assad's Syria and intimidates the regime recently? According to the regime's point of view, it seems that it is this political Islam that is ready to follow a civil, reformational, non-violent and non-exclusionary approach. The regime does not want such an Islam to come to the public and gain attention, because allowing such Islam to be publicly heard would inevitably and inescapably lead to the change of the authority-equation, which the regime resorts to and relies on as a ruling entity that habituated emphasizing its absolute antagonism with religious fanaticism.

On the other hand, which Islam is giving the regime the impression that it opts to benefit from in this case? Radwan Ziadeh gives a plausible answer to this question when he points out that the Ba'thi regime, which is supposed to reflect secular ideologies, have mirrored in its last decade's political methods a closer association with the Islamist militarized movements. Al-Assad the son made strong alliance with the Palestinian Hamas and the Lebanese Hezbollah, as well as he maintained special relations with the Turkish Justice and Development Party, the Islamic Labour Front in Jordan and others in the region. The goal of this closeness, as Ziadeh continues, is one and only: preventing the moderate Islamist branch of the Muslim Brotherhood from returning to the country.[173] In light of the regime's embrace of the *Jihadi* movements in the region, the answer then would be that the regime decided to exploit the fanatic and extremist Islamism (though it stands at the very opposite with it ideologically) because it believes that such an Islam needs the regime's logistical and political help; which, in return, would enable the regime to use this help as a card in its political negotiations and deals-cutting. It seems that such an Islamist option costs the regime much less than the high price it thinks it will be paying, if it turned positively toward the moderate and peaceful Syrian political Islam.

173 Ibid., p.155. Ziadeh describes this policy as "a strategy for survival that consists of building useful alliances against unforeseen circumstances."

This previous pragmatist, Machiavellian logic substantiates the argument of those who suggest that the Syrian regime's real war is not actually with the West, but with the moderate political Islamism and its possible presence in Syria. The confrontational and violent fanatic Islam cannot threaten the regime's popularity, because it cannot gain public attention and support in the country anyway. By nature, the fanatic, confrontational and *jihadi* Islamism is an esoteric and secretive activity. It does not function in the light, and it does not attend to the people's civil and daily life concerns, nor does it know how to face the shortages of such concerns or its corruptive abuse. It does not know how to do this, because it is ideologically an eschatological movement that seeks the apocalyptic end of this reality and the future other-life in eternity, disregarding the present situation of human race. It is, in other words, a movement that aims not at gaining power and ruling authority, but rather its total annihilation and eradication.

The most dangerous thing in the regime's reliance on secret alliances with fanatic terrorist Islamism is that the first victim of this gambling game is going to be Syria the country and the Syrian people; Syria the state and Syria the nation. This is what seems to be at the core of the nature of the latest events in Syria and the regime's brutal reaction to the people's uprising. If the regime won this war which had it unleashed in the first place, and continued its usual secret alliance with Islamist *jihadism* and its projects in the region, the Syrian society will lose an important chance for the birth of a domestic, moderate and pluralist Islamism that respects the secularity of the republic's power structure, sides with authority devolution, and stretches a positive and brotherly hand to the minorities under the umbrella of a civil, democratic dhimmitude-free and society based on human rights. In its resort to violence and cracking down solution by the help of 'terrorists' insertion and fanatic threat' conspiracy theory, the regime may actually be sacrificing the Syrian religious, ethnic and cultural mosaic. Exerting security solution and using the violent hand against the people's uprising, even if there are some minority groups among the rioters, who opted for fire and fighting back, would not protect the country from fanatic Islamism and would not keep the countries mosaic, plurality and long tradition of secularism intact. It will rather push the frustrated and depressed population towards the corner of fanatic religiosity. It will more radically foster the presence and consolidate the role of fundamentalist religious institutes, whose ideologizing discourse of hatred and revenge would become the people's last refuge in the face of the failure of the voices of reason, reconciliation and dialogue in society.

If the Syrians fear any possible dangerous civil war in the name of religion in Syria, it is a fear that stems, first of all, from distrusting the regime's discretion, open-mindedness and concern about the public interest when it comes to its relationship with the people and the majority's nature and rights in the country. Their fear has proven itself to be justified in light of how the regime reacted to the people's just and urgent move in the streets. If there is an Islamist threat that lurks in Syria at this stage, we should realize that the regime's opting for violence and armed force against it has succeeded in fertilizing its soil, rather than plucking it out at the roots. The only solution against such a threat is listening to the quiescent majority's voice, which calls on the regime to make a courageous self-correction and even self-dismantling move, and to grab the historical chance of bringing all the Syrian street's societal and political spectrums together and launching a real and realistic reformation and rebuilding campaign. The Syrian citizens, from all religions, ethnicities and sects, believe today that time has come for all the components of civil society, whether at the top or at the base of the pyramid, to realize that there is no salvation for Syria except by building a moderate, pluralist and non-confessional political public square, wherein the 'other' gains its proportionate share of representation, participation and freedom. Only then can one hold all the political movements, Islamist or religionist or otherwise, accountable for their agendas and can assess its success or failure in carrying its patriotic duties. Joining the hand of the ruling side with the hand of the Syrian political public square is much better than laying the fate of the country under the mercy of the high prices, which the mosaic of Syria would find itself paying to the fanaticism and religious and confessional hatred that may originate from any violence and armed encounter.

Chapter 4: The Christians and the Call for Change: Reflections on Syria (2)

In this chapter, I would like to continue my discussion from the previous one by speaking in further detail about the Christian stance on the recent uprisings in Syria. As a Christian, protestant Syrian citizen, I am used to hearing foreigners ask me about the Christians' condition in Syria and how they feel about the country's situation. As I already started showing in the previous chapter, this general inquiry is almost always followed by the specific question: does the Christian community suffer from persecution in Syria? Moreover, very recently and in of the latest uprising, I am also asked: do the Christians feel threatened by the outcomes of the people's rebellion against the present regime, and what future they envision to come out of the changing situation? In the following paragraphs, I will try to offer a brief descriptive insight on Syria as I and my fellow Christians see it and always wish it to be, as well as on what would be the Syrian Christians' general standpoint toward the recent riots against the Ba'thi regime there.[174]

As I pointed out in the previous chapters, the Christians' immigration from the Near East is also a challenge in the life of the Christians in contemporary Syria. Syria also suffers from the Christians' departure from the country, and the Syrian society witnesses the same challenges and questions, which the immigration of the Christians puts before the governing regimes of the neighbour countries, like Iraq, Egypt, Jordan, Palestine and Lebanon. Syria is also losing a substantial component of its society, despite the fact that the Christian Syrians, the residents and the expatriates alike, have never quit declaring Syria the most secure Arabic and Islamic sphere for the Christians of the region. Nevertheless, what makes the Christians' situation in the Arab world those days a case-study worth pondering more than ever before, are the recent uprisings that beamed almost all-over the Arab world and radically shocked its long unchanged, static foundations from east to west and from north to south.

The Christian people need to speak about their presence in Syria, and the relation of the country's conditions to their life's various political,

---

174 I rely in writing this section on an article in Arabic language I was asked to contribute to a file on contemporary Syria. See: Najeeb G. Awad, "Nafs Al-'oyon Al-Mubllalah, Nafs Al-Hawa' Al-Maleḥ," (The Same Wet Eyes, the Same Salty Air), in www.o2publishing.com N. 125, April. 1,2011.

economic, cultural and sectarian dimensions, within the framework of their identity as a group of people, who belong to a non-Christian-majority (Muslim) society. The Christians also need to discern this presence in its spatio-geographical nature, which in turn underpins the Christians' escape and emigration from the Arab world. The Christians opt for departure not because they do not feel affiliated to the Syrian land or because they deny any role in its fate and best interest, but actually because they cannot rid their imagination of the image of an open, pluralist and biocenotic Syria, in which they always believed and wherein they have grown up. This mosaic context is what foreigners witness when they visit Syria, and it is what makes them leave the country with a conclusion like the following:

> In Syria, open conflicts are rarely shaped along religious cleavages. On the whole, the various religious groups live peacefully next to one another or ever together, whereas in other countries in the region such as Jordan, Egypt, Iraq, and even in the politically more open Lebanon, religious communities withdraw into separate shells, cut themselves off, and become encrusted.[175]

When the Syrian Christians sense any threat or decay to this image, they, obligatorily not voluntarily, rapidly seek refuge in other countries around the globe. The main reason, in other words, for the Christians' emigration from Syria is not an Islamist fanaticism or religious persecution. It is rather the potential transformation of the Syrian society from a pluralist and inclusivist context into a monolithic and hegemonic environment; the change, that is, that can be caused by the ruling power, and not necessarily, in Syria's case, by the society's larger community.

I reflect on the living experience of my homeland while I personally reside as an emigrant abroad. I left my costal hometown, Lattakia, when I was nineteen years old, to find myself moving between Lebanon, England, America and finally Germany in the ensuing two decades. Despite my physical remoteness, and like other Syrian emigrants, I have never stopped visiting my hometown, and, more importantly, I have never quit tracing the news of Syria's sociological and civil developments and changes. With every visit, I wish to witness new changes capable of informing me whether or not my country is dynamically moving on the

175 Wieland, Syria: Ballots or Bullets? p.34.

international track of progress toward the future, with other nations on the globe. Yet, and with slight greediness, I also cling to the hope that the one and only thing that would never vanish from the Syrian arena, but would remain one of its unchangeable, everlasting features, would be the pluralist Syria; the beautiful mosaic which contains therein all the imaginable religious, sectarian, confessional, ethnic, gender and cultural affiliations. Every time I visit Syria, this wish not only makes me keen on mingling with my old friends, but also to build up new friendships with people from the different societal segments, which Lattakia beams with: Muslims and Christians; Protestants, Orthodox and Catholics; Arabs, Armenians and Turkomans; Sunnites, Alawites and Murshidites; religious and atheists; indifferents, agnostics and secularist people. This is Syria which I left once, and I still visit and fear for from ungratefulness, greed and evil ambitions. I worry that Syria will lose its pluralist, non-exclusionist and biocenotic sphere, because of any hegemony, corruption, intolerance and suppression that can be created by narrow political, religious, societal and privative interests.

This is also the same Syria in the eyes of thousands of Christians, who emigrated, escaping from life's difficulties, rulers' suppression, state's corruption and public demagogy. This pluralist image has not merely originated in the Christians' minds since the past forty years, as if it is an achievement of the recent ruling political system in the country. It is rather a genuine expression of a mosaic life sphere, which Syria has always enjoyed, and whose presence has even been more conspicuous and more constitutive of the Syrian society than it has been during the Baʿthist regime's era. The credits of this pluralist and tolerant sphere's existence in Syria are to be ascribed to the Syrian people and to no one else.

I would not be surprised if quite a few of the Syrian Christians, if not other Arab Christians as well, withstood my previous belief in the tolerant and moderate nature of Islam in Syria and confronted this belief by recalling stories from the region's past, when the Christians were subjected to violent, atrocious deeds from the Muslims. The emphasis on the Syrian Muslims' moderation and religious tolerance aims not at beautifying or veiling the dark moments in the history of the Christian-Muslim relations and coexistence in Grand Syria. Like any story of interreligious, intercultural and interethnic existence in any other part of the world, there were chapters in the Christian-Muslim story of coexistence in the Arab world, wherein death and violence were the prevailing characteristics of the events.

In his book on the Christians' and Jews' conditions in the Ottoman era in Grand Syria and Egypt, Bruce Masters pauses at the nineteenth century and detects therein the radical social change that emerged out of the Sultanate's reforms of its institutions and its creation of new organizing and governing bodies to resonate with the growing economic, political and ideological presence of the European influence in the Ottoman Empire. These changes, Masters postulates, alarmed the Muslims throughout the sultanate's Arab territories about the collapse of the old order. This aroused the Muslims emotionally and deeply seeded fear in them, lest that the rules they lived under, and which they once believed to be immutable, are now weakened, if not about to be demolished. The outcome of this disturbing fear and arousal was a series of violent riots that led to a enormous loss of life against the Christians: the violence against the Christians in Aleppo 1850, Mosul 1854, Nablus 1856, the famous civil war of 1860 in Lebanon and the subsequent riot in Damascus and then the events of Egypt 1882.[176]

While remembering these tragic occasions by the Christians of the region is any easily practiced habit even today (people usually recall drastic stories of the past faster than they do the joyful ones), figuring out the real reasons of these interreligious sectarian outbursts is a truly significant, yet much more demanding and challenging task.[177] Some of the contemporary local, Arab historians would evade attributing this clash to any inherent religious hatred that can be innate to the Muslims or the Christians of the region, and would rather view these sectarian outbreaks as the result of direct or indirect manipulation by the Ottoman authorities according to a 'divide-and-rule' strategy.[178] Or, they will consider it an

176 Masters, Christians and Jews in the Ottoman Arab World, p. 130 (pp. 130-168).

177 Ibid., pp.131ff. See also some other literature on this question, like Jeremy Salt, *Imperialism, Evangelism and the Ottoman Armenian 1878-1896*, (London: Routledge/Curzon, 1993); and Benjamin Braude and Bernard Lewis (eds.), *Christians & Jews in the Ottoman Empire: the Functioning of a Plural Society:2*, (New York: Holmes& Meier Publication, 1982).

178 for example, Kamal Salibi, "The 1860 Upheaval in Damascus Seen by al-Sayyid Muhammad abu'l-su'ud al Hasibi, Notable and Naqib al-Ashraf of the City," in *Beginnings of Modernization in the Middle East*, William Polk and Richard Chambers (eds.), (Chicago: University of Chicago Press, 1969); and and Samir Khalaf,

outcome of some European “stirring up [of] ethnic tensions to advance imperial ambitions.”[179]

Tracing the real causes of these violent confessional clashes is not the purpose of the present brief historical survey. What matters here is to realize that the Muslims’ occasional violence against their Christian compatriots is far from being the defining title of their coexistence in Grand Syria; nor is it something that either one of these two communities took for granted or treated as a common factor. Rather, both communities often searched for ways to maintain peace and positive acceptance relationships between each other. The history of the nineteenth century’s Syria tells us, as Masters notes, that the tragic events of 1850 in Aleppo and 1860 in Lebanon had consecutively, “a sobering impact on the Muslim elites throughout Syria.”[180] These Muslim leaders were, for example, the ones who prevented the ordinary members of their Sunnite community in Aleppo from hurting the Christians or abusing their properties. The British Consul of Aleppo at that time, J.H. Skene, writes in one of his official letters to his government that Aleppo’s Muslim *‘ulama’* (religious thinkers and leaders), “rebuked the Muslims who had accosted Christians on the street and preached sermons highlighting the equality of all humankind before God.”[181] Masters narrates how the Christians and Muslims worked together to maintain peace and extinguish any religious abuse in Aleppo in the following lines, which are worth to be cited in full.

> In the summer of 1860 as rumours of the fighting in Lebanon reached Aleppo, the city’s poor Muslims began to agitate against perceived Christian privilege once again. The governor [usually Muslim] met the threat with a firm show of force, apparently having learnt from the fatal mistake of his predecessor in 1850 not to let things get out of hand. The Christians has also absorbed a valuable lesson from the past and they offered ‘protection’ money to potential rioters. Further damp-

---

Persistence and Change in 19th Century Lebanon, (Syracuse: Syracuse University Press, 1979).

179 Masters, *Christians and Jews in the Ottoman Arab World*, p. 131.

180 Ibid., p.171.

181 David Gillard; David Throup and Michael Partridge (eds.), *British Documents on Foreign Affairs: Reports and Papers from the Foreign Office Confidential Print*, (USA: University Publications of America, 1995), Vol. 1, Prt. I, Sec. B, pp. 1-3.

ening the tensions, the Muslim notables organized patrols in the Christians quarters in a demonstration of civic responsibility.[182]

The events described above and the Christians' and Muslims' reactions in Aleppo both clearly show the following: first, the Muslims' insolence toward the Christians was not because of their religious faith or confessional identity, and it was not exerted by religiously-oriented or fanatic groups. It was rather a situation of an exposition of certain communities in the city to social and economic pressurization. These Muslims who accosted Christians on the streets were from the poor, lower-class community of Aleppo, while the Christians, being mostly merchants and educated, represented a rich and high-class community in the city. Secondly, what the Christians needed to do to calm down these reactions was not by any means to give p their religious affiliation and converting to Islam. It was rather important to financially contribute to the the attempt of improving the pressurizing economic conditions of the city's poor pockets. The case was, in other words, far from any religious persecution. Otherwise, no moderate, tolerant and inclusive characteristics could have been expressed in the Muslims' group-forming activity to protect the Christian quarters of the city.

The moderate and tolerant position towards the Christians did not only prevail in the Syria of the nineteenth century. It also characterized the Muslims' view of the Syrian Christians during the twentieth century, notwithstanding the rapid rise of political Islam and its ambitious endeavour to become the ruling power in the post-World War II and post-Ottoman Syria. In his book on the dynamics of power and political strife in modern Syria, Radwan Ziadeh offers a brief yet precise and valuable narration of the history of political Islam in the twentieth-century Syria. Ziadeh opines that political Islam has always played a prominent role in the post-Ottoman Syria, from the state's independence onward. The expansion of this role, Ziadeh maintains, is witnessed to a significant extent during the 1960s and 1980s, when the waves of violence started to break out between the Muslim Brotherhood and the security forces of the political ruling authorities.[183]

According to Radwan Ziadeh, the beginning of the organized Islamist work in Syrian society was actually far from any purely politically-driven

182 Masters, *Christians and Jews in the Ottoman Arab World*, p. 171.
183 Ziadeh, *Power and Policy in Syria*, pp. 129-156.

intentions. It first started with the Syrian religious scholars' attempt at establishing charitable societies to serve the population's humanitarian, educational and social needs. Later on, however, these societies, as Ziadeh explains, turned into expressions of, "the desire of religious scholars to recover their influence in the wake of the Ottoman state having introduced regulations that accorded value to non-religious knowledge, thus undermining their moral power."[184] What were originally established as organisations for promoting education and schools with an ambition of reforming society according to Muslim values and ideals, turned into major players in the political destiny of the country since the early half of the twentieth century. They concentrated primarily on mobilizing and organizing the public against the government, whenever the latter promoted or permitted what these organizations' managers and founders deemed contrary to Islam. The educational and intellectual contributions of these charitable societies, Ziadeh continues, played, since then, an influential political role in the country's history, like the central role it played in achieving Syria's independence in 1946.[185]

Within the context of the now independent Syria, the role of the Islamist organizations has intensified and grown stronger in the political and parliamentary life of the country. Organizations like the Islamic Cooperation Society, the Islamic Orientation Association, the Association of Islamic Charitable Work and the Ethics and Benevolence Society started to gain so much power and entertain a noticeable mobilizing ability in the society; so much so that its growing political interest reached the level of fighting for power and competing for authority with other political movements and ideologies in the country.[186]

---

184 Ibid., p.130. See also on the historical background of the challenge of reforms to the role of religious leaders in Grand Syria's society David Dean Commins, *Islamic Reform: Politics and Social Change in Late Ottoman Syria* (Oxford: Oxford University Press, 1990); Roderic H. Davison, Reform in the Ottoman Empire, 1856-1876, (Princeton: Princeton University Press, 1963); Şerif Mardin, *The Gensis of Young Ottoman Thought* (Princeton: Princeton University Press, 1962); and Moshe Ma'oz, *Ottoman Reform in Syria and Palestine, 1840-1861* (Oxford: Oxford University Press, 1968).

185 Ziadeh, *Power and Policy in Syria*, p. 131.

186 Ibid., pp.132-133. On these organizations in Syria, see also 'Abd al-Jabbār H. al-Jubūrī, *al-Aḥzāb wa-al-jam'īyīat al-Siyāsiyah fī Sūriyah min Awākhir al-Qarn al-Tāsi' 'Ashar Ḥatta 1958*, (The Political parties and Societies of Syria from the Late Nineteenth Century to 1958), (Baghdad: al-Ḥurria House, 1980).

The political role of these societies reached its peak of influence and extension in Syria's political life with the rise of the Muslim Brotherhood. This organization was the outcome of the merging of two Muslim youth groups from Homs and Aleppo, who joined forces in 1936.[187] In the following decades, the Muslim Brotherhood would prove itself the main and most influential Islamic political front in the country, whose popularity among the commoners lay in its consistent and prudent carefulness about shaping its political agenda and achieving its power-gaining goals with methods that are congenial with the Syrian factual, political, religious, ethnic and sectarian diversity and mosaic.[188] It is in the Muslim Brotherhood that we see a primary example of an Islamic organization, wherein politics is central to its discourse, rather than auxiliary to other-purposes mission.

This political mission would unveil on the ground, on the other hand, its religious roots and foundational presumptions during the parliamentary negotiations concerning the content of the republic's constitution of 1950. At the time, the Muslim Brotherhood fought for the constitution's declaration that the state religion of Syria is Islam, initially disregarding the ramifications of this step on the country's religious and sectarian minorities. When the Brotherhood would later on win the majority-vote, it needed to include this statement in the constitution, the then-leader of the organization, Muṣtafa al-Sibāʿī, would propose an amendment to the article concerned, wherein the constitution would grant respect to all religious beliefs in Syria, and would guarantee freedom of ritual practices and the preservation and observation of each religious sect's personal and private laws.[189]

One of the unfortunate and one-sided approaches to the Muslim Brotherhood's role in Syria's modern history is to attenuate this role to the drastically bloody phase, which this organization entered into with the Baʿth party's ascension to power since 1963; the phase that during the 1980s witnessed the bloody, brutal war between the Brotherhood's *jihadi* wing and al-Assad's regime and left the country with thousands of dead

187 Ziadeh, *Power and Policy in Syria*, pp. 133-150.

188 Ibid., p.134, which, according to Ziadeh, marks the Syrian Muslim Brotherhood's difference from its sister-organization in Egypt. This contextual-difference factor, Ziadeh adds, shows that "despite the overall intellectual supervision based in Egypt, the Syrian Muslim Brotherhood developed a political discourse independent of the official Egyptian line."

189 Ibid., pp.135-136.

citizens, thousands of prisoners, immigrants or with unknown fate and a very deep political, social and Muslim-Muslim rift that has not been abridged until this very moment.

Chasing after the history of the Muslim Brotherhood in Syria is definitely a topic that merits a separate, comprehensive study. The point I wanted to make from the previous exposition of the history of political Islam in Syria during the nineteenth and twentieth centuries is that the Muslim view of minorities and their relation to other religious groups in Syria was not driven by religious, doctrinal and discriminative premises, but was rather influenced by more rampant, internal and external, political, economic and societal circumstances, with a more dominant role to be ascribed to politics over other factors in the past century. The Islamic charitable organizations', and the following Muslim Brotherhood's, interaction with, and attitude towards, the Syrian context were both far from directed against the Christians or aimed at treating them as a '*dhimmi* group', with all the expected persecution and discriminating implications that follow from this labelling. They were actually directed against those other political parties and philosophies that are different from the ones these Islamists feel at home with. Moreover, even when the Muslim Brotherhood succeeded in making Islam *de jure* the religion of the state, their leader, and one of their most important historical intellectuals and theorists, Muṣtafa al-Sibā'ī,[190] called on the parliament for granting, by constitution, religious respect, freedom of practice and relative legislative autonomy to the religious minorities. In conclusion, it is this historical background that validates the claim that, on the social and religious levels, the Muslims of Syria are moderate and tolerant, and that the modern history of Syria shows that religious persecution has not truly been the political Islam's optional means for achieving any ambition. This is at least true at the level of the Muslims' relationship with the Christians of the country.

The shores of the Syrian, above-mentioned tolerant and moderate mosaic world is stricken those days by the tsunami of the Arab uprisings and public riots against the ruling regime's tyranny, oppression and dictator-

190 for this Islamist thinker's thought look at Muṣtafa al-Sibā'ī, *'Shtirakiyyat a*-Islam (The Socialism of Islam), (Damascus: Damascus University Press, 1959); al-Sibā'ī, *Akhlaquna al-Ijtema'īyah* (Our Social Morals), (Beirut: Islamic Office, 1987); and al-Sibā'ī, *Hāza Ma 'Allamatni al-Ḥayāt* (This is what Life Taught me), (Beirut: Islamic Office, 1987).

ship with their catastrophic outcomes of humiliation, poverty and total and comprehensive corruption that devastated the people for more than four decades. I vigilantly and anxiously look at the latest drastic and devastating blood bath in Syria's revolution, holding on to my belief that the beautiful Syrian mosaic will pass this storm without damage, but will rather emerge out of it brighter and stronger. Syria, which has always been the mother of all its children, will remain so in the coming years as well. I can, nonetheless, sense the pulse of the Christian public square in Syria during the latest catastrophic events in the country. I know that the Christians will not rush down to the streets *en masse*, and none of their clerical or lay representatives would participate in the uprisings and speak on behalf of them. I do also know, however, that the Christians of Syria lean on the longevity of Syria's mosaic and they do not envision any secure or possible existence in the country apart from it. They, like other citizens in this country, are eager for change and reformation; for building a free and democratic civil society; for a decent and prosperous life; for national reconciliation and for a country that respects and preserves the dignity and integrity of its inhabitants.

The Christians' contribution to the political, rebellious movement of the Syrian public square tends to be in general privative and individualistic in nature, with a genuine and honest critique and call for reformation, yet far from a bluntly and explicitly opposing and offensive tune. In their standing in the midst of Syria's complex, political and societal developments and stormy events – and in light of their minority situation and their resentment from any power-gaining ambition (contrary to the Lebanese Christians, for instance) or any obligatory need of societal recognition (like the Christians in Egypt strive for) – the Christians are traditionally reflective in their political position in the country of two groups:

1-the first is a group that is occupied with a serious fear from the jurisdictional and political outcomes of any political change that could occur in the country. More specifically, they reflect deep intimidation from the prevalence of an Islamist, political and constitutional, ruling alternative. While they are reconciled with the fact of the dominantly Islamic cultural identity of the Syrian nation, they are quite concerned, lest the change of the recent regime would lead to a crude islamization of the state's constitution and civil moral code, as well as to a possible Islamic endeavour to treat the Christians once more with an implicit, yet real and influential, *dhimmitud* attitude. This fear drives them to resorting to a Machiavellian position in their view of the riot and makes them sympathize with the regime and justify its hegemony in what one can describe as a reflection of features of the 'Stockholm syndrome'. Driven by this fear, the members of this group tend to express their wish for the remaining of the recent political status quo. They do this not because they fail to perceive the regime's corruption and hegemonic nature, but because they cannot whatsoever imagine themselves dealing with any alternative that, in their view, will lead to suppressing the Christians by means of their minority-status.

2-The second group, on the other side, principally shares the first group's the fear from *dhimmitud* and the islamization of the state or the constitution. Yet, its main concern and occupation is with the daily-life affairs and the stable availability and supplementation of material resources. It is a group that is generally adiaphorous to politics and power-struggles. It is not ready to get involved in any clash that may take place between the regime and any opposition activity, and it will not have a clear standpoint with or against each of the aforementioned clashing sides when they collide. Rather, it does not pay attention to the subject of political reformation per se, because it primarily holds no conviction that such a reform, if it ever happened, would make a real difference and cause a true pivotal change on the public level of societal living. This group's members would always recall how the regime brutally terminated the Muslim Brotherhood's attempts against it in the eighties, and they point at the regime's consistent oppression against the free thinking and human rights activists, most of whom are either dying in jails or are rigorously oberserved and bullied by the security forces.[191] This group, therefore, leans on an attitude that is noticeably pragmatist in nature, and busies itself with the daily goodwill of the family and its survival.

One can estimate almost equal followers to the above-mentioned positions among the Christians of Syria, the inhabitants and the immigrants alike. However, this fact does not stand against emphasizing the existence of lively and patriotic intellectual interactions between the Christians in the country and their compatriots, and that the outcomes of such interactions are versatile and multi-faceted in nature and extent. In the midst of

---

191 It has been estimated that in Syria there is one secret service (Mukhber) member for every 153 citizen over the age of fifteen: Wieland, *Syria: Ballots or Bullets?* P. 38; and Alan George, *Syria: Neither Bread Nor Freedom*, (London: Zed Books, 2003), p. 2.

this intellectual variety, numerous are also the Christians who believe that what threatens the pluralist and tolerant structure of Syria and equally stands against its freedom, change and progress indistinguishably lays its negative consequences over all the segments of Syrian society. Every disease that infects the internal situation of the country will deplete all the society's civil body and will not demarcate the ruler from the ruled, the strong from the weak, and the majority from the minority. Its disastrous ramifications will permeate, instead, through all the religions, the ethnicities, the sects and the sexes. Every corruption, fragmentation and clash that infects the country's body will leave negative and demolishing impacts on all the citizens, the immigrants included.

Reckoning with the aforementioned danger is what makes many Syrian immigrants, Christians included, believe that they have to serve Syria's safety and contribute to its future change and evolvement, especially during the latest uprising movement, and despite their residence abroad. The Western public, scientific and intellectual circles have recently enhanced their interest in conversing with the immigrant Syrians and Arab Christians about the Christians' situation in the Arab world and their position towards the latest events against al-Assad's ruling regime.

In the past months, I was asked by many friends and academic colleagues, German and other Westerners, about the public uprisings in Syria and the Christians' role therein. Some of them recited before me the popular claim that the Syrian Christians are not exposed to religious persecution like their brothers and sisters in Egypt and Iraq, for example (see my discussion of this view in the previous chapter). Therefore, as this opinion usually concludes, the Syrian Christians uniquely enjoy a secure, prosperous and ideal life among the Muslims and that they must support the Assad's Baʿath regime and be grateful to it because of this, and thus maybe stand with the regime against the rioters and their demands.[192] I always comment on this claim by stressing that the absence of any religious persecution in Syria against the Christians is correct. However, the credit of this religious security is not to be primarily given to the ruling political system. It is rather the fruit of the pluralist and mosaic legacy that is inherent to Syria's social history and the tolerant and moderate Islam that is deeply characteristic of the Syrian people. The absence of religious persecution is to be attributed to the positively open, horizontal

---

192 One of the recent articles I read, which entertain this view is in Philip Jenkins, "Death Warrants of Ancient Christianity."

coexistence between all the segments of Syrian society in the past and the present, and not during a specific ruling era.

Only because of this moderate Islam in the country, Philip Jenkins is not far from truth when he says that, "over the past century [to say the least] Syria regularly served as the last refuge for Christian communities who had been largely destroyed elsewhere in the Middle East." Jenkins is, nevertheless, quite inaccurate in his appraisal when he claims that the Baʿth's rule in Syria since 1960s "meant the dominance of the nation's religious minorities." To the contrary, and as a matter of fact, "the classic police state with a penchant for assassination whenever it sees fit," which Jenkins points to,[193] looks to those who oppose it and stand critical towards its misconduct with exactly the same merciless and brutal eye, and it rewards those who question its all-pervasive restrictions and abuse with jail, whether they were Sunnites, Christians or even Alawites, and whether Islamists, Communists, Marxists, Syrian nationalists, Pan-Arabists, Liberal Secularists or even Baʿthists.[194]

On the other hand, even if the Syrian Christians pride themselves on the absence of religious persecution in Syria, they clearly know that there are other dimensions of oppression and pressurization which do not differ in features and influence from those of persecution. These dimensions actually invite us to broaden the spectrum of our understanding of 'persecution' as a practice and they enable us to perceive the negatively influential presence of such a broad phenomenon of persecution in Syria. In Syria there is a political, economic, cultural, and civil oppression and abuse that radically shatters the country and lays indiscriminatively its destructive and dehumanizing influence and results, not only on the Muslims, but also on the Christians and all the other inhabitants of the country, the regime's confessional community (the Alawites) included. This fourfold persecution needs to be addressed seriously and its dangers need to be dealt with. This persecution puts the entire population of the country in a situation that can, as Alan George eloquently states, be caustically

193 Jenkins, "Death Warrants of Ancient Christianity."

194 for recent articles on interesting single examples of how the Syrian regime arrests people for their political opinion regardless to their background, religion or age, read Yassin al-Haj Saleh, "Prisoner of Damascus," in www.nytime.com 10, April, 2011; Radwan Ziadah, "Why Syria Will Be Next," in www.all4syria.info 10, April. 2011; and Mike Giglio, "The republic of Fear: Recent Protests in Syria Have Brought Brutal Government Crackdown – and Renewed Paranoia Among Dissidents," in www.newsweek.com 3, April. 2011.

described as, "a certain equality of misery."[195] It is because the Ba'thi regime has stubbornly and hubristically refused to acknowledge these four elements of persecution and to concede the urgent need for surgically eradicating the situation of misery that now makes the Syrian people screaming along the streets of almost all the Syrian cities: 'the people want to put down the regime'. And, it is for the sake of maintaining this fourfold oppression upon the people that the regime decided to respond to the street's demand of change and call for freedom with fire and blood, so far causing the death of over 14.000 citizens (normal citizens and army and police officers alike) and forcing an allegation that the rioters are fanatic *salafis*, who attempt at taking over the rule and turning the country into an Islamist caliphate, on the media and the public-opinion as a justification of its brutality and virulence.

Neither the Christians, nor any other group in Syria can anticipate what would be the political, societal, legislative or civil outcomes of the recent riots and the regime's bloody and brutal crackdown of the demonstrations. Yet, the Christians, and the Muslims too I would say, dream that tomorrow's Syria would remain the beautiful mosaic that they know. They yearn for the remaining of Syria as an oasis of moderation, pluralism, coexistence and the acceptance of the other. Therefore, they wish to see Syria emancipated in all its components from every kind of vertical oppression and tyranny by means of upholding its mosaic that is rich in many forms of positive, horizontal coexistence. Therefore, and along their belief in change, freedom, justice, democracy and truth, the Arab Christians in general, and the Syrians in specific, remain alarmed, lest any public uprising for the sake of obtaining these rights may convert into an oasis of violence, vengeance, anger and hatred, or appears eventually to be just an endeavour to snatch the stick of oppression and domination from its recent holders, instead of breaking the stick and erasing its marks altogether. From their long and complicated historical experience of living in a multi-religious, multi-ethnic and multi-sectarian world, the Christians have already learned that what starts with blood and fire ends with similar blood and fire, and that the vicious circle of death is a bottomless hole, and that what was built upon hatred and grudge does not vanish, but lurks under ash buried as coal, waiting for the right time to burn everything.

195 A. George, *Syria: Neither Bread Nor Freedom*, p. 1.

The Christians dream that the outcome of any change in Syria would give birth to a genuine civil, pluralist, democratic and secular state that treats people on the basis of citizenship and qualifications, under the rule of civil law and the principle of human rights, not on the basis of religious, non-civil legislation (be it even a Christian one). Thus, the Christians of Syria are hesitant to adopt positively, and enact factually, the idea of supporting any attempt for rebellion that is energized by any tribalist, nomadic, exclusionary, fundamentalist, judgmental, condemnative, retaliatory, religionist, backwardly or discriminative discourse or 'number-one declaration'. They believe that such alternative discourse or agenda would steal the mosaic identity from Syria, and would drown the nation in a whirlpool of oppression and counter-oppression, mobilizing and counter-mobilizing. Let us realize, after all, that the continuous devastating, bloody experiences of the Iraqi and the Egyptian Christians, despite the collapse of the dictatorial regimes in these two countries, seriously gnaws on the Christians in Syria and makes them count to thousand before saying: 'this uprising represents the Syria we belong to'.

In the first part of this chapter, I argued that the Christians in Syria would not get involved in a direct confrontational challenge against the regime, no matter how corrupted and tyrannical it was, because it will care much more about the preservation of the mosaic of the Syrian society and the social, cultural and religious tolerance that has always characterized it. This is the Christians' general and consistent view of their life and role in the country. In the remainder of this chapter, I will move from the general into the particular and purport to demonstrate the Christians' specific position towards the latest uprising that took place in the country since March, 2011.[196] The question I intend to answer before bringing this chapter to an end is: what have the latest developments of the riot in Syria revealed about the population's different positions, and where would the Syrian Christians stand between the clashing sides? I have already started constructing an answer to this question in the previous chapter. In this one, however, I will delve deeper into this answering attempt and elaborate on it in a broader and much detailed sense.

---

196 A short version of this chapter has been published in Arabic as Najeeb G. Awad, "Amma Baqi al-Nas fī Sūriyya fahum 'al- 'Aghlabiya al-Sākinah'," (The Rest of the People in Syria are 'the Quiescent majority'), in www.o2publishing.com no.128, 6, March. 2011.

The beginning of developing an answer to the above-mentioned question actually lies in answering another prior one: where does the majority of the Syrian population, Christians, Muslims, non religious, etc, stand in relation to the clash between the regime and the rioters on the streets? Answering this basic question would offer, by the nature of its content, an answer to the main inquiry of this Chapter.

I was writing these chapters in the spring of 2012. Over 13 months have passed by now since the uprising in Syria began. The regime's reaction to the people's demonstration fluctuated radically during that time. It started with an admittance of the people's fair demands and valid objections and requests. Yet, it rapidly shifted from a positive assent and acknowledgment into, first, a very negative, suspicious, and, later, strenuously brutal and completely violent strike-back. During the past months the regime made it clear to all the local and international observers that it deals with the uprising as a Sunnite fanatic-*salafi* enemy, who is launching a war against the regime's confessional sect (the Alawites) and aims at establishing an Islamist caliphate instead. Through this conspiracy, anti-terrorism theory, the regime justified its brutal and merciless crackdown of the protests, thus far causing over 14.000 casualties.

This bloody, catastrophic turn and the various reactions of the Syrians to it, has revealed to the observer quite early that the Syrian people are divided into three segments: one segment is blindly supportive and ferociously defensive of the regime. It even wishes the regime to continue using an iron, terminating fist against the rioters, and it lays its whole existence per se on the regime's salvation from its plight. This segment, however, represents a minority.

On the other hand, there is another segment that is absolutely, unconditionally and unreservedly supportive of the street's uprising. It defends this uprising in whatever form it may take and at any cost the people may pay. The followers of this group appeal to the people on the streets to maintain their rebellion and they call for its raving, despite all the possible vagueness and mistakes that may stem out of such a rough and non-calculated escalation. These mobilizers opt for this counter-violent and counter-aggressive reaction, because they also lay their fate on the final victory of the street's uprising in overthrowing the regime. This segment also represents a minority that is equal in size to the size of the previous one.

The past months, nevertheless, have unearthed the real existence of yet a third segment, which, in my opinion, made up by the majority of the Syrian population compared to the other two mentioned above, as well as it contains the biggest bulk of the Christian community in the country. I will not call this group 'silent', for it is not silent, though its voice is not loud or strong and its accent is not simmering or agitating in style. I will not also call it 'neutral', for no one can remain in neutral parity in Syria today, and no one wants to be either. In addition, this is not an impartial majority, but one that takes a real and sober position, which lies in refusing to be partial to one of the other above-mentioned two sides, because it believes that none of them echoes its own voice. Moreover, this majority is also not to be construed as the segment of the 'fearful'. For fear among the members of this group is neither different in nature, nor is it more (or less) in degree, than the fear of the regime's supporters, who are very apprehensive from the possible success of the street's uprising and the substantial change that the overthrowing of the regime would bring about. Nonetheless, the fear of this group is equal and similar to the fear of the rioters and their mobilizers from the regime's retaliation and counter-crackdown in case they decided to empty the public squares, retreat to their houses and concede to negotiation with the regime.

The third segment, then, is not silent, or neutral or exclusively fearful. It is a group that I prefer to call the 'quiescent majority', and the Christians seem to be willing stand within this majority. It is a majority that is utterly dissatisfied with the regime's perpetual reliance on its usual tyrannical, oppressive and bloody aggressive method, its condescending and hubristic attitude towards the people, as well as its systematic undermining of people's rights and underestimating of the ramifications and consequences of their suffering, bad conditions and tiredness from the recent ruling order. Yet, this is a majority that is equally saddened by, and disappointed with, the exclusionist and discriminative, simmering and agitating discourse that entices the public square's uprising and calls people to remain on the streets at all costs, and to welcome death as the passage to final victory. This is esspecially the case in light of the recently growing power of the instigation and spur that is noticeably becoming more Islamist, anathematizing, condemnatory, tribalistic, sectarian and vengeful in nature.

The Christians stand with this majority and they are also uncomfortable with the fact that the uprising people's vision is vague and imprecise and that those mobilizers, who ride the wave of the public square's opposition, are either in shortage of precise and reliable alternatives, or loaded with dangerous, disunifying and publically rejected agendas. This majority takes seriously its realization that the uprising on the street has no evidently reliable or tangible 'alternative' at hand, notwithstanding its equal perception and affirmation that the peoples have basic, essential and undeniable 'demands', which all the Syrian population aspire at and seek, and the country cannot be truly a 'state' without. Yet, this majority believes that these are still at the level of 'demands' and have not yet become tangible, complete and coherent 'alternative' for constructing a new republic, civil statehood that can preserve coexistence, plurality and unity in the country.

The quiescent majority stands astride between two equally hard choices in Syria: either the regime's opting for violence, political blindness and suicidal acrimony, on one side, or the street mobilizers' sentimental and over-reactive, religiously- and confessionally-energizing agitation of the population, on the other. Against opting for one of them, it pleads for Syria's release from the mercy of both option's mistakes and ill-visions. It hopes that a wise, reasonable and patriotic third voice may find a chance to invite the whole population to rise above any demagogic logic and to break the following three vicious circles: the physical violence and its verbal counter-violence, the vengeful fear and its suicidal counter-fear and the hatred and treason and its emotional and condemnatory counter-agitation.

The quiescent majority is failed by the regime when it sees that within the ruling circle the voice of coercion and the logic of oppression prevail over the voice of reason and reformation, the readiness to admit shortcomings and the intention for change. It seriously questions the conspicuous contradiction, which one can spot between the president's promises, decisions and decrees, and the conducts of the governmental media and security forces and their persistence in all the procedures that defy and militate clearly against the declared reformation-decision.[197] This major-

---

197 The decentralization of the decision-making in Syria has been noticed and pointed at by scholars in the past years. For example, in his book on Syria during the rule of Bashar al-Assad, Carsten Wieland says the following on this matter: "the plural 'centres' is the keyword that describes the situation in Syria after the death of Hafez al-Assad. His westernized son, Bashar, who initially studied in London to become an ophthalmologist, lacks his father's charisma, craft and experience. Beyond this, important funding sources that had used to buy the loyalty of key players and critics have disappeared. A single and undisputed centre of power is a thing of

ity asks in a calm yet rational voice: who rules Syria now and who decides its fate, and which clumsy, bloodily fatal game is the whole country pulled into by these authority-holders?[198]

On the other hand, the quiescent majority affirms that the rebellions' intentions and motives are reliable and trustworthy in their nature and goal. It knows that those who occupy the public squares in Syria's cities are innocent and sincere normal citizens, whose screams stem from the heart of the whole population's thirst for justice, freedom, human rights, decent life, prosperity and dignity. However, this majority is seriously worried when it hears the discourse of those who ignite the population and purport to dictate and orchestrate the mass' movement, especially when they continue to pressuring the people to remain on the streets non-restrictively, despite the bloodshed and the increasing amount of casualties, and prevent them from giving the regime's reformation promises' any chance, during which the people can examine and discover the sincerity or deception of the regime. The quiescent majority hears the discourse of the street's extremist mobilizers. It trembles from, and abhors its exclusionist, tribalistic, divisive, vengeful and inflaming approaches that manipulate people's sentiments and implement the noble, by now

---

the past in Syria….those in the opposition who had hoped for liberalization when Bashar took office are exerting pressure, but they no longer face a homogenous authority. Syrians are being ruled by different power centres that are blocking and fighting one another": Carsten Wieland, *Syria, Ballots or Bullets?* pp. 7-8.

198 In his recent book on the ruling-game in Syria, Radwan Ziadeh opines that "getting to know what mechanisms underlie decision-making in Syria is a highly intricate and difficult task. This is due less, for example, to the complexity of the process than it is to the secrecy that surrounds a given legal formula, which inevitably results in different research projects proceeding from different viewpoints": Ziadeh, *Power and Policy in Syria*, p. 14 (pp. 14-35). Scholars' opinions about the ruling mechanism in Syria varies and swings between 'one-man-show ruler' proposal and a 'ruling closed-circle' one. See for example, Patrick Seal, *Assad of Syria: the Struggle for the Middle East*, (Berkeley: University of California Press, 1989); Lucian Peterlan, *Hafez al-Assad: the Career of a Combatant*, Ilias Bdewi (trans.), (Bamascus: Tlas Publishing House, 1987); Moshe Ma'oz, *The Sphinx of Damascus: A Political Biography*, (New York: Weidenfeld& Nicholson, 1988); Steven Heydemann, *Authoritarianism in Syria: Institutions and Social Conflict 1946-1970*, (Ithaca: Cornell University Press, 1999); Hanna Batatu, *Syria's Peasantry, the Descendant of its Lesser Rural Notables and Their Politics*, (Princeton: Princeton University Press, 1999); Volker Perthes, *The Political Economy of Syria under Assad*, (London: I.B. Tauris, 1995); Eyal Zisser, *Decision Making in Assad's Syria*, (Washington: Washington Institute for Near Eastern Policy, 1998); and E. Zisser, *Assad's Legacy: Syria in Transition*, (London: Hurst & Company, 2001).

terrifyingly excessive, sacrifices of their casualties and martyrs in its verbal violence and hatred.

Yes, Syria has not strolled down to the streets *en masse*, and the largest portion of the Christians in the country did not actively protest with others in search for freedom and change. And yes, the majority of the Syrian population, the Christian community included, is definitely not standing unreservedly and slavishly beside the regime and it does not want it to remain the statically same. The majority of this country's Christians and population, to the contrary, is still standing in the shadow of its deep concern, sadness and wishful thinking and is resorting to its inactive position. More importantly still, many Syrian Muslim, Christian and secularist intellectuals stand within this majority's circle, because they read nothing but a vain and void strife that does not promise any alternative, and does not feature any foreseen hope between the line of the latest events and radical developments. If we look at the position of Syria's intellectuals from beyond the framework of the governmental media's treason mentality and the people-arousersing, inflaming discourse, we would realize that the Syrian intellectuals were not at all silent or impartial. They just evaded both the involvement in the regime's justification of its violence and brutality, and the endorsement of any fanatic and confrontational exploitation of the rioters' blood and sacrifice. Many of the Syrian intellectuals, Muslims and Christians, who have always been known as the first opposing front against the regime's corruption and hegemony – even when the regime's power, dominance and external support were at their peak – stand with the quiescent majority and stretch their hands toward the rational, objective and dialogical members among the two clashing sides. These intellectuals pay a very high price for this position, as they simultaneously suffer from the regime security forces' intimidation and persecution, as well as face the accusations, blames and attacks of the extremist mobilizers of the riots.

Whereto is Syria moving from here? This is the most difficult question. The quiescent majority realizes more clearly by the progress of time that the events of the public squares alone will, unfortunately, decide the answer, despite the fact that neither the people on the streets, nor the members of the regime can actually either tell us how these events will end, or can decide such an end by themselves. The only remaining hope is to enable the public squares to listen to a voice that is different from the voices of, both, the regime's hard-line members and supporters, and the streets' confrontational, fanatic and extremist mobilizers. This different voice is today the voice of the quiescent majority and the intellectual opposition members within it. This voice, nevertheless, needs the aid of the media-centres, the thinkers and authors, and the decision-making circles in the Arabic and international societies, to start finding its way to the ears and minds of the rioters. This voice needs a pulpit, from which it can address, mediate and build bridges between the reasonable and wise people of the regime and the rioters. On the other hand, the noble and innocent heroes, who went down to the streets, before any one else, need a parallel dialogical and political interaction to accompany the peaceful, patriotic and honest movement of the common citizens. Everyone in Syria, who believes in change, freedom and a future, should support the voice of the quiescent majority and help the intellectuals therein to establish a contact with the wise and reasonable in the two other groups, so that Syria can truly step away from an impending black hole that is about to swallow the whole republic, as the latest events in the country show.

Part III

The Arab Christians and the Promise of a Contextual Discourse

Chapter 1: A Possible Arabic Contextual Theology: Why?

Every now and then, one can hear in the Arab Christian communities some individual theologian conceding the necessity of developing a contemporary theological discourse that can relevantly and meaningfully speak to the Arabic world's cultural, socio-political and multi-religious context. Until this very moment, however, the Arab Christian theologians, though very few in number, have not yet started developing any detectable and reliable comprehensive and fully-fledged theology that stems contextually from the questions, existential conditions and struggles of the inhabitants of the Arab world. The call has already been aptly raised. The fulfilment, nevertheless, has yet to witness its visible dawn.

It is my belief that one can validly affirm, in the light of the latest historical and pivotal changes that are striking the Arabic region and transforming it forever, that developing an Arabic contextual theology is more than a necessity. The public scene may not be ready to realize the necessity of a *theology*, or any theological discourse, at this very moment. There are Arabs, Christians and Muslims alike, who would even argue that religion is one of the main problem-generators in the region. They would wish for a disenchanted and rather secular futural Arabic public-square, wherein religion plays no role whatsoever, or at least exerts as minimal as possible an influence, in the sociological-political, cultural and societal life of the people. Religion is considered by quite a few Arabs as not only the opium but also the core divisive factor in the region. In the light of this, proposing that the Arab Christians in the Near East ought to develop a theological stance on their role and existence in the Muslim-majority seems to be an outdated voice from the dark past of Arabic history, a hardly irrelevant call for today's Arab world.

The above notwithstanding, it is my belief that the aspects of such a Christian theology in the Arab context would gain evident significance not only in the coming years, as the Palestinian Lutheran theologian Mitri

Raheb perceptively emphasizes,[199] but more significantly in the very near future, as the Arab uprisings have started to seed their roots in the Arab region's soils and their fruits are about to show themselves gradually on the scene.

I can imagine that an invitation for pursuing such a theological discourse may be misunderstood by the non-Christians, Muslims and Jews, or even be misused by the fundamental, charismatic and evangelistic Christians of the area. I, therefore, stress here that this is not a call for developing a religious agenda for evangelizing and proselytizing the Arab societies or for making their members 'followers of Christ'. Nor is this a call for changing the Christian biblical and theological principal of separating religion from state. The Christians in the Arab world have always reflected their fear from the possible negative and discriminative consequences of any Islamization (and Judization) of the state on the basis of Islam's association and unification of religion and statehood. So, attempting at replacing such Muslim association with a Christian one would be the least appropriate project and the least needed proposal in the region.

What is meant by calling to develop an Arab Christian Contextual Theology is inviting the Christians to be more active by contributing to the life of their Muslim-majority (and Jewish-majority) homeland from the dimension of their religious particularity and this particularity's intellectual kernel with its epistemic ramifications. It is, more specifically, an invitation for a qualitative and particular involvement that is derived from, and inspired by, the values of truth, love, reconciliation, other-acceptance, altruism, relationality, hope and peace which the Christians ultimately learn from the life, ministry, death and resurrection of their faith's epicentre, Jesus of Nazareth, and which they always interpret, at least in the East, inspired by, and thinking after, the church's theological thought.

As I stated at the beginning of this chapter, though no fully-fledged, complete Arabic Contextual Theology has yet been produced, there are some Arab Christian theologians who pointed at the necessity of such a theological contribution and invited others to pursue its development. In the ensuing sections, I shall be pointing at some of these voices as I elaborate further on my view of the reasons and purposes of developing an Arabic Christian Contextual Theology.

---

199 Mitri Raheb, I Am A Palestinian Christian, p. 43.

In his attempt at suggesting an agenda for such a Christian Arab theological contribution to his twenty-first century's Palestinian context, the Lutheran theologian Mitri Raheb elaborates on the implications of such a theological contribution to the life of the Arab world. Mitri argues that in such a religiously moulded discourse, faith and politics cannot be separated. Anticipating the possible misreading of his point, Mitri does not stop at marrying politics and faith. He further emphasizes in an explanatory manner that no blending of politics and faith is to be concluded from his claim, for drawing the demarcating boundaries between politics and faith is to be strictly maintained at the same time.[200] They are supposed to enrich each other's perspectives and serve together in speaking to the concerned context as two sides of one and the same coin, namely the goodwill of the human being. Neither politics nor faith, then, must use the other as a tool for achieving its own ultimate goals or turn the other into an instrument in the service of its discourse and agenda's domination in societal and civil life.

Mitri's qualified claim is not irrelevant to the recent scene of the Arab world. It is a fact that in the conflicts of the Arab world, the latest uprisings included, politics is never out of the picture but almost always part and parcel of the problem. At the same time, the Arab world's context, in its Christian, Muslim or Jewish societal segments, is inherently religious in nature and religiosity has never left the public square or been thrown to its far, shadowy margin. Be that as it may, religion is an inescapable contributor to the solution of any conflict in the region, and its role is essential in any change and reformation attempt. From this angle, one can say that the Christians are expected to make a contextual theological contribution, not only toward peace and justice in the region, as Mitri Raheb correctly maintains,[201] but also toward the establishment of new states and civil societies that are shaped after plurality, democracy, the rule of law, human rights, freedom and coexistence.

A Christian Arabic contextual theology like the one I propose, must, moreover, be also able to contribute to the understanding of the role of religion in human life, especially in the light of the attempt of the Islamist fundamentalist groups in the Arab world to replace the falling dictatorships with Islamist states and to apply the Sharīʿa law as the state's constitution or sole source of legislation. If these groups succeeded in their

200 Ibid., p.43.
201 Ibid., p.43.

endeavour, the Arab uprisings would turn a moment of hope and future for the people, into a cause of transforming the region's mosaic, colourful context into a monolithic and entirely Islamic setting. This, if happened, would force the members of other social and religious groups either to desert the area for good, or it might turn them into people who are imprisoned in their non-Islamic religious affiliations; into citizens whose civil and nationalistic identity is totally reduced to this religiosity, and who are then forced to survive by paying the high price of their religiosity, which lies in seeking always the satisfaction and the mercy of the dominant majority.

The beginning, therefore, of evading such a drastic consequence would be redefining the concept of 'religion' and re-marking the boarders of its role and relation to human life and to human rights in the civil public-square. Mitri Raheb eloquently and accurately expresses this need when he states that the concept of religion is often given a political content in the Middle East. This mixing of religion with state not only distorts religion's true role in society. It, more seriously, misuses God's name when it uses God as a surrogate. By 'surrogate' Raheb points to the position of those who, when living in politically and socially unstable and oppressing circumstances, retreat to God and to religious zeal as their last resort, dreaming of an after-life Utopia instead of facing reality and changing it. Religion in this case converts, as Raheb states, into "an escape in imagination out of the real world into a better and more peaceful world. Fear, hopelessness, and frustration are used as whips to drive people to God – which really means to a particular political option, even if it appears in 'non-political' lamb's clothing."[202]

Now, despite my aforementioned explanation and Mitri Raheb's support of it, one may still like to raise the following question: why do you insist on calling for developing an *Arabic* contextual theology? Is it out of a sheer linguistic reason (i.e. it is an address to the Arabs), or is there another more substantial reason for this? On the other hand, why do you believe that such a discourse must be *theological*; why not a political, cultural or purely intellectual one? The first question invites me to look at the issue of the Eastern Christians' relation to the external Arabic-Islamic setting, in which they live and to which they belong. While, the second question makes me look at the relation of religion with culture as this relation is reflected in the conventional attitude of the eastern Christian theologians to their non-theological context in the Arab world. In the

202 Ibid., p.44.

coming paragraphs, I would like to reflect briefly on these two dimensions as an attempt at showing why it is incumbent for the eastern Christians, should they begin to play a responsible role in the Arab world, to present an Arabic contextual theological discourse to their Arabic-Islamic societies.

In their call for a pluralist, inclusive civil-society and state, the youths of the latest Arab uprisings, whether consciously or unconsciously, not only deconstructed the previous Arabic totalitarianism and hegemonic politics and authoritarianism. They also put an end to the traditional trends of identity-formation that characterized the old Arab society's construction process. In the last century, the national identity-formation process played the central role in the stabilization and solidification of the independent Arabic states. However, one of the consequences of this centralization of identity-formation was, as Nicola Pratt notices, "the erasure of national difference in order to construct unity within the nation-state."[203] By calling for constructing a post-collectivist, pluralist civil society, nevertheless, the youths are actually, even if indirectly, moving toward redefining, "the nation to include the previously marginalized voices – on the bases of class, gender, region, religion or ethnicity."[204] In other words, these rioters are actually shaking seriously the historical nationalistic, cultural, linguistic and ideological constructions of national identification; of, that is, what did it used to mean to be Syrian, Lebanese, Iraqi, Egyptian, etc, but, more dramatically still, what did it used to mean that one is an 'Arab'.

Famous among the Arab intellectuals is Lawrence of Arabia's challenging and intriguing saying at the beginning of the past century, "the first difficulty of the Arab movement was to say who the Arabs were."[205] This difficulty not only stands before re-constructing an Arab, pluralist identity that would include all the minorities of the Arab-speaking region. It equally challenges the invitation for an *Arabic* Christian contextual theological discourse and demands a clarification of the term 'Arabic' in such a phrase. In what sense would this contextual theology would be Arabic? What does it mean that the called-for discourse is Arabic and not

203 Pratt, *Democracy and Authoritarianism in the Arab World*, p. 145.

204 Fred Holiday, *Nation and Religion in the Middle East* (London: Saqi Books, 2000), p. 31.

205 Lawrence of Arabia, *Seven Pillars of Wisdon: A Triumph* (Middlesex: Penguin Books, 1965), p. 31.

otherwise? From where does the necessity of an Arabic identity to such a theology stem?

The question about the identity of theology takes us to a more fundamental question about the identity of the one who is invited to compose such a theology. It, more specifically, brings us to the epicentre of one of the most complicated and still understudied topics in the life of the eastern Christians: who are the Christians of the Arab world, and how are they to identify themselves in the Arabic context?

The Lebanese philosopher Charles Malek once asked, "is a Christian Arab possible? Is a Christian Arab culture possible?"[206]The Christians in the Arab world have either attended to the question by rejecting its sceptic accent and affirming unreservedly their Arab identity. Or, they ignore the question altogether. Beyond these two extremes stand rare attempts at reflecting on the issue of identity in principle and its relation to the Christians in the Middle East.

One of the local Arab scholars (a student of Charles Malek) who wrote on the subject of identity from a Christian-Arab context is the Lebanese, Protestant theologian, George Sabra. During the past twenty years, Sabra published numerous Arabic and a few English essays on the issue of being a Protestant Arab in the Middle East and on the Protestants, as western missionary-planted communities, and their image in the wider Middle Eastern non-Protestant and non-Christian Arab circles.

One of Sabra's most important contributions on the Christians' identity in the Muslim Arab world is an essay he wrote in 2006 entitled, "The Two Ways of Being a Christian in the Muslim Context of the Middle East." Far from proposing a specific identity or understanding of the Christians' self-identification in the Arab world, Sabra opts for reflecting on what he describes as, "the basic orientations or fundamental attitudes of Christians in response to their Muslim context," and as the, "pre-given, basic outlooks which shape and colour the views and accounts of Middle Eastern Christians concerning their experience with Islam."[207]

There are two fundamental attitudes or pre-given outlooks which Sabra pinpoints in the present Christian scene in the Arab world: one follows the slogan, "avoid estrangement from Muslims at all costs," and the

---

206 Charles Malek, "The Near East: the Search for Truth," in *Foreign Affairs*, 30, 1952, pp. 231-264, p. 260.

207 George Sabra, "Two Ways of Being Christian in the Muslim Context of the Middle East," in *Islam and Christian-Muslim Relations*, 1(17), pp. 43-53, p. 43.

other the slogan, "save Middle Eastern Christianity at all costs."[208] Being part of the Muslim world since the seventh century, the eastern Christians found themselves confronted with the task of rescuing their communal and religious identity and maintaining their existence despite being a minority. Some of them decided to do this by turning their faces, Sabra states, towards the east and inclining toward embracing their Islamic life-setting. Whereas, others endeavoured to protect themselves from the surrounding situation and to maintain their identity and freedom by looking west and trying to connect to the larger Christian community there.[209] These two choices, Sabra notices, became the two main components of the history of the Christians in the Arab-Islamic context since that era.

Sabra observes in today's Middle Eastern scene the existence of the aforementioned options incarnated in Christians who are keen on emphasizing their Arabic identity, 'Arab Christians', and other Christians who resort instead to an eastern title, 'Eastern Christians'. The former group, according to Sabra, tends normally to address the Arab Muslims and convince them that the Christians share with the Muslims the strife over the same, common cause. This 'common-cause claim' served its followers well during the past century, when the followers of the two religions fought for Arab nationalism over-against Ottomanization, western colonialism and Zionism. Additionally, in this group's view, Arab and Islamic culture, Sabra points out, "is warmly embraced as the natural home and world of Arab Christianity."[210]

On the other hand, the eastern Christians stand, as Sabra explains, on the very opposite river-bed of the Arab Christians. They do not focus on the commonality and unification between them and their Muslim compatriots, though they do not necessarily antagonistically withstand co-existence and cooperation. They rather prioritize and treat as their main cause, "the freedom and integrity of Christian existence in the Middle East," which eventually, Sabra opines, drives them to find in the west an aid and tutelage from the threatening insecure, "living among a non-

---

208 Ibid., p.44.

209 Ibid., pp.45-46.

210 Ibid., p.47. One of the prominent exponents of the 'Arab Christians' options, according to Sabra, is the Roman Orthodox Bishop of Mount Lebanon, George Khodr. See on the latter's view of this trend George Khodr, "Al-Masīhiyya al-ʿArabiyya wal-Gharb," (The Arab Christianity and the West), in *Al-Masīhiyyun al-'Arab: Dirāsāt wa-Munāqashāt*, (The Arab Christians: Studies and Discussions), Elias Khoury (ed.), (Beirut: Mu'ssasat al-Abhath al-ʿArabiyya, 1981).

Christian majority."[211] The main driving-force of this option is the conviction of its holders, as Sabra articulates, "that Arabs could not really separate Arab nationalism and identity from Islam."[212] Therefore, these Christians find home in the wider Christian community outside the Middle East than in the local Arabic, Muslim-majority context. The main obsession of the Eastern Christians is not, thus, the anti-western sentiments, but rather Islam: "how can Christianity in the Middle East live with Islam in such a way as not to lose its faithfulness to its identity and its freedom."[213]

Sabra emphasizes that the 'Arab Christians' and the 'Eastern Christians' approaches are far from being sharply divided or standing conceptually in total tension. They rather inter-relate and "almost invariably both exist in one and the same person."[214] These two trends neither divide the Christians, nor do they draw categorizing lines between their churches or denominations, but actually permeate through the political, social, cultural and intellectual aspects of the Christians' lives in the region. And, when one asks which approach should the Christians dominantly opt for, Sabra seems to be in favour of an open-ended answer, as he concludes that both trends continue to exist equally in the Arab world and both equally cause a dilemma in the life of the Christians, since both, as Sabra concludes, have some truths in their claims.[215]

---

211 Sabra, "Two Ways of Being Christian in the Muslim Context of the Middle East," p. 48.

212 Ibid., p.48. Of those who follow this option, see the views of Albert Hourani, *Arabic Thought in the Liberal Age (1798-1939)* (Oxford: Oxford University Press, 1962).

213 Sabra, "Two Ways of Being Christian in the Muslim Context of the Middle East," p. 49. Sabra points specifically to the dhimmitude and some social coexistence concerns, stating that "the dhimmi status of Christians under Islam and the dhimmi Christian mentality that results from it are constantly recalled, elaborated on and condemned. Attention is always drawn to certain basic features of Islam which make it extremely difficult, if not impossible, for non-Muslims to coexist in equality with the Islamic majority: the non-separation of religion and state, the strict identification of God's final revelation that is valid for aspect of life with the literal content of a seven century book, and the non admission of freedom of conscience, especially, the freedom to change one's basic religious convictions, which is the ultimate basis for a full recognition and respect for the 'otherness' of the other" (Ibid., pp.49-50).

214 Ibid., p.50.

215 Ibid., p.52.

George Sabra does not offer us a clear-cut position on the Christians' relation to Arabic identity, or about whether the Christians must or must not develop such an identity in interaction with their Arabic context. He limits his essay to the description of the situation of the Christians in the Arab world, and he points at the challenges and complications they have to face in their existence in an Islamic context. Where George Sabra's reading stops, however, the reading of another Arab Lebanese theologian starts and goes much further. Like Sabra, Mosheer Basil ʿOun is a Christian (Melkite) Arab thinker who is also interested in understanding the Christian identity and role in its eastern-Arab framework. Yet, rather than just presenting the various attitudes the Christians show towards their Arabic context, ʿOun assumes the basicality of acknowledging the Arabic sphere and of addressing it from a Christian-Arab standpoint. He calls for the Christians in the Middle East to develope an Arab Christian discourse that, as he says, "corresponds with the requirements of the contemporary Arab humans' awareness and provokes in the Christians' testimony the energy of belonging to such an awareness, devising for it renewal pathways in relation to the consolidation of the loyalty to such belonging."[216]

'Oun argues that the adherence to the Arabic-Islamic awareness stems from the historical factor that the Christians who inhibited the East had started to be influenced by Islam since the seventh century AD. From that age onwards, the Christians have often felt in the depth of their theological thinking their rootedness in the Eastern context, which by that time became the East of Islam and Arabic culture. These two new elements (i.e. Islam and Arabic culture) not only affected the Christians' cultural identity, but also shaped their intellectual discourses, their legislative perspectives and their behavioural and ethical appraisals.[217] 'Oun believes that this factor causes the Christians serious confusion: they realize their inability to be an autonomous or self-ruling entity, yet they simultaneously eagerly aspire to express freely and independently their political, social and religious views, even when these latter differ from the thought of their Muslim rulers. This makes, according to 'Oun, the dialectic of freedom-conformity the central concern of every contemporary Arab

216 Mosheer Basil ʿOun, *Al-Fekr al-'Arabi al-Dini al-Masīhy: Moqtadhayāt al-Nohūdh wal-Tajdeed wal-Mo'asarah* (The Christian Arab Religious Thought: the Requirements of Revival, Modernization and Contemporaniety) (Beirut: Dār al-Taīʿah, 2007), p. 6.

217 Ibid., p.49.

Christian discourse. How can the Christians maintain their religious freedom, intellectual independence and particularity in the midst of, and not in spite of, their presence in an Arabic society, wherein the factors of the Qur'ān's religious refrentiality and the criterial role of the Arabic culture are dominant? How can they adapt their intellectual and faith witness with the requirements of belonging to such a context?[218]

During the age of the modern Arab Renaissance between the middle of the nineteenth and the early twentieth centuries, the Arab Christians, ʿOun proceeds, were faced with a new additional challenge, namely the influence of the western philosophical and political thought and its attractive relevance for the reforming and reviving of the Arab culture. The Christians believed that the Arab world's political, social, economic and cultural conditions need re-evaluation and critical reconstruction. In order to achieve this purpose, they derived many modernist western trends and principles, the first among which were the values of freedom, rationality and plurality. In the ensuing decades, they played by virtue of this adoption a pioneering role in convincing their Muslim co-citizens about the necessity of launching a Christian-Muslim incorporation and adoption of these western values and using them for ultimately fulfilling the goal of reviving Arabic thought. Within this new circle of reconciling the factor of religious particularity and cultural distinction, on one hand, with the need of reviving and reforming Arab societies, on another, the Arab Christians, ʿOun maintains, found themselves creatively re-viewing and re-thinking the issue of identity, self-understanding, tradition and legacy, the liberation of the Arabs, the nature of Arab societies, the enlightenment of reason, and the way for developing orders and structures.[219]

One of the intriguing claims ʿOun makes at this stage of his historiological narration is his conviction that the theologians among the Arab Christian contributors to the Arab revivalism were, when compared to

218 Ibid., p.50.

219 Ibid., pp.53-54. According to ʿOun, the Arab Christians can here be categorized into two groups of thinkers and authors: the 'Arab Christian Intellectuals' and 'the Arab Christian Theologians'. He concedes that the members of these two groups are not strictly divided and that their intellectual and theological contributions intertwine in terms of content, concerns and addressed challenges. However, he also points out that one should not undermine the discrepancies and sometimes stark contrasts between these two groups' approaches and discourses in terms of their issues' prioritization, their situations' analysis and their epistemological and hermeneutic methodologies (Ibid., pp.56ff).

other Christian intellectuals, the least influential and instrumental. The reason of this under-contribution lies in the fact that these theologians focused on showing the religious distinction between Christianity and Islam and their total equation of 'culture' and 'religion'. So, if Christianity and Islam are different and should be distinguished, their cultural implications and components must also be divided. The logic underneath this position is the belief that religious distinction entails cultural division. Eventually, the Arab Christian theologians, ʿOun opined, ended up paying the least attention imaginable to the Arab culture and hardly engaging intellectually with, or addressing theologically, the cultural, societal and anthropological questions of revivalism. Their discourses were narrowly and one-sidedly restricted to discussing purely religious and dogmatic inquiries pertinent to the Christian Faith's doctrinal and metaphysical differences from Islam's. ʿOun explicitly states that this segregationist mentality unsurprisingly demonstrates, "that these theologians thought that…dealing with the religious distinction between Christianity and Islam exempts them from dealing with…the cultural distinction between the two religions, since the religious distinction, in their view, overrides the cultural one."[220] By doing this, the Arabic theological text these Christians produced rarely, if ever, touch upon the bearings and implications of the Christian salvation message on the suffering realities of the Arab humanity.[221]

ʿOun suggests for defeating this shortcoming that the Arab Christian theologians must critically assess the past Christian Arab theological contribution to Arabic thought. They must, he emphasizes, highlight the fact that theological thought is inescapably linked to lived situations, so that the theologians acknowledge their responsibility of contemplating and reflecting on the real situation of the Arab societies before anything else.[222] They are supposed to depart from the political, societal and religious concerns and dilemmas in these societies' particular contexts while they try to develop a Christian Arab theological approach that can plausibly speak to the Arab world and participate in its revivalism. This alone, ʿOun believes, would furnish for a 'local' theological thinking that not only re-interprets and re-presents the general or eastern Christian doctrinal heritage, but more significantly enlightens and reconstructs, along

---

220 Ibid.57.
221 Ibid., p.58.
222 Ibid., p.63.

with Islamic thought, all the existential fields of the Arab human existence.[223]

Valuable for my concern about the question of why an 'Arabic' and 'theological' discourse and not otherwise is ʿOun's understanding of these terms and his insistence on their relevance to any discourse the eastern Christians may develop to address the progress and reformation demands in the Arab world. On 'Arabic', ʿOun accurately states that developing an *Arabic* Christian theology implies an attempt at reconciling the religious with the cultural, so that this theological discourse would reveal the rootedness of the eastern religious heritage and legacy, which the Christians claim allegiance to, in the soil of the Arabic culture and civilization: as, "the eastern signifies the religious affiliation, the 'Arab' designates the cultural adherence."[224]

On the other hand, regarding 'theological' ʿOun argues that its importance lies in its designation of a discourse that is different from any other Christian contribution which is narrowly and exclusively either political, economic, sociological or cultural in nature. The uniqueness of any Arabic Christian discourse cannot be seen from such narrowness. It lies rather, ʿOun argues, in deriving such a discourse from the wider content of the Christian faith experience, which almost all the Arabs concede its distinction from the Islamic one and its evident enrichment of the Arabic civilization in all its dimensions. Only such an *Arabic* discourse, and only if it is an Arabic *theological* one, can represent a Christian contemporary and local addition; one, that is, "characterized with the contexts of local belonging, temporal commitment and lively involvement in an active faith-testimony." "The adherence to the geographical location," ʿOun continues, "requires a courageous dependence on the communal and individual existential experience as a means for creating the concepts, developing the views, originating the claims and forming the terminologies of the theological system or construct."[225]

In the discussions of George Sabra and Mosheer Basil ʿOun, one not only finds a descriptive analytical answer to the question of 'why an Arabic and theological discourse and no else?' one further, especially in ʿOun's proposal, finds a valuable, let alone indigenous Arabic Christian invitation (though not yet a full discourse) for doing an Arabic Christian

---

223 Ibid., p.64.

224 Ibid., p.90.

225 Ibid., p.92 (pp. 90-92).

contextual theology that concurs with the one I call for in this research. My proposal in the ensuing essays stands with both feet in the stream of such an invitation and it tries to suggest certain topics that are relevant to the attempt at venturing through it. It is my belief that the invitation for developing an Arab Christian contextual theology gains much more significance and relevance in the light of the radical changes the latest uprisings brought to the Arab world.

As one carefully observes the political and sociological sophistications and fully open developments in the uprisings' aftermaths of Tunisia, Egypt, Yemen and Libya, let alone Syria, one cannot but spot a new resurgence to religiosity and realize that religious webs of meaning and world-views are gradually playing various influential roles in the rebuilding and reconstructing processes of societies and states in these mentioned Arab countries.[226] Although all the winning sides express their aspiration about building civil, pluralist, democratic and human rights-based states, some obviously influential activists and decision-making maestros are reflecting in parallel their convictions that such statehood's components and constituents must be derived from religious, doctrinal and jurisdictional sources. In other words, the socio-political re-building process is inevitably exposed to a 'theologization' attempt and is being clothed with religious garbs.

In the midst of this situation, the Christians in the changing Arab world find themselves inescapably pushed to remind the majority-Muslim victors about their human and civil rights. They base this on the particularity of their religious non-Islamic identity, and not on the basis of their citizenship and civil status. One can find real examples of such a situation in the post- but also pre-uprisings' Arab world. One vivid and compelling example comes recently from Egypt. Against the Muslim Brotherhood's ambition of deriving the country's constitution from *sharī'a*, and the *Salafi* Islamists' strive to completely islamicise the entire society and not only the state, the Copts in the country, and instead of making the highlighting and fostering of cultural and political plurality their contribution

226 For some recent articles describing the rise of this religiosity's role in post-uprisings Arabc society's, see for example Tom Henghan, "Arab Spring and the Rise of Political Islam," in www.muslimvillage.com. 1. November. 2011, Patrick Seale, "The Rise of Political Islam," in www.gulfnews.com 28, October. 2011; Ahmed H. al-Rahim, "Whither Political Islam and the 'Arab Spring'?" in *The Hedgehog Review*, Fall 2011, pp. 8-22.

to society, find themselves emphatically stressing the *religious* diversity in the Egyptian public-square. They do this because the other religious publics in that square approach the Copts from the narrow angle of their religious identity, and not from the angle of their citizenship and Egyptian nationality.[227]

Two other good examples on the Christians in other Arab countries are in Palestine and Lebanon. Faced with the serious danger of double-persecution (read my presentation of it in part II, chapter. 2) from the Muslim extremists' attempt at islamizing the Palestinian territories and the Jewish extremists' attempt at judizing the state of Israel, the Arab Christians in Palestinian territories and in Israel alike find themselves forced also to stress the religious element (i.e. Christian) in their identity over the other cultural, civil and national ones. They also inevitably address the public challenges in their life-settings from the angle of their affiliation to a non-Muslim and non-Jewish religious faith and their strong wish to reflect their particular and distinguished appraisal of how these challenges must be tackled and solved. Last but not least, the Christians in Lebanon find themselves, ever since the civil war up until now, strongly stressing their religious identity and clinging to their religious communality in order to maintain a tangible, influential and far from marginal presence in the country's scene. This stress becomes for them the only means of survival they are left with, as they experience how the other non-Christians in Lebanon's indelibly and almost irrevocably confessionalist society and state, almost always receive their intellectual, cultural and civil contributions to the Lebanese society as the contributions of 'the Christians', and not of 'Lebanese co-citizens'.[228]

227 For recent expositions on the Copts situation in Egypt after the Uprising, read Habib C. Malik, "Intolerant Arab Spring," in *Newsweek Magazine*, www.thedailybeast.com 16, October. 2001; and Fouad Ajami, "Pity the Christian Arabs: Who Will Protect them from Islamist Assault?," in *Newsweek Magazine*, www.thedailybeast.com 16, January. 2011.

228 For a valuable historical and analytical study of the situation of the Christians in relation to their Lebanese Muslim context, see David D. Grafton, *The Christians of Lebanon: Political Rights in Islamic Law*, (London & New York: Tauris Academic Studies, 2003), pp. 115-194, especially; and on the challenge of Islamism in Lebanon in general, see Robert G. Rabil, *Religion, National Identity and Confessional Politics in Lebanon: the Challenge of Islamism*, (New York: Palgrave Macmillan, 2011), pp. 59-83; 115-140, especially.

The examples of Egypt, Palestine and Lebanon show that the Arab Christians find themselves living in a specific setting, wherein one's religious background inevitably shapes, even dictates, the other's reception and perception of whatever one contributes to society, whether the contributor personally wanted to act in society from a sober, deliberate emphasis on his or her religious affiliation and beliefs or not. In this context, reading into one's views, convictions and traces of his or her religious background and ties is almost normally treated as part and parcel of the sociological and intellectual scene.

It is in the light of such a situation that I necessitate a development of a Christian theological contribution to the Arab world's new self-understanding, self-regeneration and self-transformation phase. In its stance on the addresser or the addressees, the non-Christian Arabs approaches the Arab Christians from an inevitable, and far from underminable, religious-identity perspective. They opt for this stance whether the Christians expected it, and hoped for it, or not. This means that the Arab Christians' intellectual, literary, cultural, scientific or civil contributions would be, anyway, received, read and appraised by means of religious lances, no matter how secular and scientific this contribution's content may be. If this is the case, then it would be plausible, maybe even necessary, for the Christians to develop a clearly claimed and defined theological discourse and, right from the outset, to place it consciously alongside their other already available and valuable intellectual, literary and scientific achievements. Within this framework, and to correspond with this specific nature of the Arabic context, developing an Arabic contextual theology (beside other discourses) is not an irrelevant, useless or fruitless goal.

Calling for developing a Christian Arab contextual theology is an invitation to the Arab Christian community to opt by means of its theological mind for rationalizing the political thinking of the Arab public-squares and for protecting the youths' contemporary revolution from any incalculable, incomprehensible counter-effective consequences. The Christians can practice this role by calling for freeing the religious element of the Arabs' identity from any magical world-view, or naïve understanding of the relationship with the different religious other (or even the wholly Other). But, if the Christians want their Muslim compatriots to believe in their ability to contribute this voice in the Arab world, the Arab Christians must stressfully and clearly state their intimate belonging to the

Arabic culture and their mutual share with their non-Christian co-citizens a similar thirst for freedom and justice and prosperity, as well as similar concerns about the future.

Once, Jesus asked his disciples 'who do the people say that I am?' The same question is faced by the Eastern Christians in today's Arab world: who do our Muslim compatriots and co-citizens say we are as Christian Arabs? Who are we in the eyes of the recently rebelling Arabic public squares: allies of the dictatorial regimes – who made us believe that without them in rule Christianity stands no chance of survival in the dominantly fanatic atmosphere of the Arab world, – or part and parcel of the suffering street and the oppressed people – who expect us to put our hands with theirs in building the newly rising Arab world? Answering these questions is crucial for the Christians' future in the region. Moreover, answering them from a contextual, theological point of view will be decisively functional in enabling their countries' public-squares to perceive that the Arab Christians believe in, and want to maintain, their constitutive and inherent belonging to the Arab-Islamic space. They want to maintain this belonging despite their different religious faith, and they wish to continue the mutual-influence relationship that allowed them along the centuries to enrich the Arab culture and society by virtue, and not despite, of their own religious heritage.[229]

In the remaining chapters of this part, I intend to propose some themes that are, to my conviction, constitutive to any Arabic contextual theology, which the Christians in the Arab world may one day consider developing. Far from presenting my fully-fledged, comprehensive and systematically constructed Arabic contextual theology, I am just inviting other Arab theologians to consider the promise of developing such a theology from the angle of these specific inquiries.

My arguments and proposals in the following chapters of this part, on the other hand, are not to be taken as a comprehensive or fully-fledged presentation of the content of the proposed Arabic contextual theology. Far from this, I only offer what I believe to be the constitutive elements, the founding presumptions and the basic themes such a theology must be constructed upon and composed in the light of. The grounding thesis of my choice of these elements, and of my shedding light on some questions in relation to them, is: one cannot develop a theological discourse that is derived from the intellectual teaching of the Christian faith, and one can-

229 Raheb, *I Am A Palestinian Christian*, p. 46.

not produce a Christian theological discourse that is relevant to the Arabic social, political, anthropological, cultural and religious context and challenges, unless such a discourse departs from inquiries about the Christians' political role, interreligious relationships, view of Human Rights and their role in fostering national peace. My presentation is not a theological hermeneutics on these items. It is rather a theological reflection on the *basicality* of departing from a reflection on these items for developing a Christian religious discourse on the Arab region's context. My chapters, in other words, are a fivefold *invitation* for Arab and Near Eastern theologians to pursue the task of developing an Arabic contextual theology, rather than developing a complete one myself; at least not in this book.

Chapter 2: The Arab Christians and the Question of the Political Role[230]

In theological scholarship, the discussion and interpretation of Jesus Christ's relation to politics and political action is usually linked, methodologically and dialectically, to the concept of the Kingdom of Heaven. It methodologically departs from philosophical and philological hermeneutics of the notion of 'Kingdom of Heaven', and then arrives into studying the relationship between the historical Jesus and politics. One of the general theological bearings of 'Kingdom of Heaven' is God's entrance into history in Jesus of Nazareth's person, life, mission, death and resurrection, as well as God's confrontation of, and encounter with, the historical present and the human temporality *per se*. This kingdom, which is incarnated in, and *now* represented, by means of Jesus' presence in history, has not yet reached its final and complete *telos* or *existantia* – which lies in delivering human being fully from the chains of Sin and Evil – and this fulfilment will occur at the end of days. This foundational background underpins the necessary ensuing historical and existential thinking on the role of the church and Christianity with regard to the variable social, economic, cultural but also political aspects of human life. The traditional

230 I rely in this chapter on my further elaborate discussion in my Arabic book Najeeb G. Awad, *Allah, al-'Nsān wal-Sharr: Dīrasah Lahwtiyyah-Wujūdiyyah*, (God, Man and Evil: a Theologico-Existential Study), (Damascus: Codmus Publishers, 2004), pp. 194-207.

theological point of departure in thinking about the political role of the Christians community, therefore, is not the historically-founded question on Jesus and politics. Nor is it a theological inquiry on politics as one of many other phenomena in human life, or as one of the causes of human suffering as well. The traditional starting inquiry is rather doctrinal in nature. It aims first at perceiving the church's *historical*, contextually-shaped role and then analytically probing its nature. Such a praxico-contextual concern is no less a prior and central question than the doctrinal one, since Christianity still faces the challenging question, namely should the church participate in the current worldly political decision-making activities, or should it rather dissociate itself from this involvement and be adiaphorous to the present's precursors, thereby relying solely on the hope of the futural coming of the heavenly kingdom?

The Christians generally answer the question of the church's role in the political realm in one of two ways. Firstly, some opt for a conservative suspicion about the usefulness of any churchly involvement in politics, and they reflect disbelief in any theological value for such involvement. Secondly, others prefer to side with a more radical position that consists of believing in the church's ineluctable confrontation of politics' weaknesses and eradication of its misconduct and failures, for such a duty is part of the heavenly kingdom's message. One can trace the implications and meanders of these two approaches throughout the history of theological reasoning, especially in the context of the church's relationship to the human civilizational history and its location therein.[231]

In its logical postulation and justification of its opinion, the conservative approach resorts to an interpretation of certain directories from Jesus' life in the gospel narratives. It focuses on *sayings* in these narratives that are idiosyncratic to Jesus' teaching, like, 'my kingdom is not from this world' or, 'give Caesar what is Caesar's and give God what is God's' and others, and it deems such sayings as conclusive evidences of Jesus' abso-

231 See on this A. McGrath, (ed.), *The Blackwell Encyclopaedia of Modern Christian Thought*, pp. 304-308. McGrath displays the schools of thought which developed its intellectual discourse in the light of this underpinning inquiry, starting from Christian Realism up to Liberation theology and theological passivism. He maintains that the traditional Christians standpoint has mostly drifted more toward the negative, neutral conservative approach, keeping in mind the last two centuries' cultural transformation that caused deep and multifaceted sociological changes; the thing that, eventually, provided the followers of radical Christianity with a rising and influencing opportunity.

lute indifference to this world and its politics. The followers of this approach would sometimes make rare exceptions and acknowledge a slight extent of attention to politics in Jesus' life, when paying such an attention to politics served the best interest of Jesus' call for redemption, reconciliation and the divine atonement. In either case, the world, in this approach's view, remains a mere *tool* in the hands of the heavenly kingdom; just an instrument; that is, the goodness or evilness of which is valueless and meaningless, since what counts is only that which will become the one and only reality, when the final, metaphysical kingdom takes place.

To the contrary, the more contemporary radical approach often cites other specific *actions* or *events* in the Gospels' narratives, wherein Jesus experienced or passed through certain public accidents – his death on the cross first and foremost – which one cannot construe as evidences of Jesus' political involvement and even regular practice of involvement in public affairs. According to this approach's view, the world represents a standing challenge before the heavenly kingdom, the confrontation and transformation of which the children of the kingdom must be responsible for. The promised kingdom, then, does not use the world as an instrument in its service. It rather comes into the worldly sphere and dedicates it for God. The world's significance lies in being the *goal* and not the instrument of the kingdom.

Be that as it may, delving into the details of the theological understanding of the people of God's position and role in the present world, especially in relation to politics, requires tackling the question of Jesus Christ's and his 'kingdom of heaven' message's relation to politics. In the coming paragraphs, I set before myself achieving this task. I will not touch upon the conservative approach. I will rather journey through the complex and bumpy track of the radical one. The reason behind this choice is that the radical approach's theology gains more popularity among, and enjoys the conspicuous support of, either western or eastern, Arab or non-Arab Christianities in today's world. There is almost a consensus today among theologians everywhere that Jesus was radical in his life and ministry and not far in his interests from the political concern.

It is my intention in the following sections to argue that an Arab contextual theology must busy itself with showing people in the Arab world that Jesus had an *attitude* towards politics. He did not, however, have a political stance or partiality. He even approached politics as someone fighting an evil phenomenon, and not just as someone dealing with a realistic factor, whose proper function merely requires some revision, renovation and improvement. I intend to suggest that an Arabic contextual theology that is concerned about the Arab Christians' role in their countries' political public-squares must ask: what is Jesus' attitude towards politics as a *mentality* that is generative of evil and suffering? What is, in other words, Jesus' stance on politics as an *apriori*, and not only *aposteriori*, thing? In order to see what the answering of these two questions offer the attempt at developing an Arabic contextual theology, we need to view some of the various proposals other theologians already offered concerning them.

The first proposal on Jesus' relation to politics endeavours to show Jesus' complete involvement in the political complications and affairs of his age. One of the scholars who follows this view is Ronald Sider. In his book, *Christ and Violence*, Sider studies Jesus' relation to politics within the framework of the notions of power and violence, opining that in its very occupation with power-gaining struggles, politics avail a space for violence. Sider inquires: what is the relation of the cross with power, and could the suffering-servant's follower use some power and coercion forms in her non-violent seeking of justice? What position should this follower resort to in principle: a non-violent active, or a quiet passive one?[232]Sider believes that the former position is more congenial than the latter with the New Testament's teaching.[233] Yet, he equally distinguishes between coercive force, which is based on loving and respecting the other as a being which is fully free to say 'no', on one hand, and destructive violence, which dehumanizes the other and nullifies its being, on the other. He then argues that Jesus lived and taught according to the first kind of power, and he antagonized and rejected the second.[234] This indicates, Sider concludes, that the core difference lies not in the power or its absence, but rather in the nature of this power: a violent power, or a non-violent one.

From the angle of differentiating between the kinds of power, instead of questioning power's sheer presence, one can perceive the reason behind Sider's ensuing construction of his attempt at proving Jesus', sometimes coercive, involvement in peoples affairs upon the belief in the justifiability of power-use. Sider suggests that such a use is acceptable if pass-

---

232 Ronald J. Sider, *Christ and Violence*, (Pennsylvania: Herald press, 1979), p. 43.
233 Ibid., p.44.
234 Ibid., p.45.

ing love non-discriminatively is its ultimate purpose.[235] And, since power reveals itself, according to Sider, in Jesus' actions and teachings, Jesus then was never remote from politics and its ramifications. If he happened to use force and to engage powerfully in people's life, this does not make him part ways with the message of love and redemption. It just makes his involvement directed primarily against the world's evilness and the people's suffering from the principle of power-manipulation. Sider gleans from this that power as such is not innately evil. It is rather part and parcel of God's good creation. Therefore, Christians must use power in non-violent and loving manner for the sake of achieving justice in their life-settings.[236] We need political power to resist the misuse of power in politics.

One wonders here what Sider would say about Paul the apostle's calling of the Christians to submit themselves to authorities. Does not this invitation imply quiescence and passivity before powers? Sider does not deny this biblical dimension. Yet, he also wonders if it is accurate to testify to the state and other authorities therein without criticising and challenging them whenever it is necessary.[237] Sider believes that neither Christ, nor the early church believed that obeying authorities meant blindly succumbing to them regardless of these authorities' good or bad morals and intentions.[238] Blind submission would be an ideal expression of Christianity's indifference to, and disinterest in, politics. But, if this is what the church should opt for, the Christians would not then be merely spectators, but also participants in the spreading of the evil and corruption of the authorities' abuse of politics. If Christianity opted for such an impartial and adiaphorous position, it will be standing against its own principals and beliefs. For Christianity's principal rejection of societal and political corruption, and its call for creating an alternative societal context with new values, is itself a political position, even if it was a political standpoint against politics itself.

Sider suffices with pondering the public confrontation of authority's abuse without showing whether such a confrontation, and by means of tracing its possible effects, can be seen as an evidence of Jesus' adoption of a self-existing political strategy or his hostility to an existing hege-

235 Ibid., p.46.
236 Ibid., p.55.
237 Ibid., p.57.
238 Ibid., p.59.

monic authoritarian ideology. Does Jesus' attitude towards power teach us to limit ourselves to the perception of the influences of power abuse, or does it invite us to seek alternative political interpretations of power? To take this to the Arab context, one might ask, are the Christians called to observe the ruling authority critically and oppose its power-abuse and corruption, or are they expected to subscribe to the ruling and power-gaining games in order to be able to call for a certain political view or to gain certain political rights? Sider's proposal does not go as far as answering these questions, and it does not pay attention to any real difference between 'discerning the political situation' in certain context, and 'subscribing to the political games and playing a role in them' in it, which is worth noticing.

One of those who stress Jesus' use of force and resort to violence, let alone his total involvement in politics, is Richard Horsley. The beginning of Horsley's reading of Jesus' role in politics is his conviction that the conventional belief among biblical scholars that Jesus was neither violent nor politically-oriented is no more valid or plausible.[239] Horsley explains that the initial presumptions of this belief's followers state that Jesus opposed the Zealots in Jewish society and emphasized in his teachings peace and reconciliation to the extent of turning the other cheek to those who slap us and becoming servants to those who ask from us a favour. They also interpret Jesus' crucifixion predicament, which was a political conviction according to the Roman law, as a fabricated accusation that is far from hinting at the real nature of Jesus' cause.[240] Horsley argues that this passivist understanding of Jesus' core-view is caused mostly by the contemporary influence of biblical criticism by the scholars' eisegetical attempts at over-projecting the present historical conditions on the biblical texts' context.[241] He then refers us to a prior concern that once occupied post-enlightenment thought, namely the emphasis on the irreversible separation between religion and state, or religiosity and political affiliation,[242] which, in his conviction, pushed religion eventually into the

239 Richard A. Horsley, *Jesus and the Spiral Cord of Violence*, (San Francisco: Harper & Row, 1987), p. 149.

240 Ibid., pp.144-151. Horsley insists that these assumptions lack historical foundation. He, then, opines that the synoptic gospels in specific do not offer Jesus' teachings on love as clear and direct indications of his position towards meekness.

241 Ibid., p.152.

242 Ibid., p.152.

closed circle of the internal, individual, and privative realm of awareness, restricting its role and value to the boundaries of ethics and moral conduct alone.[243] This segregation between the religious and the political is what drove the modernist biblical scholars, according to Horsley, to argue that Jesus was not concerned at all about politics, but rather maintained a conservative indifference to it.

In response to this modernist allegation, Horsley insists that this segregational logic was neither prominent during Jesus' time nor the time of the gospels' composition, before affirming that Jesus was totally concerned about the fullness of life in its totality. Jesus, Horsley opines, believed that God must put, in his time, an end to the hegemonic political powers that were controlling society.[244] Jesus' crucifixion was not an outcome of a false accusation that was prefabricated against an innocent man, Horsley says, for Jesus is part and parcel of what he was accused of since his message was not far from attacking the temple and proclaiming its abolition.[245] Jesus immersed himself in the political situations of his era, even the violent ones. He confronted them entirely, because he believed that God was inaugurating through him and his heavenly kingdom's message a war against the present political system. The politico-societal dimensions, Horsley concludes, are never aloof from the religious one. Thus, God's actions in Jesus' preaching and activities were essentially political.[246]

Horsley has a valid point in eliding the anachronistic over-projection of a specific historical (modernist) separation of religion from politics on Jesus' thought and society. Yet, he goes too far, on the other hand, in his insistence on involving Jesus in politics without clarifying the extent and nature of such involvement, or of the meaning of the word 'politics', within his discussion's framework. It is my belief that one should not coerce an inappropriate or anachronistic conception of 'involvement in politics' on Jesus' era or the gospels understanding of Jesus' attitude to-

---

243 On this in modernity, see Colin E. Gunton, *The One the Three and the Many: God, Creation and the Culture of Modernity*, (Cambridge: Cambridge University Press, 1998), pp. 41-51.

244 Horsley, *Jesus and the Spiral Cord of Violence*, pp. 153-158. With regard to this, Horsley thinks that Jesus follows the Jewish apocalyptic thought, reminding that this thought is not far from the attention to historicity and history's interpretation, as it is the case among today's scholars.

245 Ibid., pp.160-164.

246 Ibid., p.170.

wards politics. Can one say that Jesus belonged to the political world in any pragmatist, positivist sense we can think of today, for example? If the answer is yes, then Jesus' involvement in politics is no less corrupted and slippery than those whom he antagonized.

As a matter of fact, what Sider's and Horsley's proposals are in shortage of is clearly showing whether Jesus' and Christianity's interests in politics mean an involvement that makes Jesus a politician and the Christian church a political institute or not. Both scholars do not differentiate between '*interest* in politics' and '*belonging* to a political trend', and they do not reflect attention to the *nature* of the relation between Jesus and politics. Rather, they seek to prove the sheer existence of such a relationship, as well as the inevitability and certainty of its existence. By doing this, both scholars do not begin methodologically from the Jesus of the gospels or from a principal critique of politics, but instead busy themselves in arguments about contemporary conditions the church finds itself surrounded with in today's world, implementing these arguments, consecutively, in tracing the political ramifications of these conditions.

The distinction between 'interest in' and 'belonging to' may not be necessary in the context of the previous two proposals. Yet, it plays a pivotal role in the context of the attention to the *nature* of Jesus' relation to politics within the research circle of systematic theology enterprise. The famous protestant German theologian Karl Barth is one of those systematic theologians who adopt the distinction between 'interest in' and 'belonging to' for understating Jesus' attitude towards his era's political conditions. Barth principally uses this distinction to reject any possible participation for Jesus or his disciples in any political group, or their attempt at forming one by themselves. He insists that Jesus has neither adopted, nor proposed, nor made any effort to battle against any political agenda in his age.[247]

Barth concedes that Jesus was not ignorant of what was occurring around him, nor was he remote from perceiving these occurrences' impacts on people's life. He was able to do this, notwithstanding his ability to survive under the ruling systems, his resentment from adopting any political endeavour to tumble it down, as well as his disinterest in supporting any opposing calls for turning the power-balance up-side-down. In Barth's opinion, this kind of interest lies in evading affiliation and

247 Karl Barth, *Church Dogmatics*, G.W. Bromiley and T.F. Torrance (eds & trans.), (Edinburgh: T&T Clark, 1936-1977), p. 96.

discouraging violent rioting, is what made Jesus become dangerous on the political level of his society's life. His threat to the political situation stemmed, in Barth's opinion, from Jesus' profound perception of reality and his deep concern about people's goodness and salvation from the evil of a certain mentality. This made Jesus, Barth continues, put all kinds of societal authorities under question and show their limitations and brokenness.[248] The bearing of Jesus' interest in politics is, according to Barth, seen in Jesus' life and ministry that equally circle around the principle of freedom. Jesus was emancipated from all the known forms of belonging. He exceeded these forms in his personal life, yet maintained a profound perception of their influence on his society. His freedom laid not in escapism or indifference. Neither did it lay in an eager attempt at deliverance or breaking-away *from* reality. His freedom lies, instead, first and foremost in confronting this reality and in refuting the present political situation and ruling power. It was freedom *in* encountering and understanding reality, freedom *in* interest and concern and freedom *from* any preconditioning affiliation. All Jesus' life and actions, Barth states, were just 'signs', yet they were unmissable signs of his freedom and revocation of the historical setting's deflections.[249]

Despite Barth's emphasis on Jesus' intellectual and functional superiority over his era's political mentality, as well as his serious questioning of its goodness, Barth tends, nevertheless, to image Jesus as a pragmatic person, lingering on the margin of impartiality and eliding any firm or direct position with or against evil politics.[250] As if Barth, who tends to follow a Hegelian dialectic thought form, engages himself in an endeavour to view Jesus' position from a paradoxical dialectical perspective, leaning eventually on one of the sides of the dialectic at the expense of the other: he emphasizes Jesus' disengagement in political actions, on one side, and his message's challenge of the political situation, on another. Yet, the thesis of Jesus' abstinence from political engagement overrides, in Barth's dialectic, the antithesis of Jesus' concern about the political needs of the people. Ultimately, Jesus seems to be an opportunist: he stands quiescent before the dangerous and lethal political condition; waits

248 Ibid., pp.96-97.

249 Ibid., p.98.

250 Ibid., p.101. We cannot, Barth states, describe Jesus' position as a pacifist reservation indicative that Jesus did not go beyond a relative and qualitative reverence (one can often deem it a possibility) towards the ruling and acknowledged regimes.

patiently till the power and danger of this condition weaken and then grabs the chance of monopolizing the benefits of this weakness (in a fashion that is similar, so to speak, to that of the Islamists in today's Arab Spring). Such a strategy, if true, is indicative of a pure political mentality, which keeps Jesus within the circle of the political mindset of his contemporary political movements and sects (like the Hasidim and the Zealots). It even invites us to see in Jesus an eager opportunism serving the purpose of self-fulfilment and personal benefit. It is not my belief that Barth himself would want to claim this for Jesus. Yet, purporting to maintain the thesis and antithesis of the dialectic proportionately in perspective is by no means an easy task.

What matters more than combining and juxtaposing 'Jesus' disengagement in politics' with 'Jesus messages'' relevant challenge to his era's politics' is to realize that Jesus was interested in politics, yet according to a specific bearing of the term 'politics'. Jesus had a realistic and active, and not a passive or reserved, presence before his era's political situation. This presence, nevertheless, is not a presence of identification and matching with the prevalent political thought, but rather a presence of confrontation and counter-parting. By his very emancipation from all the pragmatist political trends of thought and his circumventing of the trap of affiliating to any of the groups that were fighting over political, social and religious authorities, Jesus was able to emancipate the very *nature*, not only the means and forms, of his presence as such from the deflections and brokenness of these mentalities and adherences. He made his presence an expression of God's active and factual existence in the midst of the political mayhem and corruptions of the world's politics. Such an existence, as Gerald O'Collins correctly notices, does not lie in the notions of 'presence' and 'absence'. What counts is to see whether any possible presence is congenial with the dominant political mentality or antagonist to it.[251]

In his book, *On Being A Christian*, Hans Küng rightly states that whoever Jesus was and whatever it was he wanted, Christianity inevitably varies in the light of how each one of us understands his person and posi-

---

251 Gerald O'Collins, SJ. *Christology: A Biblical, Historical and Systematic Study of Jesus*, (Oxford: Oxford University Press, 1995), pp. 311-312 (pp. 309-323). See also O'Collins view on the notion of 'presence'. O'Collins spots two dimensions in the notion of presence, one related to the connection with others and the other is related to the distinction from them.

tions.[252] Upon this, Küng differentiates between Jesus' *affiliation* to his contemporary political body – that is, the priestly and lay leaders and the Sanhedrin – and his *interest* in his contemporary political situation. Küng maintains that Jesus was not affiliate to any powerful or resourceful group in society, not even to the rabbis' society.[253] This, however, does not entail that Jesus had no interest whatsoever in any divine intervention that would create a better future and put an end to the present situation.[254] Initially, Küng does not explicate whether the meaning of 'putting an end' is negative or positive (a total annihilation and abolition of existence, or a reformation and reconstruction of it). Yet, he links the idea of 'end' to the notions of judgment and condemnation, affirming that such a judgment is not directed against the external enemies of the nation, but against the internal icon-figures of the people as such. Therefore, we spot in Jesus' life an interest in society, not only through his criticism of certain conventional religious rites and practices, but also via his blunt condemnation of the law and symbols of his whole society. As if by doing this he conveys God's condemnation per se.[255]

Jesus' interest in politics, then, is never distant from the historical truth, as much as his dissociation with any political movement, whether with or against the ruling order, is no less congenial with the historical truth. Jesus never remained silent about the phenomena of exploitation, injustice, corruption, hypocrisy and oppression, and he challenged the authorities on different occasions. At the same time, this does not make Jesus, as Küng correctly conceives, a member in a rebellious, revolutionary movement, nor does it transform the heavenly kingdom's message into a political agenda with religious orientation.[256] Jesus was not a propagator of a political philosophy who seeks popularity and power. Thus, and contrary to what some recent theologians, like Sider and Horsley, think, his revolutionary ministry is free from any form of violence. Jesus' power laid in the radical questions he raised against the political notions of power and authority. Küng, therefore, is right in pointing

252 Hans Küng, *On Being a Christian*, (Garden City: Doubleday & Company, 1976), p. 177.

253 Ibid., pp. 178-180. In support of this view see also Martin Hengel, *The Charismatic Leader and His Followers*, (Edinburgh: T&T Clark, 1987), pp. 42-50.

254 Küng, *On Being a Christian*, pp. 180-181.

255 Ibid., p.182.

256 Ibid., pp.186-187.

out that the politico-sociological revolution was not for Jesus an alternative of the present political system and structure.[257]

This differentiation between 'belonging to the world of politics' and 'interesting in political ramifications' is a basic hermeneutic key to interpret the historical Jesus' life and identity without drifting into one of two extremes: either stating that Jesus was totally negligent of the political situation and hermetically sealing himself from it, or striving to prove that Jesus did depict, in his life and ministry, an example of a political activist and dissenter, and that his message is loaded with a political call for uprising and riot.[258]

The above attention to the difference between 'interest' and 'involvement' in politics needs now to move one step forward into another, no less fundamental, inquiry about the nature of politics that Jesus could have lived and practiced in his life. In his book, *The Politics of Jesus*, John Yoder argues that denying any relation to Jesus with politics, and calling for segregating the church's life from the world's, both stem from the belief that there is only one and single bearing to 'politics', which is the one that is proliferated around the world today. It is today's forms of inquiry that shape and construct what is to be deemed a 'political position' and what is not. Be that as it may, one is left with only two choices: either blindly and slavishly succumb to the prevailing understanding of politics and abide by its ready-made rules, or refuse this subduing and withdraw from the political game, considering politics as such either valueless or dirty and opting instead for mere personalist concerns and privative worries.[259] In other words, this belief sets a radical division between Jesus' message and politics: one either follows Jesus' message and parts ways with politics, or deems Jesus' following insufficient and succumbs to the dominant political thought, seeking in it another resource which might be capable of providing what Jesus does not.[260] Yoder persuasively argues that such a division is superficial and implausible, for it denies any

---

257 Ibid., p.189.

258 Ibid., pp.189, 192. Küng reminds us how many rebellions adopted Jesus as an example of their resistance and revolutionary action, like Chi Guevara, Camilo Torres, Martin Luther King, Ghandi and others.

259 John Howard Yoder, *The Politics of Jesus*, (Grand Rapids: W.B. Eerdmans Publishing Company, 1994), p. 82. Yoder states that such two-options mentality goes back to the western ethical theologian Ernst Troetlsch, pointing at the same time that it exists in the eastern theological circles as well (Ibid., pp.105-106).

260 Ibid., p.106.

third-option possibility that lies in re-defining 'politics' itself in a manner that can create a new theological approach able to challenge the prevalent secular one.

In relation to the attempt at developing an Arab contextual theology that is relevant to the question of the Arab Christians' political role in their Muslim-majority countries, one can derive from Yoder's previous suggestion the conviction that the Arab Christians are not supposed to be coerced to follow the political equations and power-struggle rules that are prevalent in the Arab societies, because there should not be one, single understanding of politics, according to which their political role should be assessed or decided upon. They are not inescapably called to reckon with a political rule by blindly and slavishly following a certain political agenda and supporting it unreservedly. The Arab Christians can also, if not more urgently, consider developing a political role that departs from a confrontation of a specific political view and agenda, the corruption, evilness and destructive influence of which are clearly seen and experienced. They can, that is, consider developing a political interest that lies in a serious and genuine attempt at working for changing certain evil and hegemonic situations by means of proposing an alternative, politically-, socially- and contextually-oriented, view.

Opting for this might certainly be very costly. Because Jesus opposed his contemporary, dominant thought and confronted those who represented it, and because such an attitude had ineluctable political implications and ramifications, Jesus' fate was death. If the Arab Christians are, like their brothers and sisters around the world, followers of Jesus, they must then know that being Christ-like demands becoming more, and not less, attached to societal life and its relation to the power-games and authority-struggles. As Yoder says, the key-figure of Christianity did not say 'you have your politics, while I am busy with another more significant thing'. He rather said 'your definition of the civil and social and all the societal connotations of human being have all been corrupted."[261]

The question, though, remains; what is the notion of 'politics', which the Arab Christians can be adoptive of and can propose to their societies civil and societal alternatives in relation to? The best answer to this question I can find in the Arab world context is the one proposed by the Lebanese, Protestant theologian, George Sabra, the Systematic Theology professor and the Academic Dean of the Near East School of Theology, Bei-

261 Ibid., p.107.

rut, Lebanon. In an Arabic article titled "The Church and Politics," Sabra tackles directly this question, departing from the relationship of politics with religious confessionalism and sectarianism in the Arab world. Sabra notices that the organic association of the religious sect with the churchly denomination makes it strikingly ineluctable to speak about the church in relation to politics. This means that the Arab Christians cannot opt for a conservative passivist and indifferent position towards the political situation of their homelands, and they cannot live in socially and politically hermetically-sealed churchly communities. The Arab Christians' life at all levels is immersed with political connotations, and it is almost always viewed by the non-Christian majority with the use of political eyeglasses. Be that as it may, the Christians in the Arab world are expected to play a role in the political developments and changes, as much as participating in the guardianship and caretaking of the political status-quo, along with their Muslim co-citizens. So Sabra concludes that interest in politics is an impending demand and a rather strictly expected requirement. What matters, according to Sabra, is which politics the Christians ought to participate in and which they should not in the Arab world.

Like Yoder, Sabra focuses on the meaning of the word 'politics' and offers two possible understandings of it. Firstly, he says, there is a sense that designates power, authority, domination, control, self-interest, leadership, centralization and hegemony. But, there is, second, another bearing which is Greek in origin that designates people's conditions, public affairs and daily-life matters.[262] In English, Sabra continues, the word 'politics' is derived exclusively and directly from the Greek *politia*, and it designates solely people's affairs and public life; whereas, the first meaning of hegemony and totalitarianism, according to Sabra, is not implied. So, when the church's relation to politics is studied in the west, there is no need to derive the understanding of political thought in this case from a prior concern about clarifying the sense that 'politics' means in the context of using the mere term. The concern shifts instead toward thinking about the forms and methods of political *activity*. It is because of this, Sabra claims, that western theologians do not spend much time pondering the bearings of the word 'politics' as such, but rather aim at proposing new ways for living and practicing politically in a responsible Christian way.

262 George Sabra, "al-Kaneesah wal-Syyasah," (The Church and Politics", in *Resalat al-Kaneesah*, 2, 1993, pp. 5-10, pp. 6-7.

When it comes to the Arabic language and context, however, Sabra warns that the case is different. For, one needs primarily to state clearly the meaning one implies in the word 'politics' (*Syasah*, in Arabic) before speaking about the political practice and role. Sabra then shows that although the earliest meaning of the word *Syasah* in Arabic was derived directly from the Greek *politia* and carried its designation of 'public-affair and civil-issues', the latter, and still dominant, meaning of the word in today's Arabic language carries different philological connotations and roots. In Arabic, the word *Syasah* comes from the Arabic root '*Sasa*', which is a word used primarily to speak about riding horses, controlling them, domesticating them and readying them for riding. It designates in other words, the second abovementioned meaning of 'politics': control, authority, domination and power-exertion.[263]

The significance of Sabra's argument stems from his attempt at showing that, opposite to the western case, the Christians' criticism of politics in the Arabic, eastern thought must not stop at the methods and forms of political action. It must rather inaugurate a serious and profound reconsideration and re-definition of the *meaning* of the word '*Syasah*' (politics) as such. Such a proposal is very relevant to the concern about developing a contextual theology on the Arab Christians' role in their societies. If politics means domestication, ruling-games, power-gaining and authority-control, this is definitely not what should be the meaning of politics in such a theology. The Arab Christians, as the community of Christ in the region, must not play a role in a political view that is designative of authoritarianism and power-control. Such a view would be, as Sabra eloquently states, "the biggest trap for the humans and the greatest temptation to the believer and the church."[264] This is the more so in the case of the Arab Christians, for it will place this religious minority at the mercy of a disproportionate and unbearably costly competition with the Muslim, more influential, resourceful and capable majority.

Yes, Jesus had an interest in politics, but not in its authoritarian form. He was rather political in his interest in public-affairs, in the needs of the people and their difficult conditions. The Arabic contextual theology I am calling for developing here is one that asks the Arab Christians to play a political role that basically lies in caring for the people's needs and dedi-

---

263 Ibid., p.6. In Arabic, Sabra says, the word 'Syasah' comes from the action of the stableman and it implies 'handling people's affairs, that is ruling them'.

264 Ibid., p.7.

cating their power and resources in the service of their nations' freedom from the evil of the hegemonic and authoritarian notions and presumptions of 'politics'. Politics in its original Greek meaning, not the Arabic one, namely serving the public-needs and attending to the public-affairs, is what the Arab Christians' political role must be.[265]

From George Sabra's approach, one concludes the insufficiency of talking merely and narrowly about Jesus' relation to politics or his dissociation from the political world and its evil. One must purport to show that the nature of politics, which Jesus lived and imaged in his person, follows the Greek and not the Arabic sense: caring for people's life and living their suffering and pain with them in order to eradicate it. The Arabic contextual theology that does not chase after the meaning of '*Syasah*' may find itself misunderstood and misread by the non-Christians of the region, who might think that the Christians in their stress on Jesus' interest in politics are defending an authoritarian and power-gaining political agenda. In order, therefore, for such a theology to elide this misunderstanding, it needs to reveal the negative and deconstructive elements in the authoritarian and power-centred meaning of '*Syasah*', and not only in the political authoritarian and hegemonic practice.

Once Jürgen Moltmann pointed out that the intertwining of Jesus' history with the history of the poor, hungry and oppressed is totally different from his history's intertwining with the history of the rich and the powerful.[266] This saying might not be far from truth, for such a differentiation leads to a distinction in the meaning of the word 'politics' as such. For the oppressed, many of whom are in the Arab world, the political Jesus would make sense as one who dedicates his life for the sake of the suffering and tyrannized, of the poor and hungry, for the brutalized and tortured. For the powerful, on the other hand, the political Jesus would make sense as a miracle-worker, as a heavenly ruler and as a charismatic, populist street-motivator. The more genuine and useful political understanding of Jesus, nonetheless, lies in viewing his personal history as a unique, peaceful, yet also as a courageous uprising against the authoritarian, su-

265 Ibid., p.9. "The Church must be committed to the service of the humans' affairs in society and the world, for the God it worships committed Himself to the world and the human person, especially when He incarnated in Jesus Christ and became human."

266 Jürgen Moltmann, *The Church in the Power of the Spirit: A Contribution to Messianic Ecclesiology*, 2nd ed., (London: SCM Press, ltd., 1998), p. 17.

pernatural, and oppressive meaning of power and politics. The political Jesus is the one who calls the Christians to stand firm with the public fight against the transformation of '*Syasah*' from 'caring for the people's affairs and situation', into 'controlling and dictating the people'. If theology is the discourse of the Christian community on meeting the God of Jesus Christ, and if this discourse is directed to the multifarious levels of societal life, the Christian community must found its political view and role on a theological prolegomenon, and not allow the contextual conditions and situations to politicize this role and construct it as it requires and pleases.[267]

267 Ibid., p.15.

Chapter 3: The Arab Christians and the Question of Interreligious Relationships[268]

One of the main items in any promising Arabic contextual theology is the issue of the stance of the Christians toward the non-Christians, Muslims, non-religious or otherwise, groups in the Arab world. Within the framework of these relationships' question, moreover, the question of the relationship of Christianity to Islam (not yet to Judaism, due to the political complications of the Israeli-Palestinian conflict in the region) occupies the centre-stage. Usually, the first thing the issue of the relationships between the various Muslim and Christian sects and confessions in the Arab world invite the mind to think of is interreligious dialogue, more specifically the question: how can the Arab world's Christianity and Islam launch a dialogue of mutual understanding that leads to co-existence between each other?

The more significant issue in relation to this attention to interreligious dialogue, especially Christian-Muslim dialogue, should actually be on the core-questions and key-concerns and purposes that occupy the centre of attention in the context of the religious thinking in the Arab world, as well as they shape the dialogue between the religions and decide its ultimate outcomes and goals. As an answer to such an inquiry, I would like to argue in this chapter that the interest in the interreligious dialogue, which intensified since the last two decades of the past century onwards in the Arab region, reveal to me that the noticeable readiness of many Muslim and Christian intellectuals and decision-makers in the Arab world to participate in international and local conferences, table-talks and activities circling around the issue of religion and its role in the contemporary world affairs originates principally from a serious concern about the possible failure of the Christians and the Muslims in the region to maintain their life together in peace, reconciliation, mutual-acceptance and

---

268 An Arabic version of this chapter has been published earlier as Najeeb G. Awad, "'Ab'ad min al-Ḥīwar: Hal Yakfī Ḥīwar al-Ta'ayoush bayn al-'Adiyān?" in *Al-nashra of the Royal Institute for Religious Studies,* Jordan, N. 35, 2005, pp. 4-9. Also on a pneumatic-trinitarian proposal on a theology of religions relevant to the Arab world see Najeeb G. Awad, "Hall Yukhalliṣ Allah Ghayr al-Masiḥiyyīn? Fī Kawniyyat al-Khalāṣ al-'Īlāhī," (Does God Save the Non-Christians? on the Universality of the Divine Salvation) in Naḥwa Lahūt 'Arabī Mū'aṣer (Toward a Contemporary Arabic Theology), Andrea Zaki (ed.), (Cairo: al-Thaqafa Publisher, 2007), pp. 341-445.

tolerance. It is my proposal in this chapter that, far from occupying themselves with purely doctrinal or theological discussions and debates on the differences between Christianity and Islam as religious and intellectual discourses, both the Arab and the Christian interlocutors busy themselves in their meetings and correspondences with discussions on how can the members of the two different religions continue living in the region without, for example, the stronger among them subduing the weaker to its influence and pre-conditions, or without the prosperous and more educated and cultured side among them seclude itself by virtue of a societal ranking and elitist mentality from the other and create rifts and internal dividing boarders within the society, or even without the side that once ruled the region in the name of its religious identity and heritage attempting to invoke this authoritarian past and drive the ruled minority into a serious fear from experiencing persecution and religiously-driven pressure and discrimination that are reminiscent of what was once called 'the status of *dhimmitud*'.

In the ensuing parts of this chapter, I will view how Arab intellectuals approach the above-mentioned key-concerns by touching upon one specific collection of papers that were presented by a group of Arab Muslim and Christian intellectuals in an international conference on religious tolerance and dialogue. In these papers, these intellectuals share their views about the issue of Christian-Muslim relationships in the world in general, but in the Near East in specific. My selection of the papers of this specific conference does not aim at denying the value and importance of the documents and statements that generated from other various activities and venues which took place on the same theme.[269] I allow myself to

269 For some other conferences and activities on interreligious dialogue for the sake of fostering coexistence that were organized by various organizations in the Arab world, see, for example, Michael S. Bos, "Dialogue and Coexistence: A Seminar on Muslim-Christian and Arab-Western Relations," published in Arabic in *al-Tasamoh*, 2(5), 2004, pp. 328-334. look also for the charter that was adopted by the Arab Working Group on Muslim-Christian Dialogue in Cairo, Egypt on December, 20, 2001, which states that it calls clearly for prioritizing a dialogue of life between cultures and civilizations: AWG, "Christians and Muslims Together: A Charter for a Dialogue of Life and Common Action," in http://hiwar-net.usj.edu.lb/chroniques33.htm , 21, December. 2011. On the other hand, some other conferences and workshops have been organized and held in the Middle East on interreligious dialogue, with the concern about the exigencies of life and the need for common practical work for fostering interreligious acceptance clearly in mind, like the Colloquium on Mutual Views and Changing Relations between

select the documents of this conference in specific because I attempt at merely pointing at an example that serves the purpose of verifying this chapter's following main thesis: up until recently, the concern about interreligious dialogue in the Arab world was primarily and dominantly shaped after, and driven by, a prior interest in, and zeal about, producing common-understanding between the Muslim and the Christian representative figures which could practically guarantee a peaceful and secure co-existence atmosphere between the members of these representatives' communities. And in so far as the Christians are concerned, these dialogues were considered by the representatives of the Christian minority in the region as unmissible venues, wherein they might convey to the Muslim majority this minority's serious and perpetual concern about enjoying a safe, tolerant and plural life-setting in the Arabic region. It is my belief that the conference's collection of papers, which I will talk about next, would serve the purpose of mirroring how this focus on co-existence in the region occupies the centre-stage in the Arab intellectuals' approach to interreligious relationships. It will display before us calls for making the goal of dialogue the exigencies of life that religions share, rather than the resolution of religious differences; calls, that is, for turning it into 'dialogue of life', rather than 'dialogue of beliefs'.[270]

In 1997, a Christian-Muslim dialogue conference under the title 'One World for All' was held in Vienna, and witnessed a vast and serious participation from Arab leaders and scholars. The main question this confer-

---

Christians and Muslims, University of Balamand, Lebanon, 27-29 August. 1997, and the consultation on "Cooperation in Christian-Muslim Studies" that was organized by MECC in Balamand University, 29-31. August. 1997. On some other similar activities, read the report-like chart of Tarek Mitri, "Christian-Muslim Relations," in http://www.wcc-coe.org/wcc/what/interreligious/cd31-06.html , (Consulted on 11, November. 2011, 14:00 pm).

270 This attempt at transforming interreligious dialogues into dialogues on life's exigencies instead of debates on intellectual and doctrinal convictions has become recently a worldly orientation. Tow examples of international scholars who foster this hermeneutics of dialogue would be seen in Abraham Joshua Heschel, *No Religion is an Island: Abraham Joshua Heschel and Interreligious Dialogue*, Harold Kasimow and Byron L. Sherwin (eds.), (Maryknoll, NY: Orbis Books, 1991); Hans Kung, Heinrich von Stietencron: Josef van Ess; and Heinz Bechert , *Christianity and World Religions: Paths to Dialogue with Islam, Hinduism and Buddhism*, (Mayknoll, NY: Orbis Books, 1999), pp. 14-26; and Hans Kung, *Islam, Past, Present and Future*, John Bowden (trans.), (Oxford: Oneworld Publications, 2007), pp. 654-660.

ence dealt with was: do the Christians and the Muslims, in the light of each religion's claim of truth-owning, believe that a political and sociological plurality is possible by virtue of a mutual admittance of the other's equal rights, and would they concur with the call for achieving this plurality by the help of practicing cooperative operations for the sake of all's goodwill?[271] I take the Vienna conferences' documents in support of my chapter's above-mentioned thesis because in its conceptual and practical dimensions, the conference's key-question reflects authentically the main concern in the issue of interreligious relationships in the Arabic east as I claimed it to be above. One can realize in the conference's contributions of the different Arab speakers a central, if not an exclusive, attention to, and worry about, the challenge of co-existence in peace and brotherly spirit in the midst of a multi-religious society, the historical, whose ethnic minorities' anthropological and cultural roots dig in the soil of the land as deep as so many centuries before the arrival of Islam to the Arab region. This historico-ethnic factor makes the main attention of the Arab east's religions, as the Arab speakers' contributions suggest a down-to-earth, life-oriented and societal, rather than intellectual, theoretical or dialectical-apologetic, in method and orientation.

This is, again, what one can extract from the papers and contributions that were presented in Vienna's abovementioned conference. Most of the contributions focus on proposing views and visions which might make political and sociological variety the foundational originator of a possible religious pluralism, which the religions would practically become a reality on the ground. Rather than spending the dialogue in debating the proper conceptual and intellectual understanding of pluralism, the Arab contributors in this conference would actually reveal their proneness to dedicating any religious dialogue for bringing the two counterparts into an agreement and commonality about the best practical means and methods for applying pluralism in the real life of the society. The interreligious dialogue here plays the role of strategies-making facilitator, rather than mere ideas-sharing and notions-contesting stimulator.

This is, for instance, what the paper of Indraows Bachta calls for when it argues that the main purpose of the Christian-Muslim dialogue is, "to enable the people to co-exist in dignity and justice and to share the re-

271 See the introduction of the book of Indraows Bachta and 'Adel Teodor al-Khoury, *'Alam Waḥed LlJamī'* (One World for All), (Jounieh: Paulist Press, 2000), p. 7.

sponsibility of openness toward all people's initiatives and problems."[272] The main requirement of any dialogue between religions, Bachta continues, is to aim at working on the basis of an awareness of a common responsibility towards the world and towards, first and foremost, one's own society and co-citizens therein. Rather than a theoretical or intellectual approach to the components and constituents of the needed dialogue between the members of different religious groups in society, Bachta suggests a more pragmatist alternative by calling for a dialogue that is structured upon a praxical concentration. According to this concentration, the followers of every religion are expected to explicitly recant condemning other religions' supporters and to sincerely propose actual, societal procedures that would reveal this recanting in practical conducts. Such praxis-centred dialogue demands, as Bachta then stresses, a total and exclusive attention to the common ground and the similar moral values and practices among the various religious beliefs. The goal of any interreligious dialogue, according to this view, is creating an encounter-chance for developing a political and social working-plan to transform the multi-religious and pluralist context into a co-existence sphere.[273] The ultimate goal, in other words, is responding primarily to challenging and impending national ethical, political and societal factors and necessities in the Arabic societies.

The Egyptian ex-minister of religious endowments, Maḥmūd Ḥamdī Zaqzūq, concurs with Bachta's view and argues from a similar perspective in his contribution to the Vienna conference. He also restrains himself from departing from crudely Islamic theoretical and theological presumptions and convictions on non-Muslim religions. Instead, he structures his paper's thesis on a practical, contextual discussion that aims ultimately at fostering the same idea of establishing one, unified and unifying context for all nations and peoples. In such a context, religions and

---

272 Indraows Bachta, "al-Baḥth 'an Subul Jadidah Ela Mas'olyyah Moshtarakah," (In Search of New Ways for Common responsibility," in *'Alam Waḥed LlJamī'*, pp. 19-26, p. 22. For various points of views on the issue of the Christian-Muslim co-existence in Lebanon as an example of interreligious possible existence in the Arab world, see Fadhūl Abulnaṣr (ed.), *Hawajes al-Massīḥi al-Lubnāni: Maqalat wa Ḥywarāt*, (The Fears of the Lebanese Christian: Essays and Dialogues), (Beirut: Bayssan Publishers, 2001); and Albert Mansour, *Qadar al-Massīḥyyen al-'Arab wa Khayarohum*, (The Fate and Option of the Arab Christians), (Beirut: al-Jadeed House, 1995).

273 Bachta, "al-Baḥth 'an Subul Jadidah Ela Mas'olyyah Moshtarakah," p. 23.

other fields of human knowledge alike participate equally in making the longevity and success of such a context-creation a reality.[274] Zaqzūq concludes from this that the issue of interreligious dialogue must not be studied in isolation or pursued from pure doctrinal and theological perspectives. It must rather be tackled and practiced as part and parcel of wider context of issues that are related to the people's practical, societal, political, cultural and existential living-conditions. Some of the practical issues this dialogue must offer praxical co-existing strategies on are globalization, cross-culturalism and human rights. This entails, Zaqzūq adds, that the foundational question for any interreligious dialogue should be: in a globalized and interconnected context, is it possible to establish a true religious and cultural pluralism, guaranteeing thereby a factual and effective acknowledgment of the general rights of every human being, regardless of their religious convictions and affiliations?[275]

Worth the attention in the context of his praxical interpretation of interreligious dialogue is Zaqzūq's alluding to his rejection of religious relativism, which the pluralist school of thought in Theology of Religions, Comparative Religions and History of Religions believes in and totally supports. Zaqzūq opts for an absolutist approach to religious truths, calling instead for a dialogue that is strictly conducted between religions that share a common understanding of the absolute truth. He evades, that is, supporting the pluralist view that grounds religion in the historical soil of human experience. He also elides reflecting any stance on the scholarly construal of any religiosity a human expression of a relative rational awareness, which does not necessarily point at or stem from an *apriori* self-existing absolute, metaphysical reality. Zaqzūq's leaning on a prioritization of praxicality as definitive of the ultimate purpose and orientation of any interreligious dialogue aims in principle at protecting religiosity and religious understanding from any presumptive epistemological validation of relativism and reliance on a pre-conceptual belief in the relativity of religious truth. In this standpoint, Zaqzūqis is not far from echoing a common position between many Arab-eastern voices that foster interreligious dialogue. The latter also dominantly support a praxis-centred interpretation of interreligious dialogue, and call for prioritizing, if not exclusively focusing on, the pragmatic and existential common-

274 Maḥmūd Ḥamdī Zaqzūq's word in Vienna conference in *One World for All*, pp. 27-32, p. 27.

275 Ibid., p.28.

ground between Islam and Christianity. They build this stress upon their belief that both Christianity and Islam agree that religion is an attitude towards an absolute truth, inspired by *Allah* (Islam) or revealed from God (Christianity), and not at all a relativist human-made expression of privative and personalist convictions.

In the above-mentioned approach, the concentration on Christianity's and Islam's concurrence on the belief in 'absolute truth' seems to be at the expense of the no less significant and necessary reflection, in my opinion, on the theological and jurisprudential differences between Islam and Christianity with regard to each one's interpretation of this notion of 'truth' and each understanding of absoluteness and its relevance to this claimed 'truth's absoluteness', as well as whether or not the previous interpretations and understandings truly demonstrate commonality between Islam and Christianity. Instead of following this conceptual and epistemological necessary track, many scholars in the Arab east agree upon emphasizing and prioritizing the praxical, life-oriented approach to dialogue. They believe that this approach alone serves the purpose of the Christian's and the Muslims' convergence and intermingling around the matters of life, existence and togetherness.

This concern helps us to perceive the driving-force behind Zaqzūq's and others' emphasis on the role of religion in educating people on the culture of peace.[276] This also explains why scholars like Bachta and Zaqzūq would conjecture that the mission of interreligious relationship lies in defending the human person's principal rights of free life, free-choice religious belief, free thinking and reasoning, properties-possession and family-protection.[277] These elements replace, as constituents of interreligious dialogue, other theological and intellectual points of departure, like a deep understanding of God, human nature and the relation of God with the world in each religion.

The same prioritization of co-existence and praxical interaction between the religious communities in any interreligious dialogue is detected too in the contributions of the theologians and the clerical figures who participated in the Vienna conference. This is, for example, evident in the address of George Khodr, the Orthodox Bishop of Mount Lebanon, to the

276 Ibid., p.30.

277 Ibid., p.31. A similar approach to the role of religion and interreligious dialogue in today's world characterizes the thesis of the late Moroccan king al-Ḥasan II in the same conference: *One World for All*, pp. 37-45.

conference. Khodr also departs in his approach from the issue of the practical co-existence and the exigencies of life. He considers the issue of daily co-existence constitutive and foundational within the traditional societal and political framework of the Muslims' reading of the Christian-Muslim relationships. For Khodr, these exigencies pre-conceptually underpin the radical segregation in historical Islam between, 'the house of peace' and 'the house of war'.[278] 'War' and 'peace' here do not necessarily hold in every situation militaristically inimical connotations. They rather more often designate a specific relational attitude and life-stance: either in reconciliation, tolerance and mutual-fellowship with the non-Muslims, or in mutual-scepticism, intolerance and closure.

One has to point out here that Khodr is one of the few Arab Christian authors who wrote prolifically on interreligious dialogue from a Near Eastern perspective. In some of his other writings on interreligious dialogue, Khodr concedes the belief that dialogue means first and foremost 'clarifying conversation' and not 'apologetic debate'. The latter means, in Khodr's opinion, an eager attempt at convincing the other that his or her belief is wrong. Whereas, the former is loaded with positive intentions that lie in listening and strict self-observation and avoiding any intellectual arrogance and loftiness. It lies, Khodr continues, in this flexibility and tolerance that reveal, "kinship between two formulas and unity between two apparently contrasting views."[279]

One of the aspects worth pondering in Khodr's understanding of dialogue and its purpose lies in his surmising that the dialogue's clarification-purpose must not be limited to the service of the issue of co-existence. It must also lead the different religions' followers into convergence and intermingling. Here, Khodr conceptually differentiates between 'co-existence' and 'convergence'. Khodr understands the former as a mere expression of 'societal alongside-ness, an accumulation of segments that are adjacent to each other, yet far from lively intellectual intertwining."[280] To the contrary, khodr views the latter as a total openness which takes us beyond the narrow, closed boundaries of the religious sect

278 Bishop George Khodr's speech in Vienna conference in *One World for All*, pp. 47-48.

279 George Khodr, "al-Ḥīwar bīyn al-Adyān" (the Dialogue between Religions) in *Ḥadīth al-'Aḥad: ad-Diyn wal-'Adyān* (the Sundy's Speech: Religion and Religions), (Beirut: al-Nour Publications, 1985), Vol. 2, pp. 301-302.

280 Khodr, "al-Masīḥīyyah wal-Īslām fī Lūbnān," (Christianity and Islam in Lebanon), in *Ḥadīth al-'Aḥad: ad-Diyn wal-'Adyān*, Vol. 2, pp. 305-306, p. 305.

and brings us into a realm of intermingling, wherein, "lies the straight and proper life, which the modern age requires."[281] The Intermingling and convergence with the other, according to Khodr, enables the followers of different religions to "adopt one social existence track. It is a track which we dig together, not despite our existing religious affiliations, but by virtue of them. By this, we would be working toward approximating, instead of segregating, our social and material life to our spiritual one."[282]

In his turn, the Catholic Lebanese bishop, Kiryllus Bostrus, follows in his contribution to the Vienna conference the same track in his theological understanding of an interreligious relationship. He also focuses on religious tolerance, co-existence and life-acceptance, considering them the founding elements of any interreligious dialogue that aims primarily at building a pluralist society and state. Bostrus believes that the Christians and the Muslims confess one God, though in different ways and according to different interpretations. This starting commonality must invite them, he concludes, to build together a society of love, peace and justice. In order to achieve this goal, neither the Christians nor the Muslims must view the other as a prodigal or stray enemy, but as a brother, who chose to reach the one God through a track he or she opted for upon conscious conviction. This one God, Bostrus stresses, calls all believers from all religions to cooperate with other believers, each from his or her own religious belief, in achieving the common goal of building a society and state for the human who is created in the image of God.[283]

In his view of the existence of many ways to relate to God, Bosturs reflects in essence the inclusivist approach to other religions, which the Catholic Church declared as its official *ex cathedra* position towards other religions since the Vatican II. Bosturs also reveals his deep apprehension of the methodological difference between 'theology of religions', which focuses on the relation between Christianity and Islam, on one side, and 'interreligious dialogue', which talks about the relation between the Christians and the Muslims, on another, stressing eventually the organic link between these two fields of knowledge.[284] Yet, Bosturs sticks

281 Ibid., p.306.

282 Ibid., p.306.

283 Kiryllus Bostrus, *'Afkār wa 'Arā' fī al-Ḥīwar al-Masīḥī-al-Īslāmi wal-'Aiysh al-Mūshtarak* (Ideas and Opinions on Christian-Muslim Dialogue and Co-existence), (Jounieh: The Paulist Publishers, 1999), p. 49.

284 Ibid., p.55.

clearly to the Vatican II's inclusivist and christocentric approach. He maintains the importance of discerning the principal discrepancies between religions and concedes every religion's right of differentiation and particularity. Yet, he also opines that this differentiation right does not stand against the Christian belief that, "in his person, life, death and resurrection, Jesus Christ is the final and complete revelation of God."[285]

Knowing the intricate, possibly exclusionary and apologetic bell this theological statement may ring in the airs of the Muslims, Bostrus resorts to a stronger attention to, and centralization of interreligious dialogue at the expense of theology of religions. He does this because he thinks that the issue of dialogue is more relevant and pertinent than any other to the direct, down-to-earth living situation of the same state's citizens, Muslims and Christians, in the Arab world. Bostrus does not negate the religions' intellectual discrepancies and finds no harm in adopting a hierarchical, pyramid-like relation between them.[286] He, nevertheless, primarily calls for focusing on practical convergence, life intermingling and contextual cooperation for the sake of the goodwill of all.[287] Following the Vatican II's spirit and the contemporary globalized, international concern about fostering dialogue of life and politico-sociological reconciliation between religious and cultural legacies, Bostrus argues that the citizens of the Arab world must develop an interreligious dialogue that trespasses theoretical differences and focuses on praxical and life-setting commonalities.[288] The ultimate goal of such a dialogue is, "coexistence and construction of an immune and stable society as well as improving social justice, moral values, peace and freedom."[289]

The selected papers of the Vienna conference of 1997 and the opinions and proposals they display represent in my conviction a reliable example of popular and dominantly influential Christian and Muslim approaches

285 Ibid., p.59.

286 Ibid., p.75.

287 Ibid., pp.76-77.

288 Ibid., p.61.

289 Ibid., pp.169-170. Elsewhere, Bostrus shows that after Vatican II, the Catholic church started to justify its afore mentioned approach by means of no else except the stress on the multifariousness of the ways of divine salvation: Bostrus, "Min Ḥīwār al-Dīfa' īla Ḥīwār al-Shahādah," (From the Dialogue of Defence into the Dialogue of Testimony), in *Maqalāt Lahūtiyyah fī Sabeel al-Ḥīwār*, (Theological Essays for the Sake Dialogue), Mosheer Basil 'Oun (ed.), (Jounieh: The Paulist Publishers, 1997), pp. 7-17, pp. 8-12.

in the Arab world to the issue of interreligious relationships. The focus of this praxical hermeneutic of interreligious dialogue, as we saw, is one that circles around studying and analyzing how the members of different religious groups interact with each other, negatively or positively, in relation to the challenges and issues that are inherent to their life's mutual concern and common interest. Instead of debating over the content of theological discourses, the plausibility of the religious beliefs and the possible resolutions of doctrinal differences, there is here an attempt at transforming interreligious dialogue into a promotional venue of the spiritual, moral and cultural values and requirements of knowing the other and coexisting with her. I do concede that this is not the only form of interreligious dialogue one can find in the Arab world. There are some occasions where dialogues over purely theological and doctrinal issues and differences between Islam and Christianity took place as well.[290] Yet, it is my conviction that the understanding of dialogue as a venue for discussing exigencies of life first and foremost is the dominating form of dialogue that is running in the Arab world.

The question I would like to ask in the remainder of this chapter is: is such a 'dialogue of life' approach useful and sufficient as is to serve the attempt at developing an Arabic contextual theology? In the ensuing paragraphs, I would argue that the above-mentioned approach is one-sided and far from being sufficient alone to develop a comprehensive and effective Arab Christian interaction with its predominantly Muslim life-setting.

The Christians in the region, as I stated earlier, are often occupied with developing an interaction with their Muslim context in such a manner that would eventually, as they hope, grant them safe life and secure co-existence and enable them to guarantee the life-resources that are necessary for the survival of their families. This obsession with survival and security makes the Christians, however, ready to compromise substantial components in their religious and cultural worldview for the sake of gaining the satisfaction and approval of the dialogue's Muslim counterpart.

---

290 See, for example on such theological dialogues George Khodr and Mahmud Ayoub, *Nahwal al-Jadal al-Ahsan: Mūhāwarāt Īslamīyyah-Massīhīyyah* (Toward the Better Debate: Muslim-Christian Dialogues), George Massūh and Katharine Surur (eds.), (Balamand: The Centre of Christian-Muslim Studies, 2003), and George Sabra (ed.), *Hiwār al-Haqīqa min Ajl al-Hayāt Ma'ān* (Dialogue of Truth for Life Together), (Beirut: Near East School of Theology Publications, 2004).

This eventually produces a negotiating venue over the issues of peace, tolerance, acceptance and fraternity; at the expense, that is, of developing a profound and coherent theological stancc on other religions, let alone constructing the dialogue and the co-existence concern themselves upon such a theological discourse.

Developing an Arab contextual theology on the Christian view of Islam (and Judaism) must be the foundation of any form of a conductible dialogue between the followers of these religions. Such a theology must be grounded in hermeneutics on the nature of God and His relationship with the world as Christian thought views this nature and this relationship, and as such a view drives them to treat the non-Christians in real life. Theology must not just be a discourse in the service of the present, daily-life needs and requirements of certain survival-strategy in a specific non-Christian-majority context. Theology, moreover, should not succumb to pragmatist preconditions that are shaped after the strategic purposes and best-interests of the one who dialogues with the others. Arabic Christianity, therefore, cannot base its conviction about the necessity of interreligious dialogue on the mere urgency of certain political and sociological circumstances and factors; factors, that is, that are inherent to the sociological and cultural context of the Arab world, which will compel the Christians to improvise a strategy of secure and peaceful survival and presence alongside other larger, Muslim groups. The Christian belief in interreligious dialogue must stem first and foremost from Christianity's understanding of God's stance towards other religions. Therefore, the dialogue-based call for peaceful co-existence between the religious groups is disabled and useless alone for constructing a positive and fruitful relationship with other religions. The dialogue on life must be shaped after a clear-cut theological view of the other and God's relation to this other's difference and particularity.

Dialogue as such derives its *arhce* and *telos* from theological thought, upon which the dialoguing agent constructs his or her understanding and practice of dialogue as a 'dialogue'. For example, if the dialoguing person departed from an exclusionary view that acknowledges no divine truth in other religions, he or she will inevitably inter into a polemic debate with the dialogue-partners of other religions, and she will be doing this for one and only purpose: offending the other's faith, defying its claims and then winning the dialogue-partner into the campaign of her faith's followers. In this case, such a dialogue would only depict a proselytization mission, founded on the beliefs that 1) God does not converse with the world except through one specific religion, 2) He does not reveal His reality except via narrow, limited and strictly defined means, and 3) all the forms of religiosity other than these mediums are purely false and stray expressions. Even if the terminology that is used in such a dialogical setting were words like 'reconciliation', 'acceptance', 'co-existence', 'peace', 'cooperation', etc., the conceptual and intellectual web of meanings that underpins these terms would be demonstrative of an exclusionist and discriminative theological mentality and preconception that itself needs critical scrutiny, even deconstruction.

The organic, methodological relation between 'interreligious dialogue' and its epistemological and conceptual foundations that lie in 'theology of religions', as well as the ineluctable necessity of maintaining this organic link and paying attention to its nature and implications, are the main reasons behind my invitation of the people who foster dialogue in the Arab world for searching seriously into the subject of theology of religions and developing an Arabic contextual theology on interreligious dialogue on its basis. Such an organic, epistemological link between interreligious dialogue and theology of religions can be seen, for example, in the theological minutes of the Vatican II. In these minutes, one can notice the interest of the participants in developing *first* a theology of religions, before, consecutively, and on the basis of this theology, they began to establish a down-to-earth strategy for dialogue with other religions on the exigencies of life.[291] Along the same line of argument, Christian Teroll accurately states in his paper at the Vienna conference, 1997 on religions that dialogue must be fully congenial with the religious truth

291 For a list of Christian-Muslim meetings since Vatican II afterwards, see: Alexi Jurawski, *al-Īslām wal-Masiḥiyyah*, (Christianity and Islam) translated to Arabic by Muhammad Khalaf al-Jarrād, (Kuwait: The National Council of Art, Culture and Literatures, 1996), pp. 155-158 (pp. 131-162). Mourice Bormans, *Tawjjūhat fī Sabeel al-Ḥiwār biyn al-Masiḥiyyen wal-Muslimīn*, translated to Arabic by Bishop Yohanna Mansour, (Journieh: The Paulist Publishing, 1986), pp. 161-167. On some dialogues on co-existence between Christian and Muslim students, took place between 1995-1997 as part of the activities of the Christian-Muslim studies centre in St. Joseph University, Lebanon, see *Lubnan: Taḥaddiāt al-Tafāhom al-Mutabadal: Ṭullab Muslemon wa Masīḥiyyon Wajhan-le-Wajh*, (Lebanon: The Challenges of Mutual Understanding: Muslim and Christian Students Face-to-Face), (Beirut: al-Mashreq House, 2002).

which the dialogue-partners acknowledge and attest to in their beliefs, if it must not actually emanate from this truth in the first place.[292]

The Melkite theologian and philosopher, Mosheer Basil 'Oun is principally accurate in his belief that what jeopardizes dialogue between the religious groups in the Arab world is what he calls 'the interlocutors' cultural schizophrenia': they are either only knowledgeable about religious matters, or exclusively concerned about secular and worldly issues. They are either theological interlocutors with rarely tangential knowledge about the matters of jurisdiction, economics, politics and social issues. Or, they are purely political interlocutors, who hardly hold any reliable knowledge about the matters of doctrines and theology. 'Oun is also not far from truth in realizing that this epistemological schizophrenia can only give birth to, "an impute dialogue, prone to be infected with sterile abstracts that are derived from totally hermetically-sealed fields of knowledge."[293] Be that as it may, the interreligious dialogue in the Arab world would be endangered if it is to be restricted to the dogmatic issues, apart from dealing with the public affairs and focusing on internationally acknowledged values, like equality and freedom.[294]

I side with 'Oun's emphatic call for juxtaposing the dialogue of doctrines with the dialogue of life within the context of interreligious interaction. His call is relevant to the understanding of the dialogue's inner structure and the relationship between its constituents. I, however, believe that combining doctrines and life-affairs together and making them one and the same dialogic-subject must not be the occupying alternative to the need for establishing dialogue as such on a balanced and coherent theology of religions. I drew the attention here to what lies beyond the boundaries of the dialogue alone, namely the relationship of any dialogue with its intellectual founding presumptions and primary webs of meaning.

What I propose is a transition from thinking about the best conditions and preconditions for performing a dialogue, into thinking about the pre-dialogue's breeding and founding mindset. In Christian theological terms,

---

292 Christian Teroll, "al-Ta'kīdāt al-Dīniyyah be-'Mtelāk al-Ḥaqīqah wa-'Alaqateha bel-Ta'adudiyyah al-'Jtīma'iyyah wal-Siyasiyyah," (Religious Ascertations about Possessing the Truth and its Relation to Political and Societal Pluralism," in *On World for All*, pp. 63-110, p. 86.

293 Mosheer Basil 'Oun, "So'ūbat al-Ḥīwar al-Masīḥī-al-Īslāmi fī Lubnan," (The Difficulties of the Christian-Muslim Dialogue in Lebanon," in *Maqalāt Lahūtiyyah fī Sabeel al-Ḥīwār*, pp. 187-193, p. 189.

294 Ibid., pp.192-193.

I am proposing as a methodological, prolegomenal starter for pursuing such a dialogue the following theological questions: what is the theological foundation of our understanding of the sheer concept of 'dialogue', which drives us to believe in the significance and necessity of such an activity (i.e. dialoguing) and not another? What is the theology of our understanding of the 'other', and what is the theological understanding that brings into our awareness the other's difference and makes us eventually acknowledge and concede this difference? What is the basic theological justification of our claim that the ultimate purpose of any interreligious dialogue is co-existence and unity?

In such inquiries, one can view a proposal of a scientific and methodological approach that primarily focuses on grasping the founding, principal bases of Christianity's connection to, and interaction with, other religions. After making noticeable steps on the road to developing an Arabic Christian view on interreligious dialogue, the Arab Christians need now to work on developing a Christian contextual discourse on the birth-place, the mother-fountain, of such a dialogue: an Arabic contextual theology of religions.

By arguing against the reduction of interreligious dialogue into mere dialogue on life's exigencies and co-existence, and by calling for founding any interreligious dialogue the Christians opt for pursuing with their Muslim compatriots in the Arab world on an Arabic contextual theology of religions, I am inviting Arab Christians to pay attention to the necessity of taking their existence in a sophisticatedly multi-religious context, like the Arab world, very seriously into consideration. I urge them to do this not only for sheer practical and pragmatic reasons, but more significantly for necessary intellectual and theological ones too. It is an invitation for the Arab Christians to go beyond the mere endeavour to develope a specific life-stance on the non-Christians and the narrow concern about guaranteeing a common, peaceful and phobic-less living atmosphere for them as a minority. I do encourage the Christians to trespass the boundaries of this concern and to construct a principal intellectual stance on their Islamic context that lies, firstly, in bridging between their theological belief and life-stances, and, secondly, in responding to the following questions: is our acceptance of Islam and our openness toward (or even rejection of) the Islamic religious experience originated from, and justified by our common sociological situation (minority) cultural bearers (we share the same Arabic cultural heritage) or political status (*dhimmies* on

Islamic land), or is this openness created by, and based on, different factors that are related to our theological thought and understanding of God's comprehensive mercy and inclusivist forgiveness and acceptance? My personal answer to this fundamental question is to be found in other writings.[295] I suffice here to say that any Arabic Contextual Theology should find in theology of religions an ideal ground and appropriate prolegomenon for developing a coherent discourse on the Arab Christians' relationship to the members of other religions, especially the Muslims, in their Near Eastern context.

Chapter 4: The Arab Christians and the Question of Human Rights

One of the most urgent issues any Arabic contextual theology must seriously consider incorporating in its discourse is the situation of Human Rights in the Arab world. Ever since the formation of the Universal Declaration of Human Rights in 1948, this declaration was not welcomed with open arms by the Arab and the Muslim worlds. The first reason was a perennial feeling that the underpinning values and thought form of the declaration's statements are strictly Christian and Jewish, or basically western, in origin and they do not represent all the religious and cultural heritages of other nations on the globe. Another reason has to do with the idea of self-sovereignty, as the Muslim and Arab countries considered the western powers' criticism of their states' undermining of Human Rights an interference in their internal affairs and a breach of the fact that 'the way a country treats its own people is a matter that is solely up to its own sovereign decision'. On the other hand, being part of the developing countries' group, the Muslim and Arabic states felt that, in light of their social, political, economic and human circumstances, the priority should not be given in their case to individual, economic or political human rights, but rather to the sole focus on, "the right of existence, the right of living and survival."[296]One more crucial factor in relation to the accep-

---

295 See in Arabic Najeeb G. Awad, "Hall Yukhalliṣ Allah Ghayr al-Masiḥiyyīn? fī Kawniyyat al-Khalāṣ al-'Īlāhī," pp. 341-445; and in English, Najeeb G. Awad, "Theology of Religions, Universal Salvation and the Holy Spirit," in Journal of Pentecostal Theology, 2(20), pp. 252-271.

296 Jürgen Moltmann, *God for a Secular Society: the Public Relevance of Theology*, (London: SCM Press, 1999), pp. 117-121.

tance or rejection of the Human Rights Declaration in the Arab world has to do also with the influence of the Islamist ideologies in Arab societies. Most of the Islamist political views on statehood and civil life would envisage actually religious-based legislation that would be, as Valerie Hoffman correctly states, "a powerful enforcer or a rigid morality that contradicts international human rights norms, particularly in relation to the rights of women and non-Muslims."[297]

Despite the mushrooming of many Arab organizations that were established for fostering Human Rights in the region since the nineties of the last century, and despite their resilient work to create a welcoming atmosphere for these rights in the Arab societies, the Islamists' criticism of this declaration succeeded until very recently in mobilizing the public opinion against tolerating these attempts and facing these organizations' work, instead, with scepticism and negativity.[298]

Is Islam as a belief in stark contrast with the norms of the Human Rights Declaration, or do these norms just represent particular veritable bastions of the human basic and natural rights and prerogatives, which Islam acknowledges and defends as well? This question needs a separate fully-fledged study of its own. Suffice it here to say that even if one admits the possibility of spotting evident commonalities and similar views about these rights and values between the Muslims' holy book and the international declaration's norms, one can not undermine the realistic fact that in the countries, where the population vociferously declares its adherence to Islam, we have, as Khaleel Mohammed admits, the worlds' most flagrant examples of Human Rights' violation.[299]

The question now is: being inhabitants of Muslim-majority states and part of their societies' public, must the Arab Christians succumb to the dominant negative appreciation and practical violation of Human Rights and side with the dominant religious criticism and rejection of the international Human Rights Declaration? It is my belief that the Arab Christians should be as far as they can from this option. They should, rather, be

---

297 Hoffman, "Islam, Human Rights and Interfaith Relations: Some Contemporary Egyptian Perspectives," p. 697. See also the study of the differences between Islamic human values and the Human Rights' standards in Ann Elizabeth Mayer, *Islam and Human Rights: Tradition and Politics*, (Boulder: Westview Press, 1991).

298 Rolf Hille, "Human Rights and Islam – Is the 'Clash of Civilizations' Already Pre-Programmed?" in *Human Rights and Islam*, 30:4, 2006, pp. 352-361.

299 Khaleel Mohammed, "A Muslim Perspective on Human Rights," in *Society*, 1. January, 2004, pp. 29-35, p. 29.

the ambassadors of this declaration's acceptance and application in the Arab world's societies. They should not, however, play this role just because the foundational elements of the declaration were derived from Christian legacy (the thing that is not necessarily the case). They must do this because the Arab and Eastern Christians, before any other, can actually pride themselves about the fact that they are historically one of the co-makers and co-designers of the international declaration of Human Rights of 1948. They were rewarded this privilege via the substantial and indelible role the Lebanese, Arab, Christian Orthodox philosopher and diplomat, Charles Malek, played in the declaration's formation.

In the following, therefore, I would like to shed light on the role of Charles Malek in the creation of the Human Rights Declaration. I will present briefly his philosophical understanding of the Declaration and its value for human existence and international goodwill. It is my belief that Malek's philosophical hermeneutics of the crucial necessity of Human Rights in establishing civil society is not only a valuable point of departure for an Arabic discourse on Human Rights. It is more significantly a proper prolegomenon for an Arabic contextual theology which endeavours to introduce Human Rights to the Arab world and show the Muslims value and fruition in adopting it.

In 1999, the United Nation celebrated the 50th anniversary of the birth of the Human Rights declaration. In the same year, the Charle Malek's Institute in Beirut, in cooperation with Naufal Publishers, issued a book narrating the story of the creation of the Human Rights declaration.[300] The book contains the detailed conversations and debates that occurred during the three years-long gatherings of the declaration preparation's committee, as they are recorded in the private papers and speeches of Charles Malek, who was then, besides his academic position as a philosopher, the Lebanese ambassador to the United Nations. The book's importance stems from being the analysis of an Arab Christian philosopher and politician of the most debatable and controversial international production in the Arab world's intellectual centres. This, to say the least, makes the book's philosophical interpretation of the Declaration's core-content and purpose, from the point of view of an Arab eastern mind, a

300 Rafīq al-Ma'lūf; Ḥabīb Malek and George Sabra (eds.), *Charles Malek: Dawr Lubnan fī Ṣon' al-'I'lān al-'Alami le Ḥuqūq ul-'Insān* (Charles Malek: The Role of Lebanon in Making the International Human Rights Declaration), (Beirut: Noufal Institution, 1998).

very efficient instrument in the attempt to make human rights part and parcel of any reformation project or new, native renaissance in the Arab world. Malek himself invites us to perceive the book's instrumentality when he shows in his analysis the epistemological and conceptual presumptions that underpin the Declaration's items. These presumptions, Malek states, invite us to go beyond the human life-setting into the human being *per se*, beyond the person's daily rights into her ontological being, beyond his status as a member in a community into his status as a self-existing, existential entity. He concludes that "freedom is the free persons, wherever they exist and whenever they are situated."[301] Here lies the significance of Charles Malek's unique contribution to the Declaration, in fact: his resilient scholarly strife in favour of intellectual analysis, rather than political pragmatism, and his insistence on making the members of the Declaration formation's committee dialogue about the philosophical presumptions and preconceptions, exceeding thereby the mere concern about the drafting mechanism and the legislation process.

In his papers, Malek states: "there is an actual danger in mixing the internal and the external matters within the human and meshing them together with the essence of the human in himself."[302] He then argues that the decisive point in any work for the sake of the human lies primarily in the definition we offer to the human nature. While most of the delegates focused on finding the most appropriate and acceptable drafting mechanism for the Declaration, Malek was relentlessly pointing at the crucial necessity of reaching into a common, international understanding of the nature of the human being, who is supposed to be granted her rights. At some occasions, he would even put aside his diplomatic fluency and state with the crude objectivity of a thinker and scholar that the mere prioritization of the human's material needs is nothing but an incomplete and insufficient perspective. For, any rights-acknowledgment for a human whose nature is vague or ill-conceived makes any declaration about this human's rights false and hypocritical.[303]

But, who is the human being in Malek's view? According to Malek, the human is first and foremost the being who thinks; "the essence of the human is his mind and conscience."[304] Any marginalization of the hu-

301 Ibid., p.119.
302 Ibid., p.152.
303 Ibid., p.166.
304 Ibid., p.214.

man's right of self-knowing, and of perceiving her needs afterwards, means turning the human person into mere mindless *something*.[305] Here lies a very significant philosophical view that is reminiscent of Martin Heidegger's existential understanding of the human being as someone who is born into this world and corresponds with his and her worldly experiences by means of thinking.[306] The human *is not*, unless her being is founded on a veneration of her mind and conscience. Moreover, there is no reverence to the human reason except by means of granting him his freedom to be what he wants to be and what actualizes his being as a human. Be that as it may, Malek concludes, the Declaration that starts with the human's essence and being and ends with her rights and duties must strictly reflect careful attention and appreciation of the human's free ability of "becoming and change."[307]

This as such brings us back to the stress of Malek's philosophy teacher, Oliver North Whitehead, on the concepts of 'being-ness', 'change' and 'eventuality', the thing that reveals to us that Malek walks in the shoes of his teacher's call for respecting every human's freedom in constructing one's self.[308] The Declaration calls for human rights without departing from the belief in the human's substantial freedom to become what she becomes, as well as to make, accept and experience change, is a Declaration that is calling for the rights of a being other than the living human one. Therefore, before one seeks to offer the human person her rights and starts to specify the terms of these rights, one must always ask, Malek stresses, "when and where are we really free and human in truth?"[309]

The above-mentioned philosophical principal serves the recent Arabic eagerness for change and reformation. The recent uprisings in the Arab

---

305 Ibid., p.221.

306 Thus notices S.E. Stumpf, *Philosophy: History and Problems*, (New York: McGraw-Hill, 1994), p. 503. Stumpf recalls Heidegger's saying that the human differs from any other being by virtue of his ability to ask questions related to his being and to the ultimate being alike. The being of the human contains an awareness of being-ness (Ibid., p.504).

307 al-Ma'lūf; Malek and Sabra (eds.), *Charles Malek: Dawr Lubnān fī Ṣon' al-'I'lān al-'Alami le-Ḥuqūq al-'Insān*, p. 127.

308 See on this A. E. McGrath, *The Blackwell Encyclopaedia of Modern Christian Thought*, 'Process Theology', pp. 472-473.

309 al-Ma'lūf; Malek and Sabra (eds.), *Charles Malek: Dawr Lubnān fī Ṣon' al-'I'lān al-'Alami le-Ḥuqūq al-'Insān*, p. 168.

world, and the rioters' call for freedom and human rights and change, all invite us to ask: who is the Arab human person today? Who is supposed to become? What does it mean to say the Arab is a thinking, free and creative being, and, before this, what does it mean to say he and she are 'human'? One of the most puzzling and saddening things in the Arab world is the fact that after more than 60 years of the Human Rights Declaration's publication, the Arab citizen's knowledge of the Declaration and its norms is noticeably poor. It is also one of the most embarrassing and unfortunate facts that the local Arab organizations for defending and promoting human rights are until this very moment, and despite the fall-down of the dictatorial regimes, who are the first opponents of the declaration in the Near East, being unable to pave the way for any possible role to the Human Rights Declaration in people's life.

The civil and political bodies in the Arab world have not yet begun to realize that the question about the self and its nature is not a luxurious mental gymnastic, which only the society's upper-class, rich and educated people entertain. It is a basic, *apriori* human inquiry, which people from all civil society's segments must ponder and dialogue about, even before beginning with inquiries about national, sectarian and cultural identity. What makes things more difficult in the Arab context is the absence of the civil and cultural institutes that are supposed, in every society, to help the people think and consistently search for answers to these questions. Where is the helping entity that will avail to the Arab citizen the necessary sphere of self-reflection after the latest political and societal radical changes that are brought forth by the Arabic spring? It is by now evident to all the Arabs that such a helping entity could never be the conventional Arabic authoritarian regimes, who, as once Edward Said eloquently said, "excel in persecuting the public by inducing the intellectuals and co-opting them in their own frameworks."[310] It is also obvious that

---

310 Edward Said, *Ṣowar al-Muthaqqaf* (The Images of the Intellectual), (Beirut: al-Nahār Publishing House, 1996), p. 33. Said's words are reminiscent of Burhan Ghaliyon's criticism of the modernization project in the Arab world. Ghaliyoun argues that one of the reason behind the failure of this project is the authoritarian state's control of the modernization process and imposing itself the sole source of power and legislation, which the Arab regimes achieved by dictating and monitoring ideologically the intellectuals in the society. See: Shams al-Deen al-Kylani, "Dawlat al-Nokhbah wa Nokhbat al-Dawlah: Burhan Ghaliyoun Namuzajan" (The State of the Elites and the Elitism of the State: Burhan Ghaliyoun as a Case-Study), in *al-Adaab Journal*, 1-2, 1999, pp. 56-63, p. 58.

this help would not be found easily in a context, wherein one can still chance upon people (predominantly Islamists) militating against the Human Rights Declaration and labelling it 'a poisonous discourse' that is reflective of the western everlasting endeavour at dominating the east. These voices would actually stand in its, "far from any truly human nature"[311] against any attempt at fostering human rights in the Arab world.

The recent condition of Human Rights in the Arab world mirrors the disinterest in this region's societies in the inquiry about the essential constituents of humanness in the human person. This inquiry is the pivotal demarcating point between treating the Human Rights Declaration as mere legislative constitution subjected to official and governmental acceptance or refusal, and buried in the historical circumstances that generated it, on one side, and treating this declaration as an intellectual and conceptual statement that aims at reminding the Arab world time and again about what has been buried of the human existence under a Machiavellian living-policy and hegemonic statehood, on another. The danger of undermining this distinction lies in the person's falling a victim to powers, the best interest of whom is marginalizing the essence of things for the sake of using any illegal means to grant alleged dignity and rights to a nebulous creature without any specific, definable being. This is what Charles Malek points at when he says, "regardless to any practical application, are not you interested in knowing that your integrity as a human consists of these and other rights? And, if you insisted that this knowledge as such does not concern you, then allow me to reveal that your humanity is incomplete, for the organized humanity defines you as a mind and the mind seeks knowledge."[312]

One of the interesting debates Malek speaks about in his papers in relation to the formation of the Human Rights Declarations is on the relation of the individual person with the community. This debate reflects the

---

311 In his introduction of the second part of the above-mentioned discussion of the Arab world's modernization project, Muhammad Jamal Barout says: "the sample of Arab modernism seems to be the first obstacle before obtaining real modernism, for this sample achieved goals that are contrary to its starting purposes and ambitions, re-generating thereby what it was in first place founded to militate against.....real modernism and its re-origination is an emancipation, not hegemony process, an openness, not an exclusion and marginalization project": M.J. Baroot, 'Introduction," in *al-Adaab Journal*, 1-2, 1999, pp. 39-63.

312 al-Ma'lūf; Malek and Sabra (eds.), Charles Malek: Dawr Lubnān fī Ṣon' al-'I'lān al-'Alami le-Ḥuqūq al-'Insān, p. 221.

background that is idiosyncratic of the Cold War between the Marxist-Communist and the Democratic-Capitalist campaigns, which was gradually rising during that time, and influenced the discussions that occurred between the members of the Declaration-creation committee. Charles Malek's papers record this discrepancy between these two campaigns via a lively controversy between the members of the committee over the logical validity of 'the individual precedes the community' and validity of the logic 'the community outranks the individual'. Malek sided then with the former logic. The main criticism this logic faced, and the Human Rights Declaration still actually faces in the Arab east till this day, stemmed from the fear that, in their focal attention to the individual person's goodwill, such rights would deny the community's importance and role in human society, thereby paving the way for individualism and disorder, ignoring the sanctity of the nations' existence as a communal entity that is shaped after ultimate and sublime imperatives and premises, and supporting, finally, the individualistic interests and availing an effective impact to privative orientations and selfish and egoistic passions over society.

I can recall here a similar debate that took place during the brief political revival in Syria that is known by the name of 'the Spring of Damascus', 2000-2001. During that time, many intellectuals and activist from the regime's dissenters and adherents alike launched a debate on the nature of the civil society that Syria needs. The two teams' opinions divided similarly into an understanding of civil society that emphasizes the individual citizen as the starting point of any approach to the communal dimensions of politics and authority, on one side, and another understating of civil society that departs from the collectivist nature of the society's leadership, down to the citizen as an active and free member in society, on another. In simple words, we had then a debate between two reforming visions: one starts from the central head down to the communal basis, and another starts from the plural basis and moves up to the head. This debate has never been completed as the regime decided then to suppress every political or intellectual activity in the country and considered any discourse on civil society other than the one that was officially certified and produced by the regime forbidden and condemned.

To come back to our Lebanese philosopher, Charles Malek argues that the most appropriate starting point in dealing with the individual-community dialectic lies in differentiating between the *nation* as a certain congregation of people, which consists of human beings who enjoy all their rights, and the *stately* or *governmental* body, which is supposed to lead and rule this nation. He persuasively shows that this basic differentiation creates an indispensable chance for viewing the nation as a group of humans, and not as a collection of instruments. Eventually, the growth, progress and prosperity of this group as a human nation become organically conditioned by the progress and prosperity of its core-component, the human being *per se*, and not by the ruling or power-devolution systems as such. The state is just a regularizing and ordering instrument of co-existence. It aids the human person in discovering its own free essence and avails to it all the required and available means for encountering and intermingling with others within the framework of a relational network we usually call 'one-nation's life'. Thus, nations originate from the heart of the human's evolvement; as, that is, an outcome of her self-growth. It does not descend on the human's existence as a premeditated legislation or a pre-tailored ideological fact, and it does not play any absolutist justificatory role in the service of any ruling power. "The human's essential personhood outranks any communal entity the person belongs to, whether in terms of rank, ethnicity or nationality."[313]

The above prioritization of the human person over the communal entity does not mean that the individual person nullifies the nation or replaces the community. The point here is about degree and not about existence: the personhood of the human person stands *above* the community's presence as a *state*. This is what Malek wants to postulate from saying "Robinson Kruzo does not exist in reality."[314] By this metaphoric statement, Malek refutes the Enlightenment's Cartesian notion of the individual self, which views the human person as a thinking, self-enclosed and self-reflecting individual.[315] Malek strictly rejects the Cartesian individualistic notion of the self, proposing instead a personalist understanding of the self, which departs fundamentally from assuming a Buberan-like (from Martin Buber) real and essential 'I-thou' relationality.[316] This is

---

313 Ibid., p.132.

314 Ibid., p.132.

315 The metaphor of Robinson Kruzo is Cartesian *par excellence* and Malek clearly stands against it. For a good brief exposition on Descartes' view of the self see: Stumpf, *Philosophy: History and Problems*, pp. 242-244; and Diogenes Allen, *Primary Readings in Philosophy for Understanding Theology*, Eric O. Springsted (trans.,), (Louisville: John Knox Press, 1992), pp. 117-125.

316 Martin Buber, *I and Thou*, (New York: Macmillan Publishers, 1987).

why Malek deliberately distracts himself from saying that the individual precedes any community, and states rather that the *personhood* of the human precedes any communality. He does not believe in a secluded, self-sufficient human person, and he does not believe that the Human Rights Declaration is a chance for the individual's abuse of its society and her undermining of the relation with the surrounding realities. The relations and interactions with these realities are essential and unavoidable for the human being to be his and her very own self.[317]

An Arabic contextual theology on human rights is one that should invite the Arab-Muslim, usually collectivist societies to reconsider their belief in the demand of the individual's melting into the collectivist pot of the community. It should show to such a society that acknowledging the person's individuation does not stand against the fulfillment of his personhood by virtue of being part of a community.[318] The individual is the basis of any society, and his existence precedes the existence of any social order. This includes the existence of the state, or any form of statehood.

The Arab mentality that is shaped after a religious, collectivist understanding of belonging needs another counter-religious discourse to show it that the ruling state, which, in the Islamic mind, speaks on behalf of the community and its religious identity, exists in the first place to serve human persons; he and she do not exist to serve it or just to blindly succumb to the state's ideology, whether political, cultural or religious.[319] Malek does not speak here about the community as an expression of a human form of existing as such. He is rather concerned about the tendency in collectivist societies to imprison the community's presence and existence within the boundaries of the state alone and reducing their meanings and forms to the culture and intellectual realm of the authoritarian side.

In the Arab world, there has been, until recently, a form of thought that totally identifies the nation with the state, erasing thereby the community's presence as a society of human individuals and transforming it eventually into a politico-economic entity in the service of the ruling

---

317 One should keep in mind here that Malek studied under Oliver North Whitehead, who says that connectivity and interaction are the substance of everything that is. See Stumpf, *Philosophy: History and Problems*, p. 440.

318 This is also what Whitehead believes in according to McGrath, *Blackwell Encyclopaedia of Modern Christian Thought*, pp. 472-475.

319 al-Ma'lūf; Malek and Sabra (eds.), *Charles Malek: Dawr Lubnān fī Ṣon' al-'I'lān al-'Alami le-Ḥuqūq al-'Insān*, p. 63.

power and its ideological agenda. We used to see this in falling dictatorships like Iraq and Egypt, Libya and Yemen and still in existing ones, like Syria, where the nation is reduced to, and totally identified with, the ruling regime, where the authoritarian ruling order is the A to Z of the community. Against this situation, an Arabic theology with the Human Rights Declaration in mind would address a deeply religious society – whose Islamic faith centralizes the notions of 'nation' and 'society' – by means of Charles Malek's emphasis that the alphabet of the nation and the community is its free and dignified human persons, and not its dogmatic and legislating thought forms which blur individuation and real personalist freedom.[320]

In this attention to individuation, the theology that aims at participating in any reformation project in the Arab world must ask the following essential question: when and how are the human persons truly free and human? Is this possible under the dictating wings of a hegemonic regime (whether like the old dictatorships or like any coming dictatorial alternatives), which decides for us what we should believe, how we should live, to what we should declare allegiance to and which identity we should adopt? Is this possible in a state that decides for us who is the friend and who is the foe, who is the trustworthy other and who is the suspicious? Or, does this real freedom and humanity lie in living in a community that exceeds in its being and boundaries the narrow realms of the political, ideological and religious discourse of the state, and despite the fall down of the dictatorial regimes, who are the first opponents of the declaration in the Near East? Is this freedom and humanity, that is, possible when we are enabled to exist, despite our different religion, culture, ethnicity, or gender within a community, wherein we can enjoy our needed space to, "highlight the true human nature, namely one's mind and spirit, to bring it forth, to protect it and strengthen its status"?[321]

These questions must be central to any attempt at developing a contextual Arab Christian discourse on human rights to address the citizen of the Arab world and contribute to his and her eagerness for societal reformation. A Theology on the human rights in the Arab context must offer some plausible answers for the question: which is for the service of the other, the state or the citizen?[322] Whose rights constitute the foundation of

320 Ibid., p.147.
321 Ibid., p.166.
322 Ibid., p.223.

the nation: the rights of the free citizen of the state, or the rights of the state's premeditated system, which makes it believe that it is the rulers' and the dominating majority's, or their religious or cultural standards', right to offer freedom to people or deny it to them whenever it pleases?

A contextual Arab Christian invitation for re-valuing the Human Rights Declaration in the Arab world should endeavor to welcome all the members and the groups of the nation into a serious intellectual dialogue-program, in order to reflect together on what truly detains the progress and development of the Arab societies and whether such a blocking factor lies in the peoples' deprivation of their natural and basic social, civil and intellectual rights as human beings, and it does not stem primarily, or only, from the political and economic oppression of the ruling regimes. The bad civil conditions of the Arab societies are ultimately humanitarian and civil, and not merely political in nature.

In the past four decades of Arab history, the Arab public was deprived of its natural basic rights in the name of the Arab countries' suffering from a consistent state-of-war with Israel and international imperialism, and the urgent need for security and stability, which the regimes often used to intimidate the population for the purpose of gaining its loyalty and support. This obsession with security produced fake and superficial peaceful-looking Arabic societies, which hide underneath, as Malek perceptively realizes, internal, dangerous and unbridgeable rifts. Security turned from a source of strength and progress into an inhibitory, strict policy, guaranteeing nothing except the longevity of the ruling regimes.

The security-prioritization logic and the forceful exertion of emergency laws deprive the public from interacting openly, freely and positively with the international human thought. The vast majority of the Arab easterners remained during the second half of the last century hermetically sealed in their strife for materialist, economic and confessionalist survival, and under the mercy of the state's unfair permissions and prohibitions. Applicable to this situation is what Charles Malek concludes from observing the Arab societies that became victims of their governments' economic, financial and security plans, saying that, "all those [in the Arab states] who emphasize the human person's rights and his primal economic needs are stressing nothing except his animalistic existence. This is crude materialism, no matter by whichever other name one calls it. Materialism is a folk philosophy for this [Arabic] age, in the presence of which defending the human as a soul and mind seems to be a difficult task."[323]

Suppressing the Arab publics under the mercy of the state's security and patriotic and economic ideologies is one of the main driving-forces that pushed the Arab youths between the 80s of the past century and the beginning of this century into seeking an outlet for the anger and despair energies either into religious fanaticism and extremism or into ethnic, geographical, cultural and nationalist exclusivism and segregation. Although, for example, the Ḥanbalite Islamic school of jurisprudence is not the most important, original and influential school of thought in Islam, yet George Ṭarābīshi is not far from the true situation of the recent Arabic public-square when he opines that this school was the most successful branch of Islamic religious thought in attracting the public and enjoying a big reservoir of followers more than any other Islamic school.[324] On the other hand, the same situation helps us to apprehend why Ibn Tymiyyah is clearly influential in contemporary Egyptian society more than a modernist and rational Islamic author like Ṭaha Ḥussein, for instance.[325] The present Muslim Arabs forgot their natural human thinking, critical and free nature, which enables them to stand on an equal objective and scrutinizing distance from all the masses' taken-for-granted ideologies, whether these latter were offered from the security-centered state or the fundamental and fanatic opposition.

In the light of the suppressive policies against the human person's individuation and free rights, it is no wonder that the most extremist Islamic religious schools of thought are becoming the most appealing final court of appeal for many youths in the Arab world. Charles Malek is quite correct, and still relevant for today's situation of the Arab world, in his conviction that, "the danger of our age is not that the society has no advocates to defend its cause, nor is it that the state is not strong enough to defend its demands before the human individual. The real danger of our

---

323 Ibid., p.165.

324 George Ṭarābīshi, *Maṣā'er al-Falsafah bayn al-Masiḥiyyah wal-Īslām* (The Destinies of Philosophy between Christianity and Islam), (Beirut: Dar al-Saqui, 1998), p. 87. Ṭarābīshi argues that the simplifying and totalitarian nature of Ḥanbalism transforms it into a totalitarian ideology.

325 Thus noticed by Muhammad Ṣayyd Rusas, "Naqdlı Ma'ayyer al-Ḥadāthah fī al-Fikı al-'Arabı," (Critiquing the Standards of Modernism in the Arabic Thought) in *al-Adaab Journal*, 1-2, 1999, p. 40.

age lies in the societal demands that may turn into a threat that can lead to the quenching of every true personhood."[326]

Any Arabic contextual theology on the Human Rights Declaration's relevance to the Arabic world would find in Charles Malek's understanding of human personhood a useful, accessible language that can show the recent Arabic people that what guarantees security and reformation, and make them possible, is the human person who is aware of her freedom and rights in their accurate and realistic form. This person alone can apprehend his or her responsibilities and perceive that it is a being with rights it naturally obtains and duties it should offer in return. Fundamentalism has witnessed rapid and broad growth in the Arab world because of the disregard and disrespect of human rights. Fundamentalism also intensified in the Arab world because of the security complex, 'maintaining the status quo' ideology and the collectivist view of unity. This led eventually to the Arab person's estrangement from his or her reality and alienation from the present. Under these conditions, all the societal institutions, like the religious institute, the school, the cultural clubs and other civil organizations inside the society lost their effective educating and enlightening role and turned from constructive means for the human's self-fulfillment into echoes of the state's discourse.

In light of the new radical and irreversible changes in the Arab world, it is necessary for the Arab Christians to recall their participation, via the Lebanese Orthodox thinker Charles Malek, in the creation of the international Human Rights Declaration, and to play a role in fostering this declaration and in reconciling their Muslim context with its items. Would the human rights subject find a deeper and more serious activation space in the coming political and societal Arab states? Would there be a new generation of Arabs who would dedicate themselves to play a historical role which might deliver their societies from despair, pessimism and visionlessness? Would the thought that calls for placing the human person ahead of the state and communal authority find listening ears among those who are about to build the new Arabic states, so that the Human Rights Declaration would be picked up from the dusty shelf and would be used afresh in the re-creation of the new Arab civil societies?

For some Arabs, there are people who already have begun to do this. For me, this is yet an answerless question. For, the Human Rights Decla-

326 al-Maʻlūf; Malek and Sabra (eds.), *Charles Malek: Dawr Lubnān fī Ṣonʻ al-'Iʻlān al-ʻAlami le-Ḥuqūq al-'Insān*, p. 146.

ration is still either a stranger or a tourist, and it has not inhibited our homeland yet. Even in the discourses of the opposing powers that rose recently out of the ashes of the fallen regimes and started promoting civil-society values, the subject of human rights is still considered as just a theoretical, purely speculative item or a theme of a declared statement in relation to a minor circumstantial event. The Human Rights Declaration has not yet been granted a central, methodological appreciation in a process of developing a road-map for the establishment of the hoped-for Arab civil society. It is a dream that such a thing would happen in the coming future in the Arab world. Yet, there is a need for an agent to invite the public to consider it. Such an agent can be an Arabic Christian contextual theological voice.

Chapter 5: The Arab Christians and the Question of (National) Peace

In the Middle East, one of the most discussed issues is peace and how the region's struggling sides can come into a peaceful co-existence and non-violent stance on each others' differences. The issue of peace is not only pivotal in relation to the Arabic-Israeli old and complicated struggle.[327] It is also a crucial demand in relation to the internal conditions and societal textiles within every Arabic country. The Multi-religious, multi-ethnic, multi-confessional, multi-cultural and multi-denominational nature of the Arabic societies bring with them negative as much as positive consequences and challenges. The positive principal result of such a multi-faceted variety is the richness, the depth and the life-forms' and co-existence settings' vividness, which these differences and particularities add to the people's thought-forms, conducts and personalities. The negative, conspicuously damaging consequences, nevertheless, are the possible identities' clashes, societal fractions, cultural discriminations, ethical condemnations and ideological and dogmatic categorizations, which such differences and particularities may drive people to develop and use against each other.[328] One can spot such negative consequences and antagonisms by means of the mere fact of 'the others' difference from me' in almost every society in the Arab world. Some of these 'clashes-

327 For the issue of peace in relation to the Arab-Israeli conflict see, for example, among the vast amount of literature on the subject Joshua Muravchik, "Listening to Arabs," in *Commentary*, 116(5), 2003, pp. 28-33; Nikolos Van Dam, "Israel and Arab National Integration: Pluralism Versus Arabism," in *Asian Affairs*, 10(2), 1979, pp. 144-150; Laura Zittrain Eisenberg and Neil Caplan, *Negotiating Arab-Israeli Peace: Patterns, Problems, Possibilities*, 2nd edi., (Bloomington, IND: Indiana University Press, 2010); Alan Dershowitz, *The Case of Peace: How the Arab-Israeli Conflict Can Be Resolved*, (Hoboken, NJ: John Wiley & Sons, Inc., 2005); and Marina Ottaway and Amr Hamzawy (eds.), *Getting to Pluralism: Political Actors in the Arab World*, (Carnegie Endowment for International Peace, 2009).

328 On the subject of peace in relation to the Arabic-Arabic relations and the intrinsic dimensions of coexistence within the Arab societies and relation of this demand with the present age, see, also among the various available literatures, for example Paul Salem (ed.), *Conflict Resolution in the Arab World*, (Syracuse, NY: Syracuse University Press, 1997); James Craig, "Arab Society: Characteristics and Contradictions," in *Asain Affairs*, 38(1), 2007, pp. 1-11; Lawrence Rosen, *Varieties of Muslim Experience: Encounter with Arab Political and Cultural Life*, (Chicago, Ill: University of Chicago Press, 2008); and Yasir Sulaiman, *Arabic, Self and Identity: A Study in Conflict and Displacement*, (Oxford and New York: Oxford University Press, 2011).

because-of-differences' create enmity and hatred and turn the Arab world into an oasis of multifarious, self-breeding violence.

Be that as it may, if the Arab Christians want to develop any contextual theological discourse to speak to the Arab world's realistic situation, then the subject of peace cannot but occupy a central position within such a conversation and role-finding attempts. And, when it comes to the inter-religious relations in the Near East, the question of peace and mutual acceptance pops up to the surface and occupies the centre of the religions interaction stage.

Both Christianity and Islam believe in peace and consider it one of the central values in the Faiths' moral discourses. Peace is a recurring theme in the Christians' religious book. It is, for example, one of the Holy Spirit's fruits: "the fruit of the Spirit is love, joy, peace, patience, kindness, generosity, faithfulness, gentleness and self-control" (Galatians 5: 22). Those who opt for making peace are blessed by God: "blessed are the peacemakers, for they will be called children of God" (Matthew 5:9). Peace is an eschatological promise God bestows upon his creation: "and I will give peace in the land, and ye shall lie down, and none shall make you afraid: and I will rid evil beasts out of the land, neither shall the sword go through your land" (Leviticus 26:6). And, God's eschatological kingdom is built upon peace and not upon victory or material prosperity: "for the kingdom of God is not meat and drink; but righteousness and peace and joy in the Holy Ghost" (Romans 14:17).[329]

The centrality of the notion of peace is not restricted to the Christians' religious scripture. It is also recurrent in the religious texts of Islam. In the Quran, there is also a divine promise that lies in God's invitation of all the believers into His holy abode of peace: "for [the believers] is the abode of peace with their Lord. He will be their protecting friend because

---

329 For some literature on the notion of peace in Christianity, see Paul Tillich, *Theology of Peace*, Ronald H. Stone (ed.), (Louisville, Ken: Westminster/John Knox Press, 1990); Marlin E. Miller and Barbara Nelson Gengrich (eds.),*The Church's Peace Witness*, (Cambridge: W.B. Eerdmans Publishing Company, 1994); James M. Childs Jr. *The Way of Peace: Christian Life in Face of Discord*, (Minneapolis: Fortress Press, 2008); John Howard Yoder, *Christian Attitudes to War, Peace and revolution*, TheodoreJ. Koontz and Andy Alexis-Backer (eds.), (Grand Rapids, Mich: Brazos Press, 2009); James Heft, "Religion, World Order and Peace: Christianity, War and peacemaking," in *Cross Currents*, 60(3), 2010, pp. 328-331; and Michael G. Long (ed.), *Christian Peace and Nonviolence: A Documentary History*, (Maryknoll, NY: Orbis Books, 2011).

of what they used to do" (*al-'An'ām* 6:127); "and Allah summoneth to the abode of peace, and leadeth whom He will to a straight path" (*Yūnis* 10:25); "peace will be for him who followeth right guidance" (*Ṭaha* 20:47). The very word *'Islām* is derived from the Arabic root *slm*, which connotes peace. In al-Bukhari's *Hadith*, the prophet Muhammad himself taught that Islam as such *is* peace, which means that peace is the prerequisite of being an affiliate to Islam. And, as the kingdom of heaven in Christianity is the kingdom of peace, in Islam paradise is also to be called the 'Home of Peace', where the people would wish only peace to each other.[330]

One can also say, finally, that both Christianity and Islam associate peace with reconciliation and with people's attitudes toward each other in real life and daily conduct, and not only with people's relation to God or to their inner self. In sum, for any Arabic contextual theology to be a relevant conversation with the Christians and Muslims in the Arab world, it needs to take peace as a notion into serious consideration and find in it a promising common ground for unity and mutual acceptance.

On the other hand, if the Arab Christians want to deal contextually with the issue of peace in the Arab world, the question of the challenge of violence must be kept always in mind and attended to directly and seriously. Peace is the reflection of people's relationships with each other. It is not how people think about themselves and the different others before them. It is basically how people *relate* to others and *act* before them and over-against them in daily-life and realistic contexts. And, as peace is about the people's conduct and relational attitudes, the opposite of peace, that is violence, is also about people's actions and behaviours towards the different others. It follows from this that theological thinking about peace is inevitably associated with, and influenced contextually and interculturally by, the absence of peaceful co-existence; that is the presence of multifarious forms of violence, in certain societal and public contexts.

Be that as it may, in the following paragraphs, I intend to propose some guiding ideas for developing an Arabic Christian contextual stance

330 For few literatures on peace in Islam, see Ibrahim M. Shalaby, "Islam and Peace," in *Journal of Religious Thought*, 34(2), 1978, pp. 42-49; Mohammed Abu-Nimer, *Nonviolence and Peace Building in Islam: Theory and Practice*, (Gainesville, FL: University Press of Florida, 2003); Majid Khadduri, *War and Peace in the Law of Islam*, (Clark, NJ: The Lawbook Exchange, Ltd, 2010); Qamar-ul Huda (ed.), *Crescent and Dove: Peace and Conflict Resolution in Islam*, (Washington, DC: United States Institute of Peace, 2010).

on the following question: what does it mean to say that the Arab Christians are called to become vehicles of peace in the midst of violent spots in the Arab world; in specific, and how can the Arab Christians be a vehicle of peace in such a prone-to-violence, versatile and complex context as the Middle East, in general?

Let me first admit that deciding what the Arab Christian ought to consider and think of under this question is not an easy or a narrowly clear-cut task. In principle, there are various ways for discussing the issue of peace in relation to violence. One can think about the nature of peace that the Arab world needs, supposing that all the Arabs or the Middle easterners agree that they really live in a violent region and experience various levels of violent syndromes in their life-settings.[331] In this case, if the Arab societies do not want to acknowledge an existence of violence in their own people's life-settings, it would be initially difficult to dry the fountain-source of such violence phenomenon. Instead of achieving this task, one would find him or herself busy with the challenge of making the other Arabs co-citizens, from all backgrounds in this case, realize the very existence of such violence and concede its dangerous impact on their lives. Generating this realization demands as such a certain discussion, analysis and presentation tracks, which this chapter should follow if I decide to tackle the question of peace and violence from this specific angle.

One can, nevertheless, touch upon the question by reflecting on violence as a notion or as a phenomenon in human life around the world,[332] making this macrocosmic framework its starting point for a following microcosmic focus, in this case, on the Arabic world's context. If this option is to be followed, then I am supposed to argue firstly why the violence of today's world is so crucial and why we have to ponder a possible

---

331 On some literatures on violence in the Arabic societies, see, for example, Kanʿān Makkiya, *Cruelty and Silence: War, Tyranny, Uprising and the Arab World*, (New York and London: W.W. Norton & Company, 1993); Magid Shehade, "Internal Violence: State's Role and Society's Responses," in *Arab Studies Quarterly*, 27(4), 2005, pp. 31-43.

332 See for example, Elizabeth Kandel Englander, *Understanding Violence*, (Mahwah, NJ: Lawrence Erlbaum Associates, Publishers, 1997); Bruce B. Lawrence and Aisha Karim (eds.), *On Violence: A Reader*, (Durham and London: Duke University Press, 2007); Douglas C. North; John J. Wallis, and Barry R. Weingast, *Violence and Social Orders: A Conceptual Framework for Interpreting Recorded Human History*, (Cambridge; Cambridge University Press, 2009).

peace-making duty the church, that is the worldwide Christian churches, should play on the globe specifically today.

This notwithstanding, I do think that violence as such is not the needed starting point for developing an Arabic Christian contextual stance in relation to peace and violence in the region. There is nothing intellectually or ontologically special or different about the violence that casts its shadows over the Arab world. It is just one form of violence that one can also be traced, though in different features and applications, all over the world, if not all over human history. When was human life not violent throughout history? When was the human ever living in an ideal, perfect peace? Violence is a curse the human should not only ponder and captivate rationally, but must first of all confront and eradicate without any hesitation or any second-thought. The world is fed up with talking about violence instead of acting against it. I assume that the Arab and Middle Eastern people on the ground hope to see the religious sides in the region developing practical stances that will lead eventually not only to a better understanding of the syndromes of violence in the region, but primarily to a more practically effective eradication of violence from the daily life of the Arabs, especially these forms of violence that stem out of religious differences or religious presumptions.

The abovementioned, rather general point of departure, is useful and every contextual theology about peace and violence can benefit from it and use it as a pavement toward the contextual discussion of the images and applications that are idiosyncratic of peace and violence in the concerned setting. However, this will not be the track my reflections' wagon would rail on. On one hand, every Arab Christian, let alone Arab Muslim, in the Near East knows more or less what the nature of peace is according to the religious and non-religious ethical codes' teachings. People do not need further theologization on the notion of 'peace' per se and its philosophical, purely intellectual and philological connotations. Nor do they, I believe, need further affirmative and persuasive arguments about the evilness, and immorality of violence and its damaging and disgraceful ramifications on the human life. And, in relation to the Arabs, who used traditionally to be silent and secretive about the forms and images of violence in their societies (driven culturally by the concept of shame), violence became their main public issue, as the falling dictatorial regimes in the region exert all kinds of violence and brutality against the people's public and utterly peaceful mass demonstrations in search for freedom, justice, democracy and substantial change. The violence of the regimes and the unimaginable excessively, let alone the indelibly, inerasable physical, psychological, intellectual, religious, sectarian and sociological scars it will leave on the Arabic body, are by all means the main subject on every media and cultural mediums around the Arab world. It almost became the daily bread of the people, and the Arab Christians are too drowned right in the abyss of suffering from this circle of violence to speak about it from any neutral or objective vantage point.

What is needed more urgently in the Arab world's very recent context is a more contextual and relational analysis of the possibility of living in peace and eradicating violence within the context of the co-existence with the different other. The rioting peaceful citizens, who suffered more than enough from the systematic brutality, torture and abuse of the Arabic tyrannical and non-human regimes, need a voice of hope and a voice of counter-violence. A voice, that is, that can seed a renewed belief in peace, reconciliation, acceptance and mutual trust. After these months of confrontation and immensely sacrificial rebellions, there will come a time when the rioting people will need to create new states and societies from the aches and rubbles of the old, collapsing ones. Then, living in peace with the different other, in a relationship free from any grudge, hatred or retaliation sentiments would be a demand, but also a challenge.

On the other hand, I also believe that in the past century, many non-governmental organizations around the world proved to the members of the international society, the Christians included, that they can sometimes be more competent than the official religious institutions in spreading, and acting according, to a very profound cultural and humanitarian understanding of the nature of peace.[333] So, rather than continue contributing theoretical and purely intellectual interpretations of peace, the religious institutions need to show that its religious discourse offers also a practical and relevant point of view about people's life on the ground, as well as the spokesmen of these religious institutions, especially in a deeply religious context like the Arab world (where the religious authori-

---

333 On the international NGO's peacemaking role around the world, see Oliver P. Richmond and Henry F. Carey (eds.), *Subcontracting Peace: the Challenges of NGO Peacbuilding*, (Hampshir, UK/ Burlington, USA: Ashgate, 2005); and Natalie Mychajlyszyn and Timothy M. Shaw (eds.), *Twisting Arms and Flexing Muscles: Humanitarian Intervention and Peacbuilding in perspective*, (Hants, UK/Burlington, USA: Ashgate, 2005).

ties still have an influential and heard voice in society) need to show how their discourse can lead their followers into acting and living realistically as vehicles of peace and reconciliation in their societies.

On the top of all the above, the pure theoretical reflection on the subject of peace in today's Arab world in specific has become empty and meaningless. The Arab-Israeli conflict, the havoc-radiating inferno of Iraq's invasion and all its drastic and costly aftermath on all the countries of the region, let alone the chaotic political feasts-wrestling between the west and the region's powers, just to mention a few, are all caused and committed by those who speak about peace and hide a dagger behind their backs. Peace, as such, became an empty concept; a diplomatic linguistic decoration, every politician or authoritative decision-maker from every background in the region likes to likes to start up with it its speech about the religions' situation. But, on the ground, peace is far from being an achievable goal, as far as the relationships between the powers who struggle over the fortunes of the area are concerned.

These previous contextual reasons make me believe that any speech about the value and nature of peace in absolutist and abstract general terms is useless merchandize for media consumption. What is needed is a practical approach to the realistic and down-to-earth need of attitudes, stances and relations of peace the different Arab religious communities, in general, and the Arab Christian groups, in specific, practice toward each other in the daily-life setting of society. The idea of practical action brings me in fact to the niche of thought I would like to propose for approaching the question of being vehicles of peace in a violent-breeding setting. Thinking coherently and perceptively about any sort of action drives us, in my opinion, to the zone of the *actor*. The action has no value or identity apart from the actor who conducts it. Even the act of salvation infers its value and profound truth from the reality and the nature of the actor who achieved this salvation in history. What I would like, therefore, to suggest as a starting point for speaking theologically about peace in the Arabic context is the personal and human image the Arab and Near Eastern Christians, who believe that something should be done to foster peace and fight violence in their homeland, reflect in their stance on every situation or condition in their Muslim-majority societies.

My main concern lies in the following question: if the Arab Christians believe that their contribution to their societies lies primarily in being vehicles of peace in a potentially violent-breeding context like the Arab world, what qualifies them to be so? From this question stems another no less crucial one: what would convince the non-Christians in the Arab world that the Arab Christians' message of peace is credible and addresses authentically the real, highly unpredictable and radically transforming present situation in the region? What makes the Arab Christians' message of peace as authentic, at least, as other similar ones in the eyes of the non-Christian Arabs?

My inquiry is about the Arab Christian peace-making citizen; the one, that is, who lives with his Muslim compatriots under the same conditions and is supposed to survive, just like his co-citizen, the same challenges and show to this other that she or he shares with everyone else in society the same sufferings, ambitions, dreams, actions and stances towards the future of their country. It is neither about peace nor about peace-making. I may even say this inquiry is about the things that would disqualify the Arab Christians from representing vehicles of peace in the eyes of the people in the Arab world.

People are usually prone to seek the things that make them appealing for the public opinion. Even when we introduce ourselves to the public as those who uphold a noble cause and who altruistically seek the goodwill of others in society, we tend to demonstrate this altruism through language, conduct and communicating skills that attract the attention of others and leave the most unforgettable impact and impression on them. Be that as it may, even when today we ask about the role the Arab Christians can play in facilitating peace in the Middle East, the question inevitably hides a personalist interest behind it.

The question about the Arab Christians' role as a vehicle of peace contains a sub-inquiry on what would qualify *our* views on peace before any others to the level of moving and persuading the people. And, since the essence of the assessment we make on the present for the sake of creating a better future lies in learning from the lessons of the past, the concern about coming to terms with the things that would make the Arab Christians a vehicle of peace, or a vehicle of anything, should be formulated in the light of ideas we infer from inquiries like the following: why did the people of the Middle East listen attentively to the Arab Christians, even those protestants among them despite their non-eastern theological origin and in spite of the fact that the missionaries, who landed on the Near Eastern shores some two hundred years ago, came from outside the Arabic cultural sphere and left their cultural values as a heritage to the locals?

What is it in the Christians' behaviours, personal characters and socio-ethical and cultural values that attracts the non-Christian Middle Easterners and persuades them about the Arab Christians' purposes and vision?

I am not going to spend the space of this chapter in developing a historiological analysis of the Arab Christians' work in the Middle East.[334] Far from this, I am just asking the abovementioned questions to pinpoint the following crucial factor. Sometimes, what attracts people, gains their support and changes their lives, are not primarily the message these Christians convey to their societies as much as the character and the attitude by which this group of Arabs conduct this conveyance. It is who these Arab Christians are as 'proclaimers' rather than the proclamation itself that sometimes occupies the central place in their influential role in society.

A few years ago, the professor of Modern History at St. Andrews University, Andrew Pettegree, wrote a significant book on the cultural and historical context, wherein the Protestant Reformation originated, and on the factors that led to the flourishing of this movement in Europe. Pettegree starts his book by raising the following crucial questions

> Why did people choose the Reformation? What was it in the evangelical teaching that excited, moved or persuaded them? How, and by what process, did people arrive at the new understandings that prompted a change of allegiance, and embedded them in their new faith?[335]

Pettegree points out that the decision of following the Protestant Reformation was not at all an easy one. It was rather a very painful and costly decision. It meant walking completely against the mainstream of society and confronting bluntly almost all the cultural, religious, societal and even political standards and convictions of the larger community. Despite this fact, many people followed eagerly the protestant reformers, listened carefully to them and laid the fate of their future in their hands. Why?

---

334 Some of the already available books on this subject are Philip Jenkins, *The Lost History of Christianity: the Thousand-Year Golden Age of the Church in Middle East, African and Asia – and How it Died*, (New York: Harper Collins Publishers, 2009), pp. 45-71, 227-246; Kenneth Cragg, *The Arab Christian: A History in the Middle East*, (Louisville, Ken: Westminster/John Knox Press, 1991).

335 Andrew Pettegree, *Reformation and the Culture of Persuasion*, (Cambridge: Cambridge University Press, 2005), p. 1.

What made people ready to make what many may consider today a suicidal move (i.e. trusting someone blindly with your life)? Pettegree's answer to this question is the following perceptive and noteworthy claim: the main driving force behind the people's trust in the reformers is their strong belief that the reformers were unconditionally prepared and totally willing to pay the price of their convictions and cause, no matter how high and fatal they were, and that they were ready to pay this price on behalf of their followers.

It is not my intention here to study whether Pettegree's reading of the roots of the Reformation's success and popularity among the people of 16th century Europe is coherently, comprehensive and historically accurate or not. I just refer to his above cited claim because it contains a relevant idea about the relation between convictions and practices. In a more slangy terms, it is a point about the significance of 'putting one's money where one's mouth is'. What do we have in Pettegree's pointed at case? We have a religious austerity that is based on a prophetic credibility. 'Religious austerity' here does not mean fanaticism. It rather connotes sincere and total commitment to a cause. 'Prophetic credibility', on the other hand, does not allude to a supernatural ability of controlling the others' destiny or an extraordinary preaching and evangelizing skills. It means a commitment to reflect what one intellectually shares with others and fights for before them in his or her very own life and being.

To bring this to the Middle East's context, how can the Arab Christians' discourse on peace gain credibility before the public when instead of peace and fellowship the Christian denominations in the Middle East, for example, demonstrate tension and enmity (if not verbal violence sometimes) between each other? The message of peace would be like a midsummer-night dream for those Muslims and non-Christians who hear a Presbyterian minister, for instance, degrading and attacking the Baptist preacher, the Orthodox priest and the Catholic father in the neighborly churches, or the Pentecostal charismatic leader blaspheming the Lutheran and the Congregationalist pastors and calling the Catholic and Orthodox clerics for repentance, and so on.

History tells us that it was a similar inner-clash factor that caused a division in the German city of Zwickau at the dawn of the sixteenth-century Reformation. At that time, the reformers' ministry in the city was beaming. And, due to the growth of the number of the church members, the council of Zwickau assigned the robust and rousing preacher Thomas

Müntzer as a colleague to one of Luther's brilliant students, Johann Egronus. The two preachers' ministry went well until Müntzer started singling out particular reformers for harsh and offensive criticism. Müntzer did not even spare his colleague Egronus from his fiery and bitter attack. Eventually, when the city council realized that people started to abandon the church and that the city community lost interest in the Reformation's message, they decided to seek a replacement to Müntzer.[336]

The Christians' history in the Near Eastern region offers such and many other similar stories about how constitutive peace is for the Christians internal life as communities. When 'one's money is not where one's mouth is', when one's relationships do not bestow credibility and authenticity upon the values and imperatives one entertains, preaching and intellectualizing about, it is not possible to transmit a message of peace to any different other, and it is unlikely that such a message will represent a persuasive voice of reconciliation or prove this voice's practical influence, no matter how big the Christians' communities could become one day in the region, or how resourceful their institutions can succeed in being or how high their leaders' rank in society become.

When it comes to the inner relationships between the various organs of the visible body of the risen Christ, peace and harmony among the brothers are a signs of maturity and healthiness, not only before themselves but also in their presence with the different others. Maturity is not just a phase the humans arrive at naturally or possess inherently. Maturity is a very demanding ambition, a very costly endeavour. We arrive at the ultimate, final destination in this process through falling into failures, making mistakes and learning from shortcomings. The Christians in the Arab world are not by-default vehicles of peace just because they are Christians. They are not so because they do not naturally become a mature community of God once they experienced redemption in his name. They have to struggle and work very hard to earn the responsibility of becoming vehicles of peace in a tormented area like the Middle East. They have to earn it by reaching a level of maturity that is capable of bringing them, first and foremost, into credible peace among each other in the region, so that their co-existence with the different other would also pave the way for realistic and down-to-earth acceptance and peaceful life.

---

336 Ibid., p.28.

In the previous exposition, I shed some light on some lessons from Christianity's history about what makes people consider the Christians as vehicles of peace and what would make the non-Christians listen particularly to them as a community with a valuable and credible message in the first place. The question I would like to reflect upon now is how the Arab Christians practice truly and effectively their role as a vehicle of peace in their Muslim-majority societies? It is my conviction that today's Middle East, if not the whole world, needs a Christian community that is ready to be a beacon of a socio-political and public voice that is characterized with both humility and integrity.

Studying the history of Christianity reveals that these two principles have not been maintained in companionship at all times through the two thousand years of the life of the community of Christ. There is time when the absence of either integrity or humility has uglied the face of the church before the world and turned Christianity into just another cocoon of condemnation and hypocrisy. On the other hand, there is another time in this long history when the church's living up to the Christian standards of humility and integrity not only laid a profound impression on the world, but also pioneered in shaping, and substantially challenging, the given standards of human life, as non-Christian thinkers, Muslims included, readily concede. I may even go further in saying that whenever humility and integrity marry in the life of a Christian person, the reality of the influence this Christian leaves on society is more evident than any influence Christianity can leave as a fixed religion or a static belief. After all, one of the major components of the phenomenon of religion, as many sociologist of religion already taught us, is the object who defines himself by her religious convictions. Additionally, walking the way of Jesus Christ does not primarily mean to talk like him, but rather to demonstrate a Christ-like match between one's *walk* and one's *talk*.

Let me give an example about this idea. Today, the term 'Islam' is for a serious number of communities around the globe a problematic and alarming term.[337] It is not necessarily so because of the Islamic Faith's

---

337 An interesting and valuable exposition of some European views of Islam is W. Shahid and P.S. van Koningsveld, "The Negative Image of Islam and Muslims in the West: Causes and Solutions," in *Religious Freedom and the Neutrality of the State; the Position of Islam in the European Union*, Shahid, W; P.S. van Koningsveld (eds.), (Leuven: Peeters, 2002), pp. 174-196, and Tareq Y. Ismael and Andrew Rippin (eds.), *Islam in the Eyes of the West: Images and Realities in an Age of Terror*, (Abingdon: Routledge, 2010). See also the interesting article on the im-

religious claims as such. Actually, many people, including a serious number of Muslims, admit that their knowledge of the core elements of the Islamic faith is in need of improvement. The term 'Islam' is alarming because of the religiously founded and dogmatically justified actions of the Muslim fundamentalists and fanatic *Jihadees* and *salafis* who present themselves as *the* Muslims proper. Those Muslims represent Islam in a way that makes millions around the globe abhor this religion. This is in fact an example of a post-modernist simulation or *memesis* of the well known Marxist and Feuerbachian allegation that religion sedates and stagnates human reasoning and creativity. It is also a belief that originates from a socio-political, if not psycho-anthropological, reading and hermeneutics of religious communities, rather than from a real comprehension and appraisal of the intellectual structure or the methodological and epistemological foundations of the Islamic religion itself.

What I want to say from the previous theoretical claims is the following: we define each other and interpret each other's religious identity by means of actions and attitudes to life and in life, and not necessarily from what the others hold as their intellectual convictions. It is the walk that matches the talk of those who call themselves religious that demonstrates the integrity and humility of the religious belief.

One of the most integrative and humble Christian persons I have had the privilege of knowing closely in my life is my theological supervisor and mentor, Colin Gunton, who was, until his sudden death in April 2003, the Systematic Theology Professor at King's College, London, UK. Being one of the known figures in his field, Prof. Gunton was the main target of many international students. Despite his important position, Colin was always humble when he met his students and discussed with them their theological ideas. He would receive their questions as if raised by theological experts. Some times, he would ask one of the students to comment on, even correct, what he was busy writing about for this or that journal, this or that conference, or this or that publishing house. He was always ready to act, and not only to talk, like a student before his students, like a humble Christian servant among others. He was someone whose walk always matched his talk.

Besides his memorable humbleness, Colin Gunton was an able debater and a prophetic defender of the scientific value and intellectual pertinence

---

age of Islam in the media of Bassil Akel, "Islam and the Western Media," in www.islamfortoday.com/media.htm (checked, 5, November. 2011, 10: 48 am).

of Christian doctrine. His relentless, sincere and integrative work was the main reason behind convincing the university about the significant contribution of theology to the education-philosophy of the religious studies at King's College.[338] During my postgraduate years at King's, I witnessed a very interesting debate between the theologians and the philosophers of religion in the department on whether teaching Christian doctrines in a secular and scientific academic setting like King's College is appropriate or not. In their writings, lectures and papers, the philosophers of religion in the department argued that philosophy of religion and not Christian doctrine is the field of study that can offer an appropriate hermeneutics of the concept of God for the modern world. In the face of this trend of thought, Colin Gunton stood up bravely to the challenge and endeavoured to show that the reality of God is part and parcel of the theological discourse. Therefore, any reliable understanding of the truth of the divine is obtainable from a study of theology and not merely from pure philosophical inquiry.

It is crucial to know that Gunton neither took an apologetic or a polemic standpoint, nor did he succumb to the intellectual conditions and claims of his colleague philosophers. He leaned, instead, on a peaceful interactive approach, yet a peaceful approach that was full of integrity, self-respect and prophetic credibility.[339] Colin never allowed his encom-

338 for some of Gunton's literature on the role of theology in the scientific setting of the university, see for example Colin Gunton, "The Indispensability of Theological Understanding: Theology in the University," in *Essentials of Christian Community: Essays for Daniel W. Hardy*, David Ford and Dennis Stamps (eds.), (Edinburgh: T&T Clark, 1996), pp. 266-277; Gutnon, "Indispensable Opponents: the Relations of Systematic Theology and the Philosophy of Religion," in *Neue Zeitschrift für Systematische Theologie und Religionsphilosophie*, 1996, pp. 298-306; Gunton, "Doing Theology in the University Today," in *The Practice of Theology, A Reader*, C. Gunton; S.R. Holmes and M.A. Rae (eds.), (London: SCM Press, 2001), pp. 441-455.

339 Within the reformed sphere, there is a recent attempt at viewing 'theology' as a discourse on faith that aims at presenting a Christian rationale that is basically persuasive, yet with integrity: H.J. Bernard Cambrink, "The Centrality of Socio-Rhetorical Interpretation to the Reformed Interpretation of Scripture," in *Reformed Theology: Identity and Ecumenicity II*, Wallace M. Alston Jr & Michael Welker (eds.,), (Grand Rapids, USA/ Cambridge, UK: W.B. Eerdmans Publishing company, 2007), pp. 91-106. Cambrink refers in this to arguments in Dirk Smit, *In Diens Vandie Tale Kona Ans? Q or Sistematiese Theologie*, (Stellenbosch: Universiteit Van Stellenbosch, 2000) and D.S. Cunningham, *Faithful Persuasion: In Aid*

passing openness toward other disciplines to shake his allegiance or to underrate his strong commitment to Christian faith. His understanding of his academic role as a theology professor in a secular atmosphere has always interweaved with his deep commitment to Christian faith as a cause in life. The key factor for him was integrity. It is this integrity that made Colin Gunton teach theology professionally, objectively and scientifically, yet also with the highest rate of commitment of someone who thinks and asks questions from the angle of faith.

How can the Christians be in their theological thinking and practice a vehicle of peace, or a vehicle of anything whatsoever, in the Arab world? By producing actions that are expressive of humility, yet also demonstrative of integrity. In one of his rather positively intriguing writings, the French thinker Jacques Ellul once dipped his finger right into the wound of today's Christianity. There is, Ellul argues, a serious problem in Christianity's attempt to make itself acceptable for and easy in the eyes of the contemporary world. By seeking acceptance and focusing on self-security, the church seems to be willing to sell so cheaply, and with no regret, its integrity. It departs far away, Ellul maintains, from the true message of Scripture that is supposed to scandalize the world, not to yield to the prerequisites of its approval. Ellul perceptively shows that the minute the church denies that, "what the New Testament really means by being a Christian is the very opposite of what is natural to us," it drags itself into the trap of choosing between two inappropriate options: 1) either revolting against the scandalizing nature of the Christian message, or 2) innovating cunning ways to fudge this nature by calling Christianity, "what is in fact its exact antithesis, and then giving thanks to God for the great favour of being [this kind] of Christians."[340] I leave Ellul's profound words with us to see for ourselves if it is applicable to the Christians in the Arab world or not. I personally discovered, to my disappointment, that the two options Ellul discloses are the first preferability the Christians, and mainly of a minority-complex and survival-obsession, clings to when it comes to playing their role in their Arabic societies.

One of the examples I may mention with this regard is related to politics. Politics is the Middle Eastern people's number-one hobby and pas-

---

of a Rhetoric of Christian Theology, (Notre Dame: University of Notre Dame Press, 1991).

340 Jacques Ellul, *The Subversion of Christianity*, Geoffrey Bromiley (trans.), (Grand Rapids: W.B. Eerdmans Publishing Company, 1986), p. 154 (pp. 154ff).

sion. This unfortunately makes politics the driving force and the criterial generator of values and imperatives in all the Arab societies. In the midst of an overtly politicized context like the Arab world, the church leaders and ministers are naturally prone and spontaneously tendentious to simulate popular politicians in the way they think, act and interact. It is no more a surprise, I should say, that the role of the church's representatives, along with the one of other public figures in society, is consistently undermined and their opinions are often ignored due to the public's, Christians and non-Christians alike, perception of a dominant, "spin, or corruption, or a lack of integrity,"[341] that is eating up the remaining hope in the existence of any honest leadership in the area. The Arab peoples on the public-squares, as the latest uprisings efficiently proved, can easily spot this spin of corruption and lack of integrity, and no eloquent oration or charismatic performance can hide it from their eyes. Even in a deeply religious society like the one of the Muslim-majority, Arabic countries, where religion and state are still organically intertwined, the person on the streets successfully and smartly, "sniffs religious humbug or double standards, particularly coming from [religious figures] who feel they have the right to tell others how they should live,"[342] or which leadership they should support and proclaim allegiance to.

One would be unwise to think that convincing people about the preciousness of peace and the danger of lurking violence in society needs only professional communication-skills and does not require integrity. A peace without an integrative peace-maker is an immoral oration. Peace without the necessary integrity for paying the high price of defending and even dying for the rights and dignity of the peace-seeking and peace-pleading society is a cheap lie, an ornamented publicity and, most dangerously, an immoral strategic pragmatism. This is why, for example the Egyptian population never reflected positive trust in the peace treaty the regime made with Israel and has not yet changed its fully and unconditional pro-Palestinian standpoint. This is also why the Syrian population is not fully confident that the Assadi regime is sincere in its secret eagerness for buying a peace-agreement with Israel and its forceful propagation of peace and reconciliation with Israel as a possible foreseen option the people should obediently, and not freely, welcome. Conveying a cul-

341 As expressed in Jonathan Lamb, *Integrity: Leading with God Watching*, (Nottingham: Inter-Varsity Press, 2006), p. 14.

342 Ibid., p.14.

ture of peace to our deeply troubled and dismal region is a 'to be or not to be' question. It is for the Christians' role in their Arab Muslim societies, "a matter of faith that works, of truth in action, of godliness in working clothes."[343]

Before bringing this chapter to an end, some thoughts need to be put in place on the following question: what would be the consequences of a Christian minority attempting to survive in its society without retaining its prophetic integrity? One of the lethal consequences of the lack of prophetic integrity in a heterogeneous society, where the minority-majority division is a factor, is the undermining of one's self-worth or the worth of the others. Thomas Martin, the lecturer of philosophy at Roberts University in South Africa, hits the core of the dark side of this degradation by studying its multi-faceted impact on the life of societies. He discovers that the attenuation of one's being and the being of others is in fact a nickname for a sort of bad faith oppression. Martin refers to John-Paul Sarter's distinction between the state of being self-concerned and the state of being other-concerning. He then argues that any assumed division of these two relentlessly mutually interrelated aspects of human beingness is a feature of serious self –deception.[344]

Martin's analysis offers us a useful tool to describe the bad faith that lies in dis-integrity, self-centredness and inuthenticity. Once we drift into a closed self-awareness and self-survival circle, the concern about peace becomes a privative, intrinsic obsession. We become tendentious to self-transcendence and egocentric pragmatism. As a religious minority, we, first, transcend beyond the daily oppression and suffering contextual reality of our majority co-citizens and resort to an imaginary super-natural heavenly promised world and wait its coming in isolation and hermetically-sealed spiritual aspiration. And, second, we dedicate all the capabilities and resources we may have solely for our own survival and continuation. In other words, the religious minority turns into a beneficiary community, whose ultimate concern is to gain approval. We see this escalating in the Middle East as the prophetic voice of the Christian minority transforms into a voice for glorifying authorities and even justifying tyranny and oppression, and as the Christians' expected theological dis-

343 Ibid., p.15.

344 Thomas Martin, *Oppression and the Human Condition: An Introduction to Sartrean Existentialism*, (Lanham, Boulder, New York & Oxford: Rowman & Littlefield Publishers, Inc. 2002), pp. 29ff.

course against corruption and societal fragmentation metamorphoses into an authoritative voice usually used to back up the secular decision-makers. This is what usually happens when the minority group leans on a self-concern option alone.

However, the alternative of this should not be retreating one-sidedly and over-passionately to the other extreme of 'other-concerning alone'. This alternative is no less preventive of the minority-community's success in playing the role of a vehicle of peace. If the first extreme of ego-centrism abolishes the Christians' attention to the world's need for peace, extreme altruism denies the minority Christians a balanced spiritual and personal integrity that stems from inner peace. External concern about the socio-political needs of the Muslim (or the Jewish, in the case of Israel) majority can sometimes become lethal for the Christian minority's cultural, ethical and intellectual otherness. The Christian minority could then turn into a slave to the circumstantial needs and requirements of the stronger and numerically larger voice in society, rather than an echo of the voice of the prophetic Messiah in it, and even against it sometimes.

Once, Paul Tillich affirmed that theology is just a discourse responsive of human needs and demonstrative of answers man seeks and wishes to find an actual expression of in his or her religious preoccupation with the divine. In other words, theology, which is supposed to be the intellectual voice and the practical guiding map of the Christians' life, does not raise questions against the human condition. It only offers answers that are compatible with certain human expectations. This entails that the one-sided concern about others and the reduction of the church's theological claims into mere social-gospel mission can sometimes turn God as such into the slave of creation.

Finally, how can the Christians develop a contextual theology that can enable them to become a vehicle of peace in the violent settings of the Middle East? Between the two extremes of self-subordinating altruism and self-protective egoism lays the option of an outgoing and active Christian minority that is characterized with a prophetic integrity; a minority, that is, that goes willingly to the cross of truth, yet not because this is what satisfies the needs and pleases the expectations of the major others, but because the cross of truth is the Christians life's *telos*, whether they liked it or not, whether the society accredited it or not and whether people think that this cross is compatible with their aspirations or not.

I end this chapter with a warning stated by Jürgen Moltamnn, who once perceptively and prophetically states that the church's institutional ministry, as well as its missionary presence in society can, "become a stumbling block for many people," when they fail in demonstrating the messianic witness of existence. "Through its order, its ministries and its organizations," as Moltmann affirms, "the church either confesses or denies the things that it has to represent." It is because of this the Christian community, "cannot leave its visible form to the power of the state or the requirements of its particular social order, if it wants to be recognizable as the church of Christ and as the people of the coming Kingdom."[345]

345 Moltmann, *The Church in the Power of the Spirit*, pp. 290-291.

Conclusion

The latest uprisings in the Arab world have hardly reached their final destination. One can easily notice that they have just begun. As I finished writing these chapters, the events' evolvement in more than one Arab country, where revolutions had already been unleashed, was still well in progress and escalation.

In Tunisia, the newly formed temporary government started to court the symbolic figures of Bin Ali's regime and to reconstruct the political and jurisdictional conditions in preparation for the coming phase. The country seems to have finally turned the page from the previous regime and is now looking optimistically to the future. The leaders and main figures of the Islamist movements and political parties have returned from exile and are now back in the country. Their groups practice their political role in public and, as one expects, efficiently and influentially shape the Tunisian society. New parliamentary presidential elections took place and the Islamists enhanced their control over the country, though they supported a pro-Human Rights and more secularist figure as a president. The aftermath of these elections and their forthcoming ramifications would certainly decide the character of the new ruling regime and the nature of the state for years, if not decades, to come. Since there are no noticeable or tangible religious minorities in the country, the coming Tunisia would not socially be much different from the one we already know. On the other hand, the political scene, though expectedly dominantly Islamist, reveals so far an insistence of establishing a democratic, civil and human rights-based system, which is unlikely to be crudely politically secularist.

The situation in Egypt is slightly similar to Tunisia, yet also particularly and more delicately different. After the overthrowing of the regime, the newly formed government and the leading military council are courting the corrupted and criminal figures of the old regime, president Mubarak, his wife and his sons included. The western powers, as it seems, started to digest the strong possibility of having a Muslim brotherhood ruling alternative in the country. They even seem to be in favour of it, as they back up the military council's attempt at running early parliamentary and ensuing presidential elections, despite their knowledge that this would give the Muslim Brotherhood an easy, comfortable and even guaranteed win of the majority of the parliament's seats and maybe also the presidential position (as I write these pages, the presidential election reached its second stage, with the nominee of the Muslim Brotherhood contesting with Ahmad Shafeek, the last Prime-Minister in Mubarak's rule) before the other rather disorganized and unprepared political parties and candidates. It seems for now that Egypt is passing through a radical, very complicated and intricate transitional phase, wherein the Islamist will reveal an unflinching thirst for power and the non-Islamist political trends in the country would ferociously stand between the formers and their hegemonic ambitions. The premature and spontaneous ambitious political views of the youths who made the revolution in the Egyptian public square indicate that enough time must pass before these views witness realization and constitutional appliance (in the latest presidential elections, the youths voices were dominantly divided between the Muslim Brotherhood's nominee, Muhammad Mursi, and the nominee of the Naserite Party, Hamdin Sabbahi, who became third in the presidential elections' first-round). These youths need serious time and a consistent political and civil interactive atmosphere to develop a fully-fledged, reliable political agenda and to reveal a political and civil maturity, which the country's public leading figures cannot but consider for constructing the hoped-for, fully democratic, pluralist and civil Egyptian republic.

Until this happens, the Islamist political trends, and despite the ferocious resistance of the traditional, left wing and liberal political antagonists and intellectuals, are gradually, yet surely, filling-in the gap and trying even to dominantly confiscate the youths' revolution and exploit it in their own monopolization ambitions. Against this attempt, the 'youths of the Revolution' tried sometimes to raise their voice by, for instance, organizing million-participant 'anger demonstrations', wherein they condemned the Muslim Brotherhood's and other Islamist groups' endeavour to reduce the multifariousness and the plurality of the uprising square into their own narrowly Islamist colour. Despite such attempts, the Islamists seem to be enjoying the upper hand in the Egyptian scene at the moment, yet they are witty enough to play the power-control game in a prudential and well calculated manner. They try at the moment to prove to the whole vigilantly observing world (especially America and Israel) that an Islamist system in rule may not be as dangerously confrontational and terrifyingly extremist and antagonistic as it is believed to be. This is why, the Muslim Brotherhood of Egypt are keen on publicizing a discourse that promotes democratic statehood, pluralist society, tolerance to minorities, human rights centralization, with a parallel rejection, however, of secularism and insistence on Islam as the official religion of the republic and the president.

The real religiously-driven danger and challenge in post-Mubarak Egypt, nevertheless, as we realize lately, comes from the Muslim fanatic salafi movements in the country. The salafis used to survive underground and to resort to secretive operations during Mubarak's opprcssive rule. As of late, they have risen up to the surface and begun to work vibrantly in public. Their initial strategy demonstrates that they are keen on inaugurating a series of highly controversial public activities in order to draw, first and foremost, the public attention to their existence and capabilities of influencing (if not disturbing) the life-rhythm of the country. Unfortunately, this attention-seeking goal was achieved by means of operating religious persecution and violence against the Coptic community. When, for example, the recent government assigned a Christian governor to the vicinity of Qenah, the salafi community of the city rioted against the decision because they considered the assigned figure as 'kafir' (infidel), and not a Muslim. They aggressively prevented the new governor from reaching his office in the municipality building. And, when the youths of the revolution demonstrated in support of the government's decision and in condemnation of any religious discrimination, the salafis faced them brutally and tried to oppress the youths' demonstration by force. The salafis, on the other hand, continued vandalizing the Christian Copts and brutally attacking them and their churches, in an indication that the social and religious persecution the Copts suffered from during Mubarak's rule is not going to vanish in the near future. We even could hear on a Youtube video one of these salafis cursing the late pope Shenudah III and the Christians by calling them 'dogs' and enticing the Muslims publicly to burn up the churches. Such a public gesture was not witnessed in this blunt explicitness during Mubark's era.

Whereto Egypt from here? This is yet to be seen. Meanwhile, the hope is that the main religious institute in the country, al-Azhar al-Sharif, and its scientific and religious body would begin influencing the society in its moderate and tolerant Islamic approach and replace the fanatic and salafi Islamist movements in shaping the future Egyptian society after tolerance, plurality and other-acceptance values. At the end of June, al-Azhar started to give signs about its intention to play such a role, when the Egyptian Grand Mufti, Ahmad al-Tayyeb issued with a big group of Islamic Azhari clerics and Egyptian lay intellectuals what is called 'al-Azhar's Document on the Future of Egypt'.[346] Far from calling for an Islamist state or applying Shari'a as the country's constitutions, the document called for establishing a "nationalist, constitutional, democratic and modern state", and stated clearly that Islam has not known in its history, civilization or even jurisdiction the notion of 'religious-clerical state', but rather called its followers to choose the ruling system they find useful for their own context and goodwill. The document also emphasized democracy, plurality and the principle of power devolution and ruling the state and society by the authority of the civil law alone. It also stressed on the freedom of thought and opinion and human rights. But, most interestingly still, it called for respecting the principle of religious plurality and freedom, calling for treating the people from all religions and confessions according to their civil citizenship only. This religious tolerance and concern about religious and confessional plurality and acceptance gain its clearest and most explicit expression in the document's item number six, which states:

> maintaining the dignity of the Egyptian nation and preserving the national pride, and emphasizing the total protection and complete respect of the worshiping places of the three heavenly religions, and granting a totally free practice of all the religious rituals and rites without any detentions or obstacles, and respecting all the various forms of worship, without degrading the people's culture or distort the traditions, and also totally caring for the freedom of literary and artistic expression within the framework of our steadfast civilization's value system.

As is, this document represents an advanced step in the history of the interreligious tolerance and dialogue between the different segments of the Egyptian society. It is yet to be seen if this document will or will not be welcomed positively by the Copts of the country and whether or not it will gain acknowledgment and gather followers among the Egyptian

346 See on this document "Naṣṣ Wathiqat al-Azhar Ḥawl Mustaqbal Maṣr," (The Text of al-Azhar Document on Egypt's Future), in www.onislam.net/arabic/newsanalysis/documents-data, 10:51 am, 20, June. 2011; and Muhammad al-Baḥrawy, "al-Tayyb Yo'len Wathiqat al-Azhar Ḥawl Mustaqbal Maṣr," (al-Tayyb Declares al-Azhar Document on Egypt's Future), in www.youm7.com , 12:37 pm, 20, June. 2011.

Muslims and succeed eventually in snatching the louder and more influential voice in the Egyptian public square from the hand of the extremists and fundamentalists.

In Libya, the situation has taken a drastic turn. At the beginning, Gaddafi insisted on resisting the uprising and turning a deaf ear to the international and Arab appeals for him to spare the blood-shed, step-down and exile from the country in peace. The following consequences of his counter-decision were the toppling of Gadaffi's regime and the death of Gadaffi himself assassinated at the hands of the rebellion fighters. All the opposition forces in the country are now occupied with rebuilding Libya and re-establishing the state according to a fixed timetable.

After al-Gaddafi's assassination, scermishes between the newly founded arm forces and the supporters of the dead dictator occurred occasionally, like the battles that took place in Bani-Walid's city. Some of the rebellion's militias, nonetheless, who are based in the eastern zone of the country refused to hand in their weapons to the elected government or to join the newly re-established national army, calling instead for independence and a confederal autonomy. On the other hand, the political trend that dominated the country and represented itself as an alternative to the previous regime has proven clearly to be of crude Islamist background. The rebellions' representatives and the leaders of the newly formed government in post-revolution Libya speak so far about opting for a democratic, human rights-based, pluralist and civil state, albeit shaped after Islamic values and principles. These terms, however, are being entertained by all the Arab uprising groups all over the Arab region at the moment, especially in Egypt where the Islamists sweepingly ruled over the executive and legislative ruling bodies in the country. In what form would such a state be applied, and what kind of democracy, plurality and civil society would stem out of such pro-democracy rhetoric in Libya and other places? This varies from one country to another and also from one uprising group to another. Libya is a crudely tribalistic society with a clear semi-civil, nomadically-shaped structure and strongly Islamist/Sunnite cultural identity. How the newly formed government in Libya might reconcile this legacy and culture with a civil, democratic and pluralist statehood, would be the most interesting phenomenon to observe, study and evaluate in the coming months.

The following question and most important one, though, is what kind of a Libyan state would we witness in the coming future? Though all the odds suggest that there is a strong probability that the political trend, which will dominate the country and represent itself as an alternative, would be of Islamist background, I believe it to be unlikely that this Islamist alternative would impose on the country a political alternative that would express any of the salafi and jihadi fundamentalist Islamic approaches. The Libyan Islamist rebellions know quite well that such a fanatic confrontational alternative would not be supported by the international society, let alone their European neighbours. Besides, the Libyan uprising's Islamists, before any other political branch in the country, were the ones who asked for the international military interference, and they perceive deeply that there will come the time when the Libyan revolution must pay back to those powers, which helped out. One of the prices would be meeting the international society's expectation of an Islamist, yet moderate, tolerant, semi-democratic and pro-western state in Libya.

In Yemen, the situation is also still rather unclear. In the beginning, Ali Abdullah Saleh clung to his ruling chair and refused to cooperate with all the attempts at orchestrating a peaceful ending and power-pass, which were initiated by the Council of Gulfi Cooperation, led by Saudi Arabia and backed by USA and Europe. Later on, he managed to cut a deal with these powers and to give up his ruling position to his deputy, granting in return a safe and trial-free exit from the country. The latest news I heard as I was writing these lines was the beginning of a ferocious, bloody tribal war in the country, in addition to ferocious bloody battles between the Yemeni national army forces and the jihadi troops of al-Qa'ida in southern Yemen. What people are looking at with aspirations and hope is the fact that Saleh's rule has ended for good and that his deputy has now been handed the presidential authority and has started the process of rebuilding the state, the thing that was welcomed by the opposition and seen as the beginning of a peaceful and gradual regime-change in Yemen. The success or failure of this hope will be seen in the coming future.

In Bahrain, the uprising seems to have been surgically cracked down by the royal regime. This latter seems to have succeeded in persuading the Arab league and the international society that, rather than being a peaceful, locally-made and nationally-driven call for reformation, the uprising was externally orchestrated by Iran via its influential links to the majority Schiʿite community in Bahrain. After successfully propagating this conspiracy theory, the Bahraini regime allowed the Saudi military troops to cross the boarders and conduct a massive and brutal crackdown against the demonstrators. As of late, the king of Bahrain used a live speech to address the entire nation, especially challenging the rioting opposition, for an open, serious and unconditional dialogue over the reformation and the future of Bahrain. This by no means implies that the potential for revolution in Bahrain has died out. To the contrary, the tense and edgy situation and the potential of another riotous irruption are just lurking under the surface as a fire underneath ashes.

The most drastic, unpredictable and horrifying developments, nevertheless, remain so far the regime's reaction and the rebellions' attempts in Syria. After first reacting positively to the people's public move and admitting the validity and fairness of their demands, the regime changed its position completely and mercilessly turned back against the public move. For months now, the regime's one and only choice is resorting to military termination and indescribable violence instead of politics and to ruthless termination of every dissenting voice instead of dialogue and realistic reformation. For the past seventeen months, the regime has resiliently deployed its armed troops to attack the rebellions and has brutally terminated the revolution in almost all the cities of Syria, killing so far, and causing the death of, over 15,000 citizens and soldiers. It is obvious that the regime does not want to change its violent option, but is rather determined to continue using force as much as it can to either abort the revolution or delay its inevitable outcome.

On the other side, this insistence on violence and this excessive amount of dead citizens has pushed some segments of the rioting population to also opt for violence and armed fighting against the regime's brutality, causing innumerable casualties among the police forces, the army soldiers and the security troops. In its media and political war with the opposition, the regime consistently exploits this brutality to justify its reinvocation of the scenario that al-Assad senior followed in 1982-83 to smash the Muslim Brotherhood's riot to the ground. Whereas, the opposition uses the regime's violence and brutality by mobilizing international opinion and societies against the regime and making America and Europe exert harsh sanctions on the regime's personnel. In between these two rather seemingly fruitless options, the situation in Syria seems to have reached a very vague stage and one feels that both clashing sides have no clear view for moving ahead at the moment.

The Christians in Syria find themselves in an unenviable, confusing situation, as they linger trapped in-between the clashing sides. They condemn the regime's violence and killing, and causing the death of over 15,000 Syrian citizens and wish it to give up oppression and opt for political and dialogical methods. At the same time the Christians are getting more and more confused and weary about the nature and main driving-views and intentions of some of the Syrian immigrant oppositions and the jihadi armed gorilla fighters, as they see them trying to ride the wave of the public movement and to enslave it by achieving their dream of toppling the regime by whatever means and at any costs, even the country's stable, tolerant, non-confessional and inclusivist societal textile. This terrifies the Christians of Syria and makes them feel that the future is so grimly and darkly bleak and vague. The end of Syria's uprising remains, as of now, completely wide open, with Syrians increasing in number who believe that the worst lies yet ahead.

Fear of a future worse situation has increased actually much earlier than the last seventeen months, specifically almost twelve years ago, after the president al-Assad gave a speech in Damascus university on the 20th of June, 2001. That speech was kind of a sign that the beginning of the regime's end has just kicked off after many years of violence and blood and false promises of reformation. The latest speech of the Syrian president during the Syrian revolution in 2012 has not trespassed the boundaries of the regime oppositions' old negative expectations and their already-developed pessimism about the former's willingness of change. This last speech, which the president gave more than five months ago also in Damascus University, failed indelibly in making any breakthrough in the country's recent crisis. It, rather, gave the Syrians and the world strong evidence of the regime's inability of changing itself or its view of the people and its relationship with them. The regime insists, as we understood from the speech, that everything that Syria has witnessed lately is a 'universal conspiracy', that the rioters are all and indiscriminately just subversive, jihadi groups controlled by external sides and that dealing with them should not be in any other way than force and military confrontation. Al-Assad totally refuses to admit the existence of peaceful demonstrators on the streets, who propagate no fanatic, confessional hatred, commit no vandalism and carry no guns and only ask for freedom and justice and the fall-down of dictatorship and tyranny. Al-Assad also refused to confess the security and army force's violence and mistakes and showed no willingness to send a reconciliation message or a sign of readiness to open a new page between the leadership and the people. He rather addressed the public square and opinion as if Syria is still in its past situation and as if the people are still resorting to their old silence. This insistence on indifference and condescension was associated, in the speech, with a monotonous and boring repetitive theorization on reformation, the elements of future planning, on the constructive and careful building-up and other slogans, the hearing of which the Syrian public square had for long time habituated without witnessing any actual changes on the ground.

During the past two months, the United Nation and the Arab League convoyed the ex-General Secretary of the United Nation, Kufi Anaan, to Syria to mediate between the regime and the opposition and reach a political solution to the entire struggle. What is known as 'Anaan's Initiative' seems to be facing a serious failure, as both the regime and the jihdi, counter-violence oriented rebellions (who are now considered to be an evident third-front, other than the opposition and the regime alike, which pursues its own agenda on how the struggle must end in Syria) do not show any serious adoption of this initiative, and as they continue, instead, their blind and bloody fight over the country's control. As I write these paragraphs, many Western countries have begun to expel the Syrian diplomats and ambassadors out, after the horrible massacre of al-Hula city, which left 100 innocent men, women and children dead and 300 injured. Though this diplomatic move sends a strong political message to the regime, it does not leave any evident reliable mark on the ground inside the Syrian scene. How will the Syrian hell end? Nobody can give any clear answer to this question at this very moment.

One can at least validly say that the forth presidential speech during the Syrian revolution does not convey to any observer anything except that, in its relation to reality, the Ba'thi regime in Syria lives in a state of denial. It refuses to concede that the events in Syria mark a substantial change and pave the way for a pivotal, fateful turn in the history of the country. This state of denial and loftiness towards reality is just a sign that the regime has begun to realize its impending collapse and that the gradual descending toward its era-end has started and will never stop or derail from its track. Even if the head of authority remains in his position, the regime that once guaranteed rule and legalized it to him has begun to fall down and will never remain the same, even if it managed to survive in power for a while. The age of the Ba'th regime has started to end, and sooner or later we will find ourselves in Syria face-to-face with the question of the identity of post-Ba'th Syria and which new Syrian state would the twenty first century witnesses therein.

Which system and society will develop in post-Ba'th Syria? It goes without saying, I believe, that this question occupies the Syrian, Arab and international circles, as it kept them busy in the case of the riots in the other Arab countries. There is no doubt, too, that many have begun to develop some possible alternatives that are most probably derived from statehood and societal experiences in other neighbourly Arab and Islamic countries in the region. The question is which of these alternatives or imaginings can apply to the sociological, religious, ethnic, sectarian and political nature of Syria?

Quite a few believe that the Turkish form is the suitable alternative for the Arab world, including Syria. Actually, Turkey itself aspires and works hard, as it seems to apply it, especially in its neighbour Syria in specific. Yet, the Turkish alternative does not work in Syria. The Turkish regime does not acknowledge its religious and ethnic minorities, does not grant them equal and just rights and it does not even admit the existence of non-Muslim groups on Turkish land. One can say that the Turkish record with regard to the relation with its minorities is exceedingly bad. On the other hand, the Turkish society in its majority is not reflected in the society of Istanbul, not even its western chunk's, attempt at demonstrating pluralism, modernity and openness towards other cultures. The vast majority of the Turkish seventy million-large community lives sociologically and culturally in a pre-modern, self-enclosed context, wherein the dominant life-setting is strictly rural and religious and hardly avails tolerance with regards to plurality, variability, and citizenship in its civil form. Aside from society, the Turkish state passes through a transitional, political and jurisdictional period, as the Islamist ruling party endeavours to slowly Islamize the state, Qur'ānize the constitution and publicize the culture of religiosity in the society. This drives one to assume that what we used to call the 'Ataturkian, Secularist Turkey' may vanish in the following two decades. Before speaking about a Turkish form that is suitable to the Arab world, we should wait to see how this Turkish form may transform and what kind of substantial changes it might witness and whether or not these changes would allow us to consider it still as an 'example' in the first place.

Neither does the Egyptian form apply to Syria. In Egypt, also, the non-Muslim minority suffers from oppression and societal, discriminative pressures that are almost methodical and systematic in nature. These go back to many centuries of religious fanaticism that is rooted in the historical, sociological, cultural and religious history of the land of the Nile. One can say that the political systems that ruled modern Egypt were not the perpetrators of such persecution, though they invested into it in their ruling agendas. After the success of the Egyptian youth's latest revolution, it seemed as if the youths gave up, for one reason or another, the political square to the religious and Islamist movements in the country, which devoured and wreaked in the fruits of the revolution, and began to show its anathematizing and violent fangs and publicly reflected its goal of establishing a fanatic, salafi alternative in Egypt. Till the days pass and the Egyptian revolution's youths, along with the liberal, secularist, democratic and leftist cultural and political movements, begin organizing its front and work substantially and influentially in the Egyptian public square, Egypt will not be a pluralist, democratic or civil example one can rely on following. And, the Christian minority in the country will continue paying the high price of the recent Egyptian situation, even after the fall of Mubarak's regime, which the Egyptian circles used to hold accountable for the religious and societal persecution in Egypt; when, that is, it occasionally, and under specific public opinion pressure, admitted its existence.

In Syria, the Iraqi example is also inapplicable. Iraq is a country with a real religious, ethnic and confessional plurality. Yet, this plurality before anything else takes in today's Iraq the image of fragmentation and demographic and confessional division. One can even say that the map of Iraq actually contains the borderlines of three states squeezed into one. Iraq has not become a state after the fall of the dictatorship in it. Its society, in addition, witnesses sharp regression into pre-modernist sociological forms of existence which invoke the collectivist and exclusivist tribal logic and religious institutes' authority, as well as dangerous and closed ethnic and confessional relationships, which succeeded so far in transforming Iraq from a republic and a state into circumstantial alliances and minor states. Iraq is an ideal example in the Arab world of the possibility of one society's falling from a state of open plurality and co-existence into a state of closed, confrontational and divisive plurality. Such an example is not what we aspire to in the Arab world, but the boogeyman we all fear.

In Syria, the Lebanese form does not apply either, despite all its features that seem inviting and attractive to the Syrian Christian community or the Arab Shi'ite one. In its recent situation and complicated circumstances, Lebanon does not represent a stately, civil form one can lean on. Lebanon is a sample of 'confessions' society' not of 'state society'. It is not ruled by means of civil contracts among the citizens. Its nature as a being is rather conditioned by the deals and shares-division between its confessional and sectarian leaders. Although the Lebanese society enjoys all the characteristics of modernity, progress and cultural variety, due to the country's historical openness to international cultures and its intellectual and media freedom. Yet, this does not mean that Lebanon has reached in its statehood-formation journey the stage of real civil society. For, Human Rights in it were replaced on the level of practice with the rights and shares of the sectarian group; democracy was replaced with unilateral political hegemony; the civil society was compensated with peaceful co-existence, while the citizenship mentality was replaced with the mentality of loyalty and adherence. The plurality, openness and civility of Lebanon militate today negatively against the country itself, as it is used in the enforcement and promotion of its confessionalism, rather than the state mentality.

The Gulfi example too does not apply to Syria. The Gulfi societies are free from religious and ethnic minorities, though they contain sectarian ones. Those, nevertheless, who belong to non-Muslim religions in the Gulfi countries are deprived of the right of free worship and they are not treated as equally as other Muslim citizens. The notion of civil citizenship has not yet developed in the Gulf world, because these countries are controlled by epistemological systems and anthropological relationships that are congenial with its purely collectivist and monolithic mentality. Its sociological textile is shaped after the culture of 'obeying the guardians' and the sanctity of the blood loyalty and kinship links, which express the tribalistic and nomadic roots of the Gulfi people's history. This is why we cannot find in the Gulfi countries the concept of 'public' or 'citizens', but the notions of 'children', 'followers' and 'nationals'. And, this is why the political mentality there is not orchestrated by the logic of plurality, equality, power-sharing and equal ruling-chances, but the mentality of inheritance, continuity, exclusivism, monism and quotas. In societies free from clear and real ethnic and religious plurality, the ruling forms of emirate or kingdom may work successfully. Yet, they definitely fail in open, pluralist and culturally heterogeneous societies.

None of the abovementioned stately or societal forms apply in fact to Syria. It is, therefore, a mistake to urkanize, egyptianize, iraqnize, lebanize or gulfify Syria. What applies to Syria is what distinguishes it from other states and makes it itself. What should take place in post-Ba'thi Syria is 'Syrianizing' Syria; bring it, that is, back to its real nature, which it lost when it was transformed into the ruling family's farm or feudal property: a stately sphere, a mosaic society that is open and pluralist par excellence. Syria cannot but be a mosaic in nature, practice and identity. What happened during the past forty years was that the 'syrianism' of Syria was obliterated by the Ba'th and Assadi regime's attempt at turkanizing or gulfifying Syria.

Syria has an active Christian minority, which goes back in its historical existence in the land more than two thousand years. It is impossible to treat this existence as temporary, circumstantial or accidental, and no Islamic rule managed during the centuries in doing this. For, the role of Christianity, culture and heritage is constructive and constitutive in the formation of Islam in Syria. It is a role that exceeds in it presence, influence and reality the role of the Christians among the Syrians in today's Syrian society. Even if the Muslim majority in Syria denied the existence of the Christian minority (the thing that is rejected by all the Muslim groups and trends of thought in the country), this majority cannot deny history and tradition and would not find any supporter in the world if they did so. And, if the Syrian Christian citizen was not used to suffer from any religious or societal persecution (contrary to his Coptic brother) because of his religion in the Ba'thi Syria, he cannot accept becoming the victim of such a persecution at the age of the Syrian public's attempt at building a post-Ba'thi, just and inclusivist state.

On the other hand, as in Syria, there are active and influential historical Muslim minorities, the existence, the role and the rights of which the Sunnite majority cannot deny, nor can it force these minorities to live squeezed in specific geographical sectors, is we see in Iraq: for example, forcing the Alawites to live on the coast, and forcing the Kurds to limit their existence to Syria's far northeast. The Syrian society has always lived in an old and complicated demographic intermingling and intertwining, and its Kurds, Alawites and Sunnites have always been linked to each other by means of blood and kinship and fate. All the regression into sectarian identification and the rapid growth of the fear from the other are just the by-products of the Ba‘thi regime, which established its whole being on ‘the fear from the other’ culture and made the threat of sectarian tension the safety-valve of its hegemony and control.

In Syria, there is also an undeniable old and deeply rooted linguistic, cultural and ethnic plurality. Syria contains Armenians, Kurds, Turkomans and Syriacs beside the Arabs. Each one of these not only has its own unique ethnic origin and cultural history, but also has its own national language, Armenian, Jurdish, Turkomani and Syriac. Even during the domination peak of the pan-Arabism ideology and prevalence of the Arabic language, and though the followers of these minorities speak Arabic and pride themselves about it, neither pan-Arabism nor the Arabization policy succeeded in erasing this rich cultural variety from Syria. Add to this, Syria has always been by virtue of its Mediterranean location an open space for the interaction of eastern and western cultures. These cultures have left their marks on the knowledge, sciences and thought-forms of the Syrian people.

In Syria too, a noticeable history of civil society and the struggle for establishing the statehood of citizenship, which was not disturbed by civil war between confessions (as in Lebanon) or societal clashes between religions (as in Egypt) or tribal, ethnic or nomadic struggles (as in Iraq and the Gulf). Add to this, the ideologies of Ba‘th and other nationalist, pan-arabist and leftist parties in the country have contributed through various phases of Syria’s modern history in spreading the idea of secularism and the principle of ‘religion is for God, the homeland is for all’ between the population’s various segments. Even if the concept of secularism is still vague and misunderstood in the public Syrian culture, yet coexisting with the different other, disregarding his or her religious and ethnic background, disregarding his or her language, confession or nationalistic views as well as living with him or her on the basis of the belief that the homeland is for all and that all are Syrians, were and still represent the general tendency and the dominating sociological and stately thought form in Syria. It is even popular and highly valued within the conservative Islamist circles in the country, for the followers of these circles were also born, grew up and lived in the same open, pluralist sphere.

All the above mentioned factors make Syria real mosaic that might be one-of-its-kind in the region. It also makes Syria the most viable and ready country in the Arab world to transform into a civil, democratic, pluralist, open and multi-cultural republic, if not even to a politically secular state. What the post-Ba'th Syria needs is to retrieve its mosaic 'syrianity' by establishing its own particular civil society and secular state. There is no future for Syria except in the secularity and democracy of its political system, the civility, citizenship, plurality and freedom of its sociological context and the reliance of its jurisdictional and constitutional system on the Human Rights declaration. Nations usually require many decades and multiple generations to create in its societies intellectual, anthropological and cultural spheres that prepare its people to live in healthy and balanced way in the shadow of secular and democratic orders and civil, plural and free societies. I believe that the Syrian society needs many decades to ready itself for political secularism and plural, civil citizenship and civil society. All we need to do is build upon that which is already a part and parcel of what makes Syria distinguished from all the other Arab countries.

Our historical, cultural, religious, ethnic, sociological and confessional mosaic is our most basic and valuable treasure. It is our winning card in the game of establishing the modern Syrian state. To give up this factual and unique weapon and waste time in importing ready-made, prefabricated samples from neighboring countries displays ignorance and naivety per se. Syria only needs us to 'syrianize,' and nothing else.

No matter how long the birth-operation of the new Arab world would take, sooner or later all that we know of the political, societal and even cultural context of the Arab world will be no more. The inhabitants of the Arab world, before any other from the international society, have no other choice except opening their eyes and perceiving profoundly and coherently the elements and ramifications of these changes, lest the future of the Arab world would be the fabrication of the external powers and of international interests and calculations, instead of their own creation. Among the Arab populations, moreover, no groups are required to beware of this pivotal, radical turn in the region more than the non-Muslim minorities.

For many decades during the past century, the Arab Christians rested relaxed with the rule of Arab dictators in countries like Egypt and Syria. They achieved their survival and gained the minimum of their rights by means of maintaining relations of loyalty, obedience, and even slavish submission to the ruling bodies, disregarding the majority-population's

(Sunnite in these two countries) suffering from these regimes and undermining this majority's feelings of animosity and distrust towards the Christians and their pacifism and fear. Now, as the old regimes are hitting the end of their presumed age, the Syrian and Egyptian Christians have no support to back up their existence and grant them peace and security in the area other than the relations they make and communion they build with the Muslim context and Sunnite community in their societies. Unfortunately, the Christians in Syria did not develop in the past four decades a real legacy of dialogue and intellectual intermingling with the Sunnites, which they might invest in and build upon in order to develop a strong communion with this Sunnite society in the coming future. This was partially because of the hegemonic regime's prohibition of any public speech on religion, politics and sexuality and its strict monitoring and suspicion about any attempt the Christians may develop at contacting any Muslim group other than the Alawite minority. But, this was also due to the Christians' unrealistic confidence that the situation in Syria is not going to witness any radical change as long as the al-Assad is in rule. In today's Syria, both the Sunnites and the Christians alike hold wrong and unfair presuppositions and knowledge about each one's intentions toward and evaluation of the other religion, each one's political, societal and cultural views and each one's priorities and choices. Though the Assadi regime allowed, even fostered, multi-religious and multi-confessional co-existence in the country, yet co-existence alone is insufficient to guarantee the creation of mutual trust, acceptance and cooperation, these two communities need to work together as one nation, as one population, in rebuilding the Syria of the future after the end of the uprisings.

It is because of the inevitable necessity of this mutuality, which goes beyond mere coexistence that I called in the third part of this study for developing an Arab Christian contextual discourse to address and dialogue with the Muslim-majority societies of the post-uprising Arab countries. It is also because of such a necessity, and since religion is part and parcel an inherent component of the Arab society and culture, both Christian and Muslim, that I call for developing an Arab Christian contextual *theology*. If religiosity is constitutive of the Arab's identity, then any discourse the Arab Christians would offer to rebuild their future societies must hold a clear religious character and contain religious dimensions in order to be addressed and appraised by the Muslims as a particular voice that reflects the voice of the '*other* Arab' in its uniqueness and non-Islamic difference.

On the other hand, I tried to show in the last part of this study that for any particular Christian theology to be relevant to the new situation of the Arab world and to resonate with the Arab youths' ambitions and values, as they were declared during the uprisings, it must invite the Muslim to sit at a dialogue table with the 'other Arab' and reflect upon these societal values and civil ambitions. In the light of these values and ambitions, I suggested as the starting point for developing this theology the following themes: the Christians political role, Human Rights, Interreligious dialogue, peace and Identity. I proposed this fivefold prolegomenon as main founding preface for the Christian intellectual contribution to the rebuilding of the Arab civil-society and public-square. Developing a theology on the basis of this prolegomenon not only discloses the particularity of the Christians, 'other Arabs'' hermeneutics of these what the youths demonstrated for recently. It, more crucially, ascertains these 'other Arabs'' sincere affiliation to the region's context and their profound and genuine perception of and involvement in this region's challenges and needs.

As Christians, these 'other Arabs' enjoy affiliation with two parallel cultural traditions. They, first, share with the west a common Jewish-Christian historical heritage, which they consider constitutive of who they are as a community, and not only of what they believe in religiously. Secondly, they belong also to a geographical and cultural womb that gave birth to them and the followers of the other, equally indigenous religion and tradition in the Middle East's history – namely Islam. It is the destiny of the Christians of the Arab world to maintain these two sides of their identity's cultural and religious coin and to live in the midst of the Arab-Islamic context as those who play the role of a 'bridge' between the Jewish-Christian west and the Arab-Muslim east, as well as the role of the protector and guardian of the Christian Arab and eastern otherness. These 'other Arabs' are not Muslims, but they do not stand over-against Islam or Islamic culture, as long as it does not deny the basic, original rights of the human being. On the other hand, they are also following many common values that western cultures consider definitive of their societal and anthropological identity, but they follow these common values and they can say that they hold a culture that is close to the West without losing their belong-ness to the east and their rootedness in the Arab-Islamic soil.

It is within this framework that the necessity of developing an Arabic Christian contextual theology to address the Arab-Islamic world and build communal relationships with its non-Christian majority gains it value and relevance.

The Arab Christians need to develop a discourse of cultural and religious reconciliation that stems from their natural and historical abridgment between two different, externally contradictory, yet internally reconcilable, human traditions. The unique contribution the Arab Christians can make to the development and progress of the Arab world toward the future lies in the fact that they, as their Muslim co-citizens, own the Arabic-eastern cultural heritage and are not parasitic intruders into it; as well as they are also original creators of the religious (Christian) and secular (Greek-Roman) tradition the west still considers its main constitutive heritage. They, therefore, have every right to claim property of both traditions, reassess them, correct them and turn them into two relevant contributions to the futural well being of the region. They are called to absorb in their intellectual and practical roles in the Arab world this twofold cultural identity in order to exceed its limitations, shortcomings and divisive elements by means of renewing and reforming it from within.

In his approach to the issue of identity, the Jesuit father Samir Khalil Samir suggests that for the Arab Christians to start playing this theological and societal role in the Muslim-majority region they must quit viewing the Muslim as a 'threatening other'. The other, Samir argues, is always, by merely being the different other, a potential threat to me. Yet, it is my responsibility to turn this other from a threat into a 'challenge' by listening to him and accepting her and doing my best to apprehend and contain everything I can in him and her. When I do this, I myself would also become a challenging, instead of a threatening, other to the Muslim, and my particular intellectual views and practical role would both become for him or her a particular theological, societal and cultural invitation, rather than an inimical offence, for viewing his and my Arabic-eastern identity as a dynamic, ever-growing, ever-inclusive and ever-adapting, rather than a static, narrow or discriminating, reality.[347]

It is this goal of calling the Arab Muslim society to walk with the Christian Arabs on the common road of building a new identity and soci-

---

347 Samir Khalil Samir, "Lahūt al-Sharq al-'Adna al-Hadīth fī al-Silah byn al-Hawiyyah wal-Ghaīriyyah," (The Theology of Modern Near East on the Link between Identity and Otherness), in *al-Mashreq*, 1(75), 2001, pp. 25-55, pp. 54-55.

ety in the light of the latest historical changes the youths' uprisings are creating in the region that plays the guiding motif of my study. The Christians in the Arab world are destined to be part of the recent uprisings, whether they participated tangibly and physically in them or not, and they are going to experience these revolutions' consequences and ramifications on the life of the region, whether they subscribed to these moves' causes or not. Sooner or later, they are going to show their Muslim compatriots where they stand and what their positions and choices are with regard to the newly rising Arab societies. Once they are asked to declare their views, the best way to do it will be by addressing the Arab society from their religious heritage, because it is the most capable treasure they own to show the Arab Muslims' the bridging capacity the Christians can play between the Arab and the western world.

Appendix I

The Christians and the Syrian Uprising: How Do We Deal with their Fears?

The question of the Syrian Christians' stance on the uprising has become since last August, 2011, one of the most controversial and ambiguous inquiries for the majority of the people in Syria's public-square. During the past six months, the opinions about the Christians' factual view and real role in relation to the uprising varied broadly. One group of people accused the Christians of supporting the regime and defending it, if not even justifying this latter's resort to the military power of arm, rather than to the persuasion power of politics. Another group accused the Christians, along other minorities in the country (e.g. Alawites, Druzes), of remaining silence and recanting from, at least, raising the voice to demand the regime to stop the violence, to seize the bath of blood and to quit the armed crackdown, or raising the voice to demand reformation and substantial change in the ruling structure of the country. Last but not least, another group of the people who are concerned about the Syrian affair tried, though quietly and with a low voice, to defend the Christians and affirm their active presence in the uprising, pointing at the evident, though individual, participation of many of the Syrian Christians in it, if not their exposition, like their Muslim compatriots on the streets, to arresting, torture, violent intimidation and consistent surveillance and pursuance from the security forces.

Within the inner circle of the Christian street, one can spot among the Christians positions toward the uprisings that are as versatile in its scope as the abovementioned external interpretations of these positions. There are among the Christians those who actually stand by the regime, as it is specifically represented by the person of its head, Bashar al-Asaad. They do not support the regime as such, for they are fully aware of this regime's shortcomings, failures and corruption. They stand, however, with the person of the president in specific, because they believe that it is still valid to hold hope in this president's fulfilment of his promises if the chance was granted to him to do so, and if he was aided in releasing himself from the legacy of the authoritarian system he inherited from his father and found himself obliged to co-exist, with without being able to reform this system or convince its members to welcome new vision s and blood. One can undoubtedly water down this belief, scrutinize it critically and logically and unearth its various flaws on the realistic and historical levels alike. But, one cannot ignore the factual existence of this opinion and the belief of a sizable group of Christians in Syria in it.

On the other hand, there is as sizable a group of reformists among the Christians in Syria, who believe in the people's demands and want to see Syria democratic and civil State-of-Law that is free from corruption, tyranny and all kinds of oppression. And, they are certainly against the historical tyrannical and hegemonic misconducts of the regime, as well as totally against the regime's recent opting for blood, violence and force and its daily killing of the unarmed demonstrators, and they would have wished that the regime had opted instead for responsible reasoning and political and dialogical option. Yet, at the same time, these Christians do not feel that the opposing sides that speak on behalf of the Syrian uprising and claim its representation of the street, especially among the opposition sides in the expatriation countries, do really represent the Christian reformists, speak their aspirations on their behalf or even acknowledge the Christian community as such as part and parcel of the Syrian textile and as a major player and substantial element in the futural, post-Ba'th, post-al-Asaad Syria.

The first reason for these Christians' fear is the Islamist history of some of these expatriate opposing sides and the bloody image, which these dissenters left on themselves during the famous events of the Eighties in Syria; these events that have never been erased from the memory of either those Syrians who paid their own blood as a price for it, or those Syrians who witnessed these events without being part of their conducting agents. The second reason for these Christians' fear is the nature and the accent of the recent discourses of some of the dissenters, who either adopt a sectarian, mobilizing, discriminating accent loaded with religious perspectives and connotations, or it reflects a mobilizing and offensively stimulating language loaded with violent, confrontational and vengeful intentions.

The Christians fear the first approach (Islamist) because it reminds them of some dark ages, wherein they lived as *dhemmi* people under the yoke of another religion's rule. They fear that if the religiously oriented opposition won the sceptre of rule, they may find themselves forced again to live with an 'other' who consider them infidel and persecute them upon this infidelity consideration. They fear in this case to suffer from what the Iraqi Christians suffered from or the Egyptian Christians still face in form of marginalization and non-stopable religious persecution, despite the Coptic youths' evident participation in Egypt's uprising and their filling-in of the *Tahrir* Square along with their Muslim brothers.

On the other hand, the Christians fear the second dissenting approach (confrontational and vengeful) because, as they think, it wants only to topples al-Asaad regime, not actually to reform Syria and re-establish its state on civil, democratic, free and pluralist foundations that grant every citizen his or her rights and factual role. They are afraid of the angry and mobilizing accent of that opposing discourse, which gives an impression of this opposition's pragmatist readiness to sell its cause to any devil that is ready to demolish the regime and help this opposition *alone* to replace it; even, that is, if allying with this devil meant transferring Syria into another Libya or Yemen and pushing the Syrian people into the swamp of an internal civil war; the war, that is, which the Christians know well that they are unable to coop with and they would have no escape from extermination if it happened. Be that as it may, these reformist Christians feel that their eagerness – which is no less strong and sincere than the one of the rebelling youths in the streets – for change is not heard in Syria and is not allowed to express itself in its own particular way. They feel that the only preconditioning possibility for them to demonstrate their particular and distinguished position is 1) either by submitting themselves to the regime's view of reformation in order to avoid this latter's oppression and evade its 'national treason' accusation; or 2) by drifting into the street-rebellion and playing the game according to the strict and almost monistic rules of some of its sides – losing thereby its voice's difference from the voices of the abovementioned opposing discourses – otherwise the street would accuse these Christians with cowardice and the denying of people's suffering. Both options are harshly bitter, and they equally push the reformist Christians (whom I believe are the prevailing majority among the Christians in Syria) to remain not silent but quiescent, and to stand still in the shadow waiting for a near salvation.

Yes, there are Christians (let alone Muslims) who still believe in the presidency of Bashar al-Asaad and in his ability of fulfilling what has he been promising to achieve if the street cooperated with him. No matter how delusional, illogical and starkly mistaken such an opinion may be for many of us, it is a factual and existing belief, and we are supposed to respect at least its holders and treat them, despite of it, as an inherent and constitutive part of Syria, which we all dream of and want. Otherwise, we will be just like the regime in its discrimination, exclusivism and other-rejecting mentality.

Yes also, there are Christians (let alone Muslims alike) who hold serious and profound fear from any Islamist or religious alternative of the recent regime. They view what happens to the Christians in Iraq as a terrifying nightmare and they are almost obsessed with what happens to the Copts in Egypt. Yes, there is fear among many Christians from experiencing one more time the difficulty and hardship of living in the shadow of a state of '*Dar al-Islam*', '*Ahl al-Dhemmah*' and under the mercy of imposing Islamic *Shari'a*; the thing, they believe, that will rip them off the sphere of free existence, wherein they can by themselves in its multifaceted particularity. Yes, this fear indelibly exists, even if we can easily crack its logic down and show its exaggerating, narrow-minded and unrealistic dimensions, especially that we live today in a historical era that is totally different from the ages of Muslim *Caliphate* and we must take seriously and profoundly into consideration the variety of intellectual and religious approaches within Islamic thought and historical narrative as such, let alone avoiding always that reading of the history of the interreligious relations in the Near East that one-sidedly and narrowly highlights the dark moments and blind itself of the many equally constitutive bright moments in the same history.

I am one of those Christians who believe that the fear from an Islamist alternative is more psychological in roots than rational or logical in nature. I also believe that fearing from the unknown makes it stronger, when, to the contrary, we are supposed to ready ourselves to deal with this unknown interactively and positively whatever it revealed itself to be. I say here, yes there are these abovementioned fears and serious concerns among the Christians in Syria. Unless we start to take them seriously into consideration, pause at them carefully and try to probe their nature and deconstruct their components – instead, that is, of offending this fear and concerns' holders and accuse them of failure and indifference (as some already did) – we will not be able to perceive profoundly, wisely and precisely why some Christians still either cling to a hopeful witnessing of some remaining goodness in the regime, or retreat back to the shadow of the sphere of quiescence, away from any material, influential and collective presence in the public square.

I write these lines as a Syrian Christian who stands fully with the people of Syria, in all its segments and components, and who believe in this people's peaceful and free rebellion and the nobility of its message, if not also the nobility and brightness of its promises. I am also one of those Christians who call their community to defeat fear from political Islam and to replace this fear with dialogue and interaction and to face one opinion with another, one approach with another, one role with an equal other, as well as to get red of hypothetical suspicion, ready-made rejection and premeditated assumption of the other's bad intentions. Since the kick-off of the revolution in Syria, I do my best in calling my brothers and sisters in Christ to fight their fear and obsessions, to rationalize their view of the situation and to remain optimistic about it.

Having said that, I do believe that there is an equal message somebody must also address to the Muslim street in Syria, in all its opposing trends, whether Islamist, secularist, leftist, rightist or liberal, but more specifically the Islamist in it. I would like to invite the internal and external spectra of opposition, especially the Islamist, to try in its turn to stretch its hand toward the Christian street in Syria and to endeavour to interact and communicate with its religious and civil, young and educated, sides and to set clearly and coherently before them its view of the religious other and its vision of this other's role and status in the Syria which we work for building via the uprising. I invite the Islamist trends of the opposition to start building bridges of self-introduction and re-introduction with the Christians. Such bridges have been demolished for four decades, and Syria never needed them as it does today. I invite them to build such direct communication-bridges with the official religious prelates, first, and lay representative, second, of this street, and not to suffice with their dialogue and contacts with few Christian individuals, who are known with their historical dissention to the regime. Although Christians in identity, these latter do not factually represent, or speak on behalf of, the majority of the Christian population, and do not have a direct influence on them.

I allow myself to urge the opposition to interact with the Christian street. I even allow myself to ask the Islamists in this opposition, in specific, to issue an official and public Code of Ethics, wherein they pledge clearly, frankly and responsibly that they will work for the sake of turning Syria into a civil, pluralist state that respects all the religions in it, and that they will protect, defend and even guarantee the rights of not only the Christians, but also the rights and life and existence of all the minorities.

Let there be such a Code of Ethics and a public pledge and commitment to it in front of the Arabic and international public opinion, and let it be an attempt to attend to the fears and concerns of not only the Christians, but actually other minorities in Syria. Let us even construe it an endeavour to break that last barrier that stands, in my opinion, between the internal Christians' real, broader and clearer contribution to the uprising and detain them from declaring a conspicuous and responsible support of the people's call for reformation and change in Syria. Let us make such a Code an instrument for snatching from the regime's hand the cards of intimidating the minorities and of warning the international circles from the Islamist bogyman that might take over.

The revolutions are not only constructed in its intellectual content on political charts and principles alone. They must be established equally on foundational ethical and moral rules and values. Therefore, let us prepare such ground for the futural Syria that will be born from the womb of the rebellion. The time has come to make a Code of Ethics to be addressed especially to the minorities, wherein we state without circumlocution and with utter responsibility, our view of them, and reveal readiness to be held accountable of it before the world, but primarily before the people of Syria, in the future.

Appendix II

The Arabic Spring and the Democracy of the Non-Democrats

In 1994, at the aftermath of the first Gulf War, as the overall features of the post-Cold War scene became clearly visible, and as many scholars reflected conviction about the delay of the Arab-Islamic world in riding the wave of democracy that stroke the shores of Latin America and Eastern Europe, the Lebanese scholar Ghassan Salame edited a book on the conditions, horizons and possibilities of democracy in the Arab world. In this volume, Salame presented a collection of essays and studies for a group of renowned academicians on the political, economic and sociological impacts of democracy in relation to the Islamic world and in the light of the growth of political Islam's prevalence over the general public scene in the Arab countries.[348]

As a title to his above mentioned anthology, Salame chooses a quite intriguingly interesting title: *Democracy without Democrats?* The significance of this title stems from its thought-provoking connotations and discussion-triggering meanings, which the reader is invited to via the main two approaches that the essay's authors display in their discussions:

the first approach that is exposed in the mentioned anthology introduces scholars who adopt an optimistic or 'accommodationist' stance on what it describes as a noticeable growing interest in, and appreciation of, democracy among the followers and supporters of political Islam. These optimists propose that the Islamist movements' leaning on democratic processes in achieving their political ambitions would eventually lead them into a full assumption of values and principals that are inherent to democracy, and it would make them concede the basicality of the voters' public mobilization, the reliance on the election ballots and the essential value of sectarian and political pluralism in relation to the game of equal, fair and transparent competition over authority.[349]

---

348 Ghassan Salame (ed.), Democracy without Democrats? the Renewal of Politics in the Muslim World, (London & New York: I.B. Tauris, 2001).

349 John Waterbury, "Democracy without Democrats? the Potential for Political Liberalization in the Middle East," in *Democracy without Democrats?* pp. 23-47: "the gamble of the accommodationists is that if one lets the Islamic groups into the democratic process, they will, within time,...prove human, enjoy power, find satisfaction in the approbation of the electorate, learn the importance of the mundane,

Opposite to the above mentioned accommodationism, other scholars, including most of the book's authors, reflect a rather skeptical stance on the Islamists appreciation and incorporation of democracy. They argue that one should not be over-optimistic about the political Islam's hospitable attitude towards democracy in the Arab world. The wave of democracy that gradually looms high in the Arabic public scene, as this view claims, is going, and sooner than later, to witness a fate similar to the one of the sea waves: at the beginning, they approach the shore high and strong, yet once they prepare themselves to hit the shore, they break down and crash so easily and their influence rapidly fades away. In other words, the careful and meticulous observer can easily find out, so the argument goes, that political Islam's adoption of democracy is no more than a purely pragmatist, beneficial strategy. Their slowly growing interest in the usefulness of democracy conceals in fact an aspiration as creating alternative hegemonic, exclusivist, monolithic political systems. It extrinsically wears a democratic-like mask and figuratively calls itself the representative of 'people's democracy'.[350] Yet underneath this figural democracy, it motivates itself by an attempt to exploit the democratic performance in the service of constructing ideological, dogmatic and collectivist statehood; this time, however, on the basis of religion and religious *asabiyya*, bestowing the authority of decision- and policy-making to theological and jurisprudential legislators and inaugurating in society an age of *shari'a*'s rule and *assabiyyah*'s discourse.[351] In sum, as the followers of this group argue in the book, the offspring of a possible

and grant grudging respect to the system that allowed them to be politically recognized" (Ibid.p.36).

350 Jean Leca, "Democratization in the Arab World: Uncertainty, Vulnerability and Legitimacy. A Tentative Conceptualization and Some Hypotheses," in *Democracy without Democrats?*, pp. 48-83: "Arab public opinion is sometimes acutely aware of that phenomenon when it chides the rulers and their intellectuals for justifying a façade democracy (*dimoqratiyya shakliyyah*), that is to say an authoritarian government masquerading as a 'people democracy'…" (Ibid.p.54).

351 On *assabiyya* in the Islamic and Arab world, see Olivier Roy, "Patronage and Solidarity Groups: Survival or Reformation?" in *Democracy without Democrats?* pp. 270-281. For a study on Ghannushi's view of the value of democracy for Islamic societies, his call for islamizing democracy and his rejection of what he calls 'liberal-secular democracy', see the study of Azzam S. Tamimi, *Rachid Ghannushi: A Democrat within Islamism*, (New York: Oxford University Press, 2001), pp. 63-104.

marriage between political Islam and democracy is 'democracy without democrats'.

'Democracy without democrats'. I cannot find a better expression than Ghassan Salame's book-title to describe what the Arab world experiences today in the Arabic Spring era. With utmost carefulness and seriousness possible, I and many other Arab and international observers, intellectuals and scholars follow up the dramatic and constructive changes that are occurring recently in Tunisia, but more significantly in Egypt. The developments that one witness in these two countries (who are the Arabic Spring's manger, but they can become its entombment-soil as well) mirror before our eyes some of the most intriguing possible political alternatives and newly-born public-squares that can regenerate themselves strongly and monotonously in other, still agonizingly rioting, public squares in other Arab countries.

Most significant in terms of presence and influence among these possibilities in the post-revolution Tunisian and Egyptian public square is the phenomenon of democracy's conversion from an imported, foreign product, into the most appreciated concept in the discourse which political Islam propagates as its stately and political operating method for re-establishing the state in Tunisia and Egypt. There is no doubt that the political Islam's interest in democracy and its attempt at repatriating it as its working method merits attention and positive appreciation, let alone originates positive expectations about the political, sociological and stately future of an Arab world that is going to be ruled, so it seems, by the islamists. Yet, this excessive support of democracy and the public overzealous about repatriating it as the political operating-tool from the islmaist movements, whose intellectual history dominantly demonstrates a total rejection and conceptual antagonism against democracy, cannot but make the observer cautiously reluctant to support unreservedly this intriguing transformation in the Islamist discourse. such an excessive support of democracy from this traditionally non-democratic political trends cannot but invite for considering the possibility that this Islamist democracy is no more than a figural façade that masquerades in essence no other than 'democracy without democrats'.

Lest I get accused of unscientific speculation and of making negative prejudices against the democracy of political Islam, I would like in the ensuing paragraphs to point at one simple case from today's Tunisian situation and two other cases from the Egyptian one. I believe that these simple cases are sufficiently loaded with worth pondering connotations that are directly pertinent to the consequences and entailments of the state of 'democracy without democrats' I detect in the recent changing scene in the Arab world.

Let me start with Tunisia, first. In the new Tunisian state, the leader of the Islamist opposition, Rashid Ghannushi became with his political party, *Islamic Nahda Party*, the predominating power in the parliament (the legislative authority) as well as the prime minister of the first officially formed governmental cabinet (the executive authority) after the revolution. Ghannushi climbed the authority chair on the shoulders of the public revolution that called for a new Tunisian republic structured upon democracy, freedom, civil society and human rights. He won the leadership battle by the weapons of the voting ballots, of a totally free and democratic electoral game par excellence. He made all the supporters of the revolution among the Tunisians and the Arabs release a sigh of relief when he publically pledged that he and his Islamist party would protect democracy and grant the civil rights democracy usually guards to all the trends and segments of the Tunisian public (especially women).

This conceded, what drives the observer to pause and makes her perceptively scrutinise whether this Ghannushian type of democracy-patronage holds behind its democratic melody a democratic singer or not is the fact that the same Ghannushi, who defends democracy and proclaims it as a basic and constitutive value in modern Tunisia, wrote in 1991 a three essays-long study on the relation between the international political system and the Islamist movements, wherein, and contrary to his recent positivity and auspice, he stated bluntly that democracy and human rights are just 'malign ideology' and a sort of a foreign secularist religiosity that is maliciously probated and supported by the colonialist west who is headed by America.[352] In his other speeches and writings during the past decades, Ghannushi has often maintained that democracy is unthinkable unless it gets first islamized and based on *shari'a*. For his followers and supporters, Ghannushi has already moved so far from his past radicalism into a more moderate and pro-democracy stance. For the non-Islamists and secularists in Tunisia, however, there are serious doubts about the genuineness of Ghannushi' change and accusations to him of

352 Aziz al-Azmeh, "Populism Contra Democracy: Recent Democratist Discourse in the Arab World," in *Democracy without Democrats*, pp. 112-129, p. 126.

being two-faced.[353] Which one between these two opinions would appear to be true? This is yet to be seen in the coming future. One can, nonetheless, still validly and safely notice that the anti-democratic and pro-*Shari'a* Ghannushi of the past is presenting himself, and is presented by many, as the godfather and guardian of the temple of democracy in today's Tunisia. Ghannushi's change of attitude towards democracy as such may be sincere. This notwithstanding, for me the question that is worth asking here is: could it be the case that what we have in his support of democracy is a realist example of 'democracy without democrats' and nothing more?

Let us look now at Egypt and take from its latest incidents two examples. The revolution of the 25th of January was unleashed by the force, actions and sacrifices of the free and brave Egyptian youths. It was the new young generation of the Egyptian nation, and not the followers of the Muslim Brotherhood or the salafis, who strolled down the streets to oppose Mubarack's regime. It was the pro-democracy and modern civil-state promoters among the Egyptian people, and not the pro-islamic and *sharia* rule, who welcomed the bullets of the regimes' forces with naked chests while calling explicitly for freedom, democracy, human rights, equality of citizenship, pluralism and even secularization. One of the godfathers of the revolution and its most influential young voices, as those who want to admit this know, is Wā'il Ghonaym. Ghonaym is today one of the heroes of the Egyptian Spring in the eyes of the revolution's youths as well as the liberal, leftist, secular and civil segments in the Egyptian public square. Yet, his name is hardly mentioned and his role is almost unacknowledged among the followers of the Islamist and salfies in the country. There is, moreover, an incident that became famous after Ghonaym himself narrated it on the Egyptian media, which reflects the deeming of the islamist and salafi publics of some religious and clerical preachers (like Yousef al-Qaradhawi) the inspirers and patrons, if not the intellectual creators, of the Egyptian Spring, and denying this to Khalid Ghonaym and some other youths. When the rebellions organized an open-air event in al-Tahrir Square to celebrate the falling down of Mubarak's regime, Ghonaym was in the square and he seemed to have wanted to give a speech in that event too. Yet, the Islamists, who started

353 Mathieu von Rohr, "The Smiling Islamist: Popular Politician Worries Secular Tunisians," in http://www.spiegel.de/international/world/0,1518,druck-791018,00.html , 10, Nov. 2011.

soon after the victory of the revolution to confiscate the achievement and try to unilaterally rape its fruits instead of the real agents of the change, wanted only the famous cleric Yousef al-Qaradhawi to address the masses in that occasion. So, in a strongly indicative move, Ghonaym was prevented by the bodyguards of al-Qaradhawi from climbing up to the speakers' stage, clearly nerved and eventually pushed to leave the square.[354] Al-Qaradhawi was presented as the main spokesman of the revolution that day: has the islamists' democracy showed up to kick the revolutions' democrats out of al-Tahrir square? A question worth asking.

What remains, nevertheless, the most significant and pivotal event lately in Egypt is definitely the outcome of the parliamentary elections. The results of the election did not only eventuate in an indelible and sweeping victory to the Muslim Brotherhood, but also in a no less sweeping, and even more shocking, rising-up to the Salafis. The democratic operation and no else led those who used to publically declare an inimical ideological, absolutist discourse against democracy into the arena of the legislative authority in the country. Those who consistently intellectually, culturally and religiously antagonized democracy in the past became its primary official spokesmen and its first public representatives in the present. More challengingly still, they became so notwithstanding the fact that they fuelled their election campaigns by a purely religious and sectarian discourse, mobilizing people behind them by means of religious *asabiyyah*. They casted strong skepticism and degradation claims against the religious commitment and adherence of their leftist and liberal competitors and made the public believe that these latter would not be genuine representatives and guardians of the Islamic identity and values of the

354 The incident is lately mentioned in Michael S. Doran, "The Impact of New Media: the Revolution Will Be Tweeted," in *The Arab Awakining: America and the Transformation of the Middle East*, Group of Authors, (Washington, DC: Brookings Institution Press, 2011), pp. 39-46, p. 45. See also the whole story narrated in "Egypt Protest Hero Wael Ghonim Barred from Stage," Agnece France-Presse, http://www.hindustantimes.com/Egypt-protest-hero-wael-Ghonim-barred-from-stage/article-663996.aspx , 18, Feb. 2011; Aimée Klingman, "Egypt Iconic Revolution Figure Wael Ghonim Barred from Speaking in Tahrir Square," in http://www.examiner.com/foreign-policy-in-national/egypt-iconic-revolution-figure-wael-ghonim-barred-from-speaking-tahrir-square , 18, Feb. 2011; and Maggie, "Wael Ghonim Barred on Stage: Yusuf al-Qaradawi and Radical Clerics Flood Back into Egypt," in http://www.maggiesnotebook.com/2011/02/wael-ghonim-barred-on-stage-yusuf-al-qaradawi-and-radical-clerics-flood-back-into-egypt/ , 18, Feb. 2011.

Egyptian nation, proving this claim by assuring the people that the *kuffar* Copts are going to vote for these liberals and leftists.[355] The very basic tools and tricks of the democratic game served very well the victory of those who neither live, nor think nor interact democratically with any other and fulfilled no primary goal than bringing them to the ruling circle.

The revolution in Egypt has started with a call and produced a publicly blatant propagation of democracy by the islamists and the non-islamists alike. Today, and after their sweeping victory, the volume of the islamists' promotion and celebration of democracy started to drop down rapidly. As if democracy has fulfilled its purpose and reached its expiry date by the end of the elections' round. There is no more any need to deal with it; it stays on-hold till the time comes when the presidential elections nock at the door and the country delves one more time into another authority-competition whirlpool. Recently, the Islamists deliberately evade mentioning democracy or talking about it in their victory's aftermath, replacing it with revived and more audible propagation of their most favorite and fundamental call for applying *shari'a* to the overall spectrums of society. As in the case of Tunisia, we observe the rapidly progressing incidents in Egypt and wonder if what we see therein is another worrying proliferation of 'democracy without democrats' phenomenon.

Seventeen years ago, Ghassan Salame and his colleagues talked about the possible option of 'democracy without democrats' in the Arab world. Here we are today witnessing what suggests that this phenomenon is gradually occuring in fact. This is not, however, what we heard the rebelling Arab youths call for in the Arabic Spring. This is not what the rioting Arabic public squares made us believe that the new Arab generations dream of. The past decades conspicuously revealed before our eyes the catastrophic results and outcomes that originated from the imaginary, artificial and mere façade-democracies of the falling previous dictatorships. Yet, the consequences and outcomes of today's reducing of democracy into mere authority-winning game and power-dividing policy would not be less catastrophic and disastrous either.

On the Islamists' latest parliamentary victory, see for example Salwa Samir, "The Islamists in Parliament," inhttp://213.158.162.45/~egyptian/index.php?action=news&id=22881&title=The%20Islamists%20in%20Parliament , 6, January. 2012; and Yasmine Fathi, "Egypt Copts React to Islamist Electoral Win," in http://english.ahram.org.eg/NewsContent/1/64/28346/Egypt/Politics-/Egypt-copts-react-to-Islamist-electoral-win.aspx , 4, December. 2011.

I have a real fear from drowning the Arabic public square in the blinding attraction of the new power-gaining game called 'democratic election'. There is a need for a strict caution lest the Arabic public square would be misguided by democracy's historical opponents (and its today's patrons), who might attempt at immersing this square in the fault of narrowing democracy down into mere methodological struggle over power, into mere electorial race for gaining autonomy, impoverishing thereby democracy from its main nature and identity as a culture and a mentality that is essentially related to social conduct and communal co-existence. I have serious fear that the investment into democracy by non-democratic minds would lead into the dawn of alternative religious dictatorships and Islamist political tyrannies in replacement of militaristic, nationalist and pan-arabist falling ones, and that this would take place in the name and by virtue of democracy, if not even under the slogan of defending and venerating it.

It is my sincere hope with innumerable other Arabs that this historical phase, which is overflowing with democracy slogans yet yearning like hill for acting democrats, would be just a transitional period, which starts with democracies without democrats, yet eventually, and despite everyone, reaches the final destination of 'democracy of democrats'. The arrival of democracy to the Arabic shores is praiseworthy, indeed. It is healthy to celebrate this arrival and to practice democracy no matter how this practice was imperfect, shallow and immature in the beginning. This is, however, acceptable just at the beginning. The dream and the most required necessity is to move from mere practicing democracy into thinking about it and reasoning from it. The dream is to reach the level of understanding and living democracy as that state of cultural identity, coexistence and social conduct that would eventually give birth to a new generation of local, indigenous Arab democrats in the nearest future.

Bibliography

Abouzeid, Rania. "Bouazizi: the Man who Set Himself and Tunisia on Fire," in www.time.com 21, January. 2011.

Abu el-Assal, Riah. *Caught in Between: the Extraordinary Story of an Arab Palestinian Christian Israeli*, London: SPCK, 1999.

Abulnaṣr, Fadhūl (ed.), *Hawajes al-Massīḥi al-Lubnāni: Maqalat wa Ḥywarāt*, (The Fears of the Lebanese Christian: Essays and Dialogues), Beirut: Bayssan Publishers, 2001.

Abu-Nimer, Mohammed. *Nonviolence and Peace Building in Islam: Theory and Practice*, Gainesville, FL: University Press of Florida, 2003.

Afifi, Muhammad El-Hadi. *The Arabs and the United Nations*, London: Longmans, Green & Co., 1964.

Ajami, Fouad. "Pity the Christian Arabs: Who Will Protect them from Islamist Assault?," in *Newsweek Magazine*, www.thedailybeast.com 16, January. 2011.

Akbarzadeh, Shahram; Benjamin Macqueen (eds.), *Islam and Human Rights in Practice: Perspectives Across the Ummah*, New York: Routledge, 2008.

Akel, Bassil, "Islam and the Western Media," in www.islamfortoday.com/media.htm (accessed 5 November. 2011).

al-Baḥrawy, Muhammad. "al-Tayyb Yo'len Wathiqat al-Azhar Ḥawl Mustaqbal Maṣr," (al-Tayyb Declares al-Azhar Document on Egypt's Future), in www.youm7.com , 12:37 pm, 20, June. 2011.

Allen, Diogenes. *Primary Readings in Philosophy for Understanding Theology*, Eric O. Springsted (trans.,), Louisville: John Knox Press, 1992.

Alston, Wallace M. Jr and Michael Welker (eds.,). *Reformed Theology: Identity and Ecumenicity II*, Grand Rapids, USA/ Cambridge, UK: W.B. Eerdmans Publishing Company, 2007.

Amos, Deborah, "Rise of Education Lifts Arab Youth's Expectations," in www.npr.org 18, March. 2011.

An-Na'im, Abdullah A. "Political Islam in National Politics and International Relations," in *The Desecularization of the World: Resur-*

gent Religion and World Politics, Peter L. Berger, et. al. (ed.), Washington, DC: Ethics and Public Policy Center/ Grand Rapids, Mich: W.B. Eerdmans Publishing Company, 1999, pp. 103-121.

'Atīq, Na'im S. "There is Another Way: the Way of Nonviolence, the Way of fidelity," in *Corner Stone*, 28, 2003, pp. 1-3.

Awad, Najib G. "Nafs Al-'oyon Al-Mubllalah, Nafs Al-Hawa' Al-Maleḥ," (The Same Wet Eyes, the Same Salty Air), in www.o2publishing.com, N. 125, 1,April. 2011.
Allah, al-'Nsān wal-Sharr: Dīrasah Lahwtiyyah-Wujūdiyyah, (God, Man and Evil: a Theologico-Existential Study), Damascus: Codmus Publishers, 2004.
"'Ab'ad min al-Ḥīwar: Hal Yakfī Ḥīwar al-Ta'ayoush bayn al-'Adiyān?" in *Alnashra of the Royal Institute for Religious Studies,* Jordan, N. 35, 2005, pp. 4-9.
"Men Ayna Ya'ti Rūḥ al-Fida' al-Filastīni? Yanbaghi an Nafhama 'Anfusana," (Where does the Palestinian Sacrificial Spirit Comes from? We Must Understand Ourselves), in *Assafir*, the cultural appendix, N. 11215, 06/02/2009.
"Hall Yūkhalliṣ Allah Ghayr al-Masiḥiyyīn? fī Kawniyyat al-Khalāṣ al-'Īlāhī," (Does God Save the Non-Christians? on the Universality of the Divine Salvation) in Naḥwa Lahūt 'Arabī Mū'aṣer (Toward a Contemporary Arabic Theology), Andrea Zaki (ed.), (Cairo: al-Thaqafa Publisher, 2007), pp. 341-445.
"Amma Baqi al-Nas fī Sūriyya fahum 'al- 'Aghlabiya al-Sākinah'," (The Rest of the People in Syria are 'the Quiescent majority'), in www.o2publishing.com no.128, 1, May. 2011.
"al-Gharb wal Badīl al-Īslamawī fil-'Ālam al-'Arabī," (The West and the Islamist Alternative in the Arab World), in www.almustaqbal.com, *Nawafez*, no. 3990, 8, May. 2011, p. 9.
"Theology of Religions, Universal Salvation and the Holy Spirit," in *Journal of Pentecostal Theology*, 2(20), pp. 252-271.
"Ma ʿAlaqat al-Thawra fi Sūriyya bel-Maūqif minal-Islām As-sīyyasī," (what is the relation of the revolution in Syria with the stance on Political Islam) in *Nawafiz, al-Mustaqbal Newspaper*, 20, November. 2011, N. 4179, p. 9.

AWG, "Christians and Muslims Together: A Charter for a Dialogue of Life and Common Action," in http://hiwar-net.usj.edu.lb/chroniques33.htm , 21, December. 2011.

Bachta, Indraows, et al. 'Adel Teodor al-Khoury, *'Alam Waḥed LlJamī'* (One World for All), Jounieh: Paulist Press, 2000. "al-Baḥth 'an Subul Jadidah Ela Mas'olyyah Moshtarakah," (In Search of New Ways for Common responsibility," in *'Alam Waḥed LlJamī'*, pp. 19-26/

Bailey, Betty Jane & J. Martin Bailey. *Who Are the Christians in the Middle East*? Grand Rapids, USA/Cambridge, UK: W.B. Eerdmans Publishing Company, 2003.

Baker, Raymond. *Islam without Fear: Egypt and the New Islamists*, Cambridge, MA: Harvard University Press, 2003.

Barth, Karl. *Church Dogmatics*, G.W. Bromiley and T.F. Torrance (eds & trans.), Edinburgh: T&T Clark, 1936-1977.

Batatu, Hanna. *Syria's Peasantry, the Descendant of its Lesser Rural Notables and Their Politics*, Princeton: Princeton University Press, 1999.

Bawer, Bruce. *While Europe Slept: How Radical Islam is Destroying the West from Within*, New York: Broadway Books, 2006.

Bayat, Aṣef. *Making Islam Democratic: Social Movements in the Post-Islamist Turn*, Stanford: Stanford University Press, 2007.

Bediako, Kwame. *Christianity in Africa*, Edinburgh: Edinburgh University Press/Orbis Books, 1995.

Beinen, Joel. *Workers and Peasants in the Modern Middle East*, Cambridge: Cambridge University Press, 2001.

Bellin, Eva. *Stalled Democracy: Capital, Labour and the Paradox of State-Separated Development,* Ithaca and London: Cornell University Press, 2002.

Berger, Peter L. et. al. (ed.), *The Desecularization of the World: Resurgent Religion and World Politics*, Washington, DC: Ethics and Public Policy Center/ Grand Rapids, Mich: W.B. Eerdmans Publishing Company, 1999.

Black, Ian. "Wael Ghonim Anointed Voice of the Revolution by Tahrir Sqaure Faithful," in www.gurdian.co.uk 8, February. 2011.

Bormans, Mourice. *Tawjjūhat fī Sabeel al-Ḥiwār biyn al-Masiḥiyyen wal-Muslimīn*, translated to Arabic by Bishop Yohanna Mansour, Journieh: The Paulist Publishing, 1986.

Bos, Michael S. "Dialogue and Coexistence: A Seminar on Muslim-Christian and Arab-Western Relations," published in Arabic in *al-Tasamoh*, 2(5), 2004, pp. 328-334.

Bostrus, Kiryllus. *'Afkār wa 'Arā' fī al-Ḥīwar al-Masīḥī-al-Īslāmi wal-'Aiysh al-Mūshtarak* (Ideas and Opinions on Christian-Muslim Dialogue and Co-existence), Jounieh: The Paulist Publishers, 1999.

"Min Ḥīwār al-Dīfa' īla Ḥīwār al-Shahādah," (From the Dialogue of Defence into the Dialogue of Testimony), in *Maqalāt Lahūtiy-yah fī Sabeel al-Ḥīwār*, (Theological Essays for the Sake Dialogue), Mosheer Basil 'Oun (ed.), Jounieh: The Paulist Publishers, 1997, pp. 7-17.

Bowman, Glenn. "A Death revisited: Solidarity and Dissonance in a Muslim-Christian Palestinian Community," in *Memory and Violence in the Middle East and North Africa*, Ussama Makdisi and Paul A. Silverstein (eds.,), Bloomington and Indianapolis: Indiana University Press, 2006, pp. 27-49.

Bshara, 'Azmi. "Arab Citizens of Palestine: Little to Celebrate," in *Tikkun Magazine* 13(4), www.tikkun.org July/August. 1998.

Buber, Martin. *I and Thou*, New York: Macmillan Publishers, 1987.

Cambrink, H.J. Bernard. "The Centrality of Socio-Rhetorical Interpretation to the Reformed Interpretation of Scripture," in *Reformed Theology: Identity and Ecumenicity II*, Wallace M. Alston Jr & Michael Welker (eds.,), Grand Rapids, USA/ Cambridge, UK: W.B. Eerdmans Publishing Company, 2007, pp. 91-106.

Carsten, Wieland. *Syria: Ballots or Bullets?: Democracy, Islamism and Secularism in the Levant*,Seattle: Cune Press, 2006.

Cavatorta, Francesco and Vincent Durac, *Civil Society and Democratization in the Arab World: the Dynamics of Activism*, London & New York: Routledge/Taylor& Francis Group, 2011.

Chacour, Elias. et. al, Mary E. Jensen, *We Belong to the Land*, San Francisco: HarperCollines Publishers, 1992.

Chaillot, Christine. "The Life and Situation of the Coptic Orthodox Church Today," in *Studies in World Christianity*, 3(15), 2009, pp. 199-216.

Chandler, Paul-Gordon. "Muslims and Copts Together," in *Christians Century*, March. 22, 2011, pp. 10-11.

Childs James M. Jr. *The Way of Peace: Christian Life in Face of Discord*, Minneapolis: Fortress Press, 2008.

Cofsky, W. "Copts Bear the Brunt of Islamic Extremism," in *Christianity Today*, 8, March, 1993.

Commins, David Dean. *Islamic Reform: Politics and Social Change in Late Ottoman Syria*, Oxford: Oxford University Press, 1990.

Cragg, Kenneth. *The Arab Christian: A History in the Middle East*, Louisville, Ken: Westminster/John Knox Press, 1991.

Craig, James, "Arab Society: Characteristics and Contradictions," in *Asain Affairs*, 38(1), 2007, pp. 1-11.

Cunningham, D.S. *Faithful Persuasion: In Aid of a Rhetoric of Christian Theology*, Notre Dame: University of Notre Dame Press, 1991.

Dalacoura, Katerina. *Islam. Liberalism and Human Rights: Implications for International Relations*, 3rd edi., London & New York: I.B. Tauris, 2007.

Davison, Roderic H. *Reform in the Ottoman Empire, 1856-1876*, Princeton: Princeton University Press, 1963.

Davies, Noel and Martin Conway, *World Christianity in the Twentieth Century*, London: SCM Press, 2008.

al-Deeb, Sami "From Dhimma Regime to One Democratic State in Palestine/Israel" in www.lpj.org 2003.

"For a Single Democratic and Secular State," in www.lpj.org 2003.

Dershowitz, Alan. *The Case of Peace: How the Arab-Israeli Conflict Can Be Resolved*, Hoboken, NJ: John Wiley & Sons, Inc., 2005.

Diamond, Larry; Marc F. Plattner and Daniel Brumberg (eds.), *Islam and Democracy in the Middle East*, Baltimore and London: The Johns Hopkins University Press, 2003.

Doran, Michael S. "The Impact of New Media: the Revolution Will Be Tweeted," in *The Arab Awakining: America and the Transformation of the Middle East*, Group of Authors, Washington, DC: Brookings Institution Press, 2011, pp. 39-46.

Duffy, Eamon. *The Stripping of the Altars: Traditional religion in England, c. 1400-c. 1580*, New Haven and London: Yale University Press, 1992.

Dumper, Michael. "The Christian Churches of Jerusalem in the Post-Oslo Period,." in *Journal of Palestine Studies*, 31(2), 2002, pp. 51-65.

Dunn, Ross. "Arab Christians Urge Israeli Compatriots to Mend Divisions," in *Ecumenical News International* at www.orthodoxnews.netfirms.com 15, May. 2003.

Dürr, Benjamin. "Farewell to A World of Black and White," in www.theeuropean-magazine.com 1. March. 2011.

Eibner, John (ed.). *Christians in Egypt: Church under Siege*, Zurich: Institute for Religious Minorities in the Islamic World, 1993.

Eisenberg, Laura Zittrain and Neil Caplan, *Negotiating Arab-Israeli Peace: Patterns, Problems, Possibilities*, 2nd ed., Bloomington, IND: Indiana University Press, 2010.

Ellul, Jacques. *The Subversion of Christianity*, Geoffrey Bromiley (trans.), Grand Rapids: W.B. Eerdmans Publishing Company, 1986.

Ende, Werner and Udo Steinback (eds.), *Islam in the Word Today: A Handbook of Politics, Religion, Culture and Society*, Ithaca and London: Cornell University Press, 2010.

Englander, Elizabeth Kandel. *Understanding Violence*, Mahwah, NJ: Lawrence Erlbaum Associates, Publishers, 1997.

Fathi, Yasmine, "Egypt Copts React to Islamist Electoral Win," in http://english.ahram.org.eg/NewsContent/1/64/28346/Egypt/Politics-/Egypt-copts-react-to-Islamist-electoral-win.aspx , 4, December. 2011.

Fawzi, M. *al-Bābā Kirollos wa 'Abd al-Nāṣir* (The Pope Kiryllous and Abd al-Nāṣir), Cairo: al-Waṭan Press, 1993.

France-Presse, Agnece, "Egypt Protest Hero Wael Ghonim Barred from Stage," in http://www.hindustantimes.com/Egypt-protest-hero-wael-Ghonim-barred-from-sage/article-663996.aspx , 18, Feb. 2011.

Frankel, Jonathan and Steven J. Zipperstein (eds.), *Assimilation and Community: the Jews in the Nineteenth-Century Europe*, Cambridge and New York: Cambridge University Press, 2004.

Friedman, Thomas L. "Pray. Hope. Prepare," in www.nytimes.com 12, April. 2011.

From Beirut to Jerusalem, New York: Farrar, Straus & Giroux, 1989.

Fuller, Graham F. *The Future of Political Islam*, New York: Palgrave Macmillan, 2003.

Gabriel, Brigitte. *The Must Be Stopped: Why We Must Defeat Radical Islam and How We Can Do it?* New York: St. Martin's Press, 2008.

al-Gawhary, K. "Copts in the Egyptian Fabric," in *Middle East Report*, Summer, 1996, pp. 21-22.

George, Alan. *Syria: Neither Bread Nor Freedom*, London: Zed Books, 2003.

Ghabra, Shafeeq N. "The Tension between East and West," in www.commongroundnews.org 29. December. 2004.

Ghadban, Najib. *Democratization and the Islamist Challenge in the Arab World*, Boulder, Colo: Westview Press, 1997.

Gigilo, Mike. "The Facebook Freedom Fighter," in www.newsweek.com 13, February. 2011.

"The republic of Fear: Recent Protests in Syria Have Brought Brutal Government Crackdown – and Renewed Paranoia Among Dissidents," in www.newsweek.com 3, April. 2011.

Gillard, David; David Throup and Michael Partridge (eds.), *British Documents on Foreign Affairs: Reports and Papers from the Foreign Office Confidential Print*, USA: University Publications of America, 1995, Vol. 1.

Gilsenan, Michael. *Recognizing Islam: Religion and Society in the Modern Arab World*, New York: Pantheon Books, 1983.

Ghosh, Bobby. "Rage, Rap and Revolution: Inside the Arab Youth Quake," in www.time.com 17, February. 2011.

Gordon, Philip H and Omer Taspinar, *Winning Turkey: How America, Europe and Turkey Can Revive a Fading Partnership*, Washington: the Brookings Institution, 2008.

Grafton, David D. *The Christians of Lebanon: Political Rights in Islamic Law*, London & New York: Tauris Academic Studies, 2003.

Griffith, Sidney H. *The Church in the Shadow of the Mosque: Christians and Muslims in the World of Islam*, Princeton: Princeton University Press, 2008.

Gunton, Colin E. *The One the Three and the Many: God, Creation and the Culture of Modernity*, Cambridge: Cambridge University Press, 1998.

"The Indispensability of Theological Understanding: Theology in the University," in *Essentials of Christian Community: Essays for Daniel W. Hardy*, David Ford and Dennis Stamps (eds.), Edinburgh: T&T Clark, 1996, pp. 266-277.

"Indispensable Opponents: the Relations of Systematic Theology and the Philosophy of Religion," in *Neue Zeitschrift für Systematische Theologie und Religionsphilosophie*, 1996, pp. 298-306.

"Doing Theology in the University Today," in *The Practice of Theology, A Reader*, C. Gunton; S.R. Holmes and M.A. Rae (eds.), London: SCM Press, 2001, pp. 441-455.

Ḥadīdī, Subḥi. "Wajeb Mulaqāt al-'Īkhwān al-Muslimīn fī Ḥiwār al-Methaq al-Waṭanī," (The Duty of Meeting with the Muslim Brotherhood around the National Charter) in www.aherwar.org no. 230, 26, August. 2002.

al-Haj Saleh, Yassin. "Prisoner of Damascus," in www.nytime.com 10, April, 2011.

Hanf, Theodore. *E Pluribus Unum? Lebanese Opinions & Attitudes on Coexistence*,

Byblos: International Centre for Human Sciences/ Friedrich-Ebert-Stiftung, 2007.

Ḥanna, Milad. *The Seven Pillars of Egyptian Identity*, 2nd ed., A.Z. el-Sherif (trans.), Cairo: General Egyptian Book Organization, 1994.

Harroub, Khalid. "Simplistic World View Quashed by Arab Spring," in www.mideastposts.com 15. May, 2011.

Hasan, S.S. *Christians Versus Muslims in Modern Egypt: the Century-Long Struggle for Coptic Equality*, Oxford: Oxford University Press, 2003.

Heft, James, "Religion, World Order and Peace: Christianity, War and peacemaking," in *Cross Currents*, 60(3), 2010, pp. 328-331.

Henderson, Randall P. "The Egyptian Coptic Christians: the Conflict between Identity and Equality." in *Islam and Christian-Muslim Relations*, 16(2), 2005, pp. 155-166.

Hengel, Martin. *The Charismatic Leader and His Followers*, Edinburgh: T&T Clark, 1987.

Henghan, Tom."Arab Spring and the Rise of Political Islam," in www.muslimvillage.com. 1. November. 2011.

Heschel, Abraham Joshua. *No Religion is an Island: Abraham Joshua Heschel and Interreligious Dialogue*, Harold Kasimow and Byron L. Sherwin (eds.), Maryknoll, NY: Orbis Books, 1991.

Heydemann, Steven. *Authoritarianism in Syria: Institutions and Social Conflict 1946-1970*, Ithaca: Cornell University Press, 1999.

Hille, Rolf. "Human Rights and Islam – Is the 'Clash of Civilizations' Already Pre-Programmed?" in *Human Rights and Islam*, 30:4, 2006, pp. 352-361.

Hinnebusch, Raymound A. *Authoritarian Power and State Formation in Ba'thist Syria: Army, Party and Peasant*, Boulder: Westview Press, 1998.

Hoffman, Valerie J. "Islam, Human Rights and Interfaith Relations: Some Contemporary Egyptian Perspectives," in *Political Theology*, 5(11), 2010, pp. 691-716.

Holiday, Fred. *Nation and Religion in the Middle East*, London: Saqi Books, 2000.

Hourani, Albert. *Arabic Thought in the Liberal Age (1798-1939)*, Oxford: Oxford University Press, 1962.

Horsley, Richard A. *Jesus and the Spiral Cord of Violence*, San Francisco: Harper & Row, 1987.

Humphrys, John. "The Arab Revolution Wrong-Foots the West," in www.today.yougov.co.uk 24, March. 2011.

Hussein, Mahmoud. *Class Conflict in Egypt, 1945-1970*, New York: Monthly Review Press, 1973.

Ībrahem, al-Ṭāher. "al-'Khwān al-Mūslimon fī Sūrriyyah…'An Qurb Marra Thaniya," (The Muslim Brotherhood in Syria..on a Close Distance, Again) in www.hem.bredband.net .

International Labour Organization, "Youth Unemployment in the Arab World is a Major Cause of rebellion," in www.ilo.org 5, April. 2011.

Ismael, Tareq Y. and Andrew Rippin (eds.), *Islam in the Eyes of the West: Images and Realities in an Age of Terror*, Abingdon: Routledge, 2010.

Jarjour, Riad. "The Future of Christians in the Arab World," in *Who Are the Christians in the Middle East?* in *Who Are the Christians in the Middle East?* Betty Jane Bailey & J. Martin Bailey, Grand Rapids, USA/Cambridge, UK: W.B. Eerdmans Publishing Company, 2003, pp. 12-21.

Jenkins, Gareth. *Political Islam in Turkey: Running West, Heading East?* New York: Palgrave Macmillan, 2008.

Jenkins, Philip. *The Next Christendom: the Coming of Global Christianity*, rev. ed., Oxford & New York: Oxford University Press, 2007.
The Lost History of Christianity: the Thousand-Year Golden Age of the Church in Middle East, African and Asia – and How it Died, New York: Harper Collins Publishers, 2009.

"Death Warrants of Ancient Christianity," in www.realclearreligion.org 11, April. 2011.

Johnson, D.W (ed.). *Acts of the Fifth International Congress of Coptic Studies*, Rome: International Association of Coptic Studies, 1993.

al-Jubūrī, 'Abd al-Jabbār H. *al-Aḥzāb wa-al-jam'īyīat al-Siyāsiyah fī Sūriyah min Awākhir al-Qarn al-Tāsi' 'Ashar Ḥatta 1958*, (The Political parties and Societies of Syria from the Late Nineteenth Century to 1958), Baghdad: al-Ḥurria House, 1980.

Jurawski, Alexi. *al-Īslām wal-Masiḥiyyah*, (Christianity and Islam) translated to Arabic by Muhammad Khalaf al-Jarrād, Kuwait: The National Council of Art, Culture and Literatures, 1996.

Kamil, J. *Christianity in the Land of the Pharaohs*, London & New York: Routledge, 2002.

Karas, Shawqy F. *The Copts Since the Arab Invasion: Strangers in Their Land*, Jersey City: American Coptic Association, 1985.

Karpat, Kemal H (ed.), *Political and Social Thought in the Contemporary Middle East*, Westport, USA/London, UK: Praeger Publishers, 1982.

Kelada, William S. "Christian-Muslim Relations in Egypt," in *The Vatican, Islam and the Middle East*, Kail C. Ellis (ed.), Syracuse: Syracuse University Press, 1987, pp. 243-262.

Kepel, Gilles. *Allah in the West: Islamic Movements in America and Europe*, Susan Millner (trans.), Oxford: Polity Press, 2004.

Kerr, David A. "A Western Christian Appreciation of the Eastern Christianity," in *Who Are the Christians in the Middle East?* Betty Jane Bailey & J. Martin Bailey, Grand Rapids, USA/Cambridge, UK: W.B. Eerdmans Publishing Company, 2003, pp. 3-11.

Khalaf, Samir. *Persistence and Change in 19th Century Lebanon*, Syracuse: Syracuse University Press, 1979.

Khadduri, Majid. *War and Peace in the Law of Islam*, Clark, NJ: The Lawbook Exchange, Ltd, 2010.

Khodr, George. "al-Ḥīwar bīyn al-Adyān" (the Dialogue between Religions) in *Ḥadīth al-'Aḥad: ad-Diyn wal-'Adyān* (the Sundy's Speech: Religion and Religions), Beirut: al-Nour Publications, 1985, Vol. 2, pp. 301-302.
"al-Masīḥīyyah wal-Īslām fī Lūbnān," (Christianity and Islam in Lebanon), in *Ḥadīth al-'Aḥad: ad-Diyn wal-'Adyān*, Vol. 2, pp. 305-306.

"Al-Masīhiyya al-ʿArabiyya wal-Gharb," (The Arab Christianity and the West), in *Al-Masīhiyyūn al-'Arab: Dirāsāt wa-Munāqashāt*, (The Arab Christians: Studies and Discussions), Elias Khoury (ed.), Beirut: Mu'ssasat al-Abhath al-ʿArabiyya, 1981. .et. al., Muhammad Ayoub, *Nahwal al-Jadal al-Ahsan: Mūhāwarāt*
Īslamīyyah-Massīhīyyah (Toward the Better Debate: Muslim-Christian Dialogues), George Massūh and Katharine Surur (eds.), Balamand: The Centre of Christian-Muslim Studies, 2003.

Khoury, Elias (ed.). *Al-Masīhiyyūn al-'Arab: Dirāsāt wa-Munāqashāt*, (The Arab Christians: Studies and Discussions), Beirut: Mu'ssasat al-Abhath al-ʿArabiyya, 1981.

Khoury, Rafiq. *Identity Cards of a Son of the Country*, Cambridge, MA: Harvard University Press, 2003.

Kilo, Michel. "Qssat ''Teqali wa-'Ttihāmi," (The Story of my Arrest and Accusation), in www.shril-sy.info 11 December. 2006. "Mata Kāna al-Īslām fī Sūriyya Oṣūliyyan?" (When Was Islam in Syria Fundamentalist?) in www.all4syria.info 25, May. 2004. "Kalīmat 'An al-Īslām wal-Oṣūlīyyah," (Words on Islam and Fundamentalism) in www.ahewar.org 23, August. 2010. "Daʿwat al-Massīḥiyyah īla al-ʿaql," (Inviting Christianity to Reasoning), in www.assafir.com , N. 11962, 13, Aug. 2011. "Ḥadīth maʿ Gibṭaṭih," (A Conversation with His Immanence), in www.assafir.com , N. 11989, 17, Sept. 2011.

Klingman, Aimée, "Egypt Iconic Revolution Figure Wael Ghonim Barred from Speaking in Tahrir Square," in http://www.examiner.com/foreign-policy-in-national/egypt-iconic-revolution-figure-wael-ghonim-barred-from-speaking-tahrir-square , 18, Feb. 2011.

Kristof, Nicholas D. "Unfit for Democracy?" in www.nytimes.com 26. February, 2011.

Kubba, Laith. "The Awakening of Civil Society," in *Islam and Democracy in the Middle East*, Larry Diamond, Marc F. Plattner and Daniel Brumberg (eds.), Baltimore and London: The Johns Hopkins University Press, 2003, pp. 28-34.

Küng, Hans. *On Being a Christian*, Garden City: Doubleday & Company, 1976.. et al., Heinrich von Stietencron: Josef van Ess; and Heinz Bechert , *Christianity and World Religions: Paths to Dialogue with Islam, Hinduism and Buddhism*, Mayknoll, NY: Orbis Books, 1999.

Islam, Past, Present and Future, John Bowden (trans.), Oxford: Oneworld Publications, 2007.

Kuttab, Jonathan and Mubarak Awad, "Non-Violent Resistance in Palestine: Pursuing Alternative Strategies," in www.palestinecenter.org 29, March. 2002.

al-Kylani, Shams al-Deen. "Dawlat al-Nokhbah wa Nokhbat al-Dawlah: Burhan Ghaliyoun Namuzajan" (The State of the Elites and the Elitism of the State: Burhan Ghaliyoun as a Case-Study), in *al-Adaab Journal*, 1-2, 1999, pp. 56-63.

Lamb, Jonathan. *Integrity: Leading with God Watching*, Nottingham: Inter-Varsity Press, 2006.

Lawrence of Arabia, *Seven Pillars of Wisdon: A Triumph*, Middlesex: Penguin Books, 1965.

Lawrence, Bruce B. and Aisha Karim (eds.), *On Violence: A Reader*, Durham and London: Duke University Press, 2007.

Leverett, Flynt. *Inheriting Syria: Bashar's Trial by Fire*, Washington: Brookings Institutions Press, 2005.

Levey, Geoffrey Brahm and Tariq Modood (eds.). *Secularism, Religion and Multicultural Citizenship*, Cambridge & New York: Cambridge University Press, 2009.

Levin, Jerry. "Historic Gatherings in Birmingham: Hear Naim Ateek Make Case for 'Justice with Mercy' for Palestine," in www.adventbirmingham.org. 2001.

Lewis, Bernard. *What Went Wrong? the Clash between Islam and Modernity in the Middle East*, New York: Perrenial/HarperCollins Books, 2003. .et. al., Benjamin Braude (eds.), *Christians & Jews in the Ottoman Empire: the Functioning of a Plural Society:2*, New York: Holmes& Meier Publication, 1982.

Long, Michael G. (ed.). *Christian Peace and Nonviolence: A Documentary History*, Maryknoll, NY: Orbis Books, 2011.

Lubnan: Taḥaddiāt al-Tafāhom al-Mutabadal: Ṭullab Muslemon wa Masīḥiyyon Wajhan-le-Wajh, (Lebanon: The Challenges of Mutual Understanding: Muslim and Christian Students Face-to-Face), Beirut: al-Mashreq House, 2002.

Macqueen, Benjamin, "The reluctant Partnership between the Muslim Brotherhood and Human Rights NGOs in Egypt," in *Islam and*

Human Rights in Practice: perspectives Across the Ummah, Shahram Akbarzadeh and benjamin Macqueen (eds.), New York: Routledge, 2008, pp. 75-88.

Mahroum, Sami. "Arab Youths, Revolutions and the Rise of the 'Second Society'," in www.knowledge.insead.edu 14. March, 2011.

Makdisi, Saree. "Beirut, a City without History?" in *Memory and Violence in the Middle East and North Africa*, Ussama Makdisi and Paul A. Silverstein (eds.,), Bloomington and Indianapolis: Indiana University Press, 2006, pp. 201-214.

Makdisi, Ussama and Paul A. Silverstein (eds.,). *Memory and Violence in the Middle East and North Africa*, Bloomington and Indianapolis: Indiana University Press, 2006.

Makkiya, Kanʿān .*Cruelty and Silence: War, Tyranny, Uprising and the Arab World*, New York and London: W.W. Norton & Company, 1993.

Malek, Charles. "The Near East: the Search for Truth," in *Foreign Affairs*, 30, 1952, pp. 231-264.

Malik, Habib C. "Intolerant Arab Spring," in *Newsweek Magazine*, www.thedailybeast.com 16, October. 2001.

Malek, N.A. "The Copts: from An Ethnic Majority to a Religious Minority," in *Acts of the Fifth International Congress of Coptic Studies*, D.W. Johnson (ed.), Rome: International Association of Coptic Studies, 1993, pp. 299-312.

Malek-Yonan, Rosie and Soner Önder, "The Baghdad Assyrian Church Massacre: Waiting for Godot!," in *Assyrian International News Agency*, http://www.aina.org/releases/20101124002721.htm , 11,24, 2010.

al-Maʻlūf, Rafīq; Ḥabīb Malek and George Sabra (eds.), *Charles Malek: Dawr Lubnān fī Ṣonʻ al-'Iʻlān al-ʻAlami le-Ḥuqūq al-'Insān* (Charles Malek: The Role of Lebanon in Making the International Human Rights Declaration), Beirut: Noufal Institution, 1998.

Martin, Thomas. *Oppression and the Human Condition: An Introduction to Sartrean Existentialism*, Lanham, Boulder, New York & Oxford: Rowman & Littlefield Publishers, Inc. 2002.

Mansour, Albert. *Qadar al-Massīḥyyen al-ʻArab wa Khayarohum*, (The Fate and Option of the Arab Christians), Beirut: al-Jadeed House, 1995.

Ma'oz, Moshe. *Ottoman Reform in Syria and Palestine, 1840-1861*, Oxford: Oxford University Press, 1968. *The Sphinx of Damascus: A Political Biography*, New York: Weidenfeld& Nicholson, 1988.

Mardin, Şerif. *The Gensis of Young Ottoman Thought*, Princeton: Princeton University Press, 1962.

al-Maṣri, Iris H. *The Story of the Copts; the True Story of Christianity in Egypt*, Cairo: St. Anthony Coptic Orthodox Monastery, 1982.

Masriya, Y. "A Christian Minority: the Copts in Egypt," in *Case Studies in Human Rights and Fundamental Freedoms: a World Survey*, W.A. Veenhoven (ed.), The Hague: Martinus Nijhoff, 1976, Vol. 4, pp. 77-92.

Masters, Bruce. *Christians and Jews in the Ottoman Arab World: the Roots of Secularism*, Cambridge: Cambridge University Press, 2001.

Mayer, Ann Elizabeth. *Islam and Human Rights: Tradition and Politics*, Boulder: Westview Press, 1991.

McGrath, Alister E. (ed.), *The Blackwell Encyclopaedia of Modern Christian Thought*, Oxford: Blackwell Publishers, 1995.

Meyers, David N. *Re-inventing the Jewish Past: European Jewish Intellectuals and the Zionist Return to History*, New York & Oxford: Oxford University Press, 1995.

Miller, Marlin E. and Barbara Nelson Gengrich (eds.),*The Church's Peace Witness*, Cambridge: W.B. Eerdmans Publishing Company, 1994.

Mitri, Tarek, "Christian-Muslim Relations," inhttp://www.wcc-coe.org/wcc/what/interreligious/cd31-06.html , (Consulted on 11, November. 2011, 14:00 pm).

Mohammed, Khaleel. "A Muslim Perspective on Human Rights," in *Society*, 1. January, 2004, pp. 29-35.

Moltmann, Jürgen. *The Church in the Power of the Spirit: A Contribution to Messianic Ecclesiology*, 2nd ed., London: SCM Press, ltd., 1998.

God for a Secular Society: the Public Relevance of Theology, London: SCM Press, 1999.

Muravchik, Joshua, "Listening to Arabs," in *Commentary*, 116(5), 2003, pp. 28-33.

Mychajlyszyn, Natalie, and Timothy M. Shaw (eds.), *Twisting Arms and Flexing Muscles: Humanitarian Intervention and Peacbuilding in perspective*, Hants, UK/Burlington, USA: Ashgate, 2005.

"Naṣṣ Wathiqat al-Azhar Ḥawl Mustaqbal Maṣr," (The Text of al-Azhar Document on Egypt's Future), in www.onislam.net/arabic/newsanalysis/documents-data, 10:51 am, 20, June. 2011.

N'ayseh, Nedhal. "Hall Yoshher Michel Kilo Īslāmaho?" (Would Michel Kilo Declare His Islam?) in www.aherwar.org 28, August. 2010.

Nielsen, Jǿrgen S. *Muslims in Western Europe*, 3rd ed. Edinburgh: Edinburgh University Press, 2004.
et al., Brigitte Maréchal and Stefano Dassetto (eds.), *Muslims in the Enlarged Europe: Religion and Society*, Leiden: Brill Publishers, 2003.

Nora, Pierre. *Zwischen Geschichte und Gedächtnis*, Frankfurt am Main: Fischer, 1998.

North, Douglas C; John J. Wallis; and Barry R. Weingast, *Violence and Social Orders: A Conceptual Framework for Interpreting Recorded Human History*, Cambridge; Cambridge University Press, 2009.

O'Collins, Gerald, SJ. *Christology: A Biblical, Historical and Systematic Study of Jesus*, Oxford: Oxford University Press, 1995.

O'Mahony, Anthony. "Christianity in Modern Iraq," in *International Journal for the Study of the Christian Church*, 2(4), 2004, pp. 121-142.

Omar, Ashraf. "Al-Zahira Al-Bouazizia wa Suqot Al-Hall Al-Amni," (The Bouazizia Phenomenon and the Collapse of Security Option," in www.alhiwar.net 19,January. 2011.

Ottaway, Marina and Amr Hamzawy (eds.), *Getting to Pluralism: Political Actors in the Arab World*, Carnegie Endowment for International Peace, 2009.

'Oun, Mosheer Basil. "Ṣo'ūbat al-Ḥīwar al-Masīḥī-al-Īslāmi fī Lubnan," (The Difficulties of the Christian-Muslim Dialogue in Lebanon," in *Maqalāt Lahūtiyyah fī Sabeel al-Ḥīwār*, (Theological Essays for the Sake Dialogue), Mosheer Basil 'Oun (ed.), Jounieh: The Paulist Publishers, 1997, pp. 187-193.
Al-Fekr al-'Arabi al-Dini al-Masīhy: Moqtadhayāt al-Nohūdh wal-Tajdeed wal-Mo'asarah (The Christian Arab Religious

Thought: the Requirements of Revival, Modernization and Contemporaniety), Beirut: Dār al-Taī'ah, 2007.

Oweidat, Nadia and Cynthia P. Schneider, "A New Arab World is Coming, With or Without U.S," in www.cnn.com 28, February. 2011.

Pace, Michelle (ed.), *Europe, the USA and Political Islam; Strategies for Engagement*, New York: Palgrave Macmillan, 2011.

Pappé, Ilan .*The Ethnic Cleansing of Palestine*, Oneworld Publications, 2007.

Pargeter, Alison. *The New Frontiers of Jihad: Radical Islam in Europe*, London: I.B. Tauris, 2008.

Peleikis, Ania. "The Making and Unmaking of Memories: the Case of a Multi-Confessional Village in Lebanon," in *Memory and Violence in the Middle East and North Africa*, Ussama Makdisi and Paul A. Silverstein (eds.), Bloomington and Indianapolis: Indiana University Press, 2006, pp. 133-150.

Perthes, Volker. *The Political Economy of Syria under Assad*, London: I.B. Tauris, 1995.

Pettegree, Andrew. *Reformation and the Culture of Persuasion*, Cambridge: Cambridge University Press, 2005.

Peterlan, Lucian. *Hafez al-Assad: the Career of a Combatant*, Ilias Bdewi (trans.), Bamascus: Tlas Publishing House, 1987.

Polk, William and Richard Chambers (eds.). *Beginnings of Modernization in the Middle East*, Chicago: University of Chicago Press, 1969.

Pollack, Kenneth M. et al., *The Arab Awakening: America and the Transformation of the Middle East*, Washington: the Brookings Institution, 2011.

Polowetzky, Michael. *Jerusalem Recovered: Victorian Intellectuals and the Birth of Modern Zionism*, Westport, CT: Greenwood Publishing Group, 1995.

Pratt, Nicola. *Democracy and Authoritarianism in the Arab World*, Boulder & London: Lynne Rienner Publishers, 2007.

Pulcini, Theodore. *Exegesis as Polemical Discourse: Ibn Ḥazm on Jewish and Christian Scriptures*, Atlanta: Scholars Press, 1998.

Qabbāni, Rana. *Europe's Myths of Orient*, Bloomington: Indiana University Press, 1986.

Qamar-ul Huda (ed.), *Crescent and Dove: Peace and Conflict Resolution in Islam*, Washington, DC: United States Institute of Peace, 2010.

Qaṣṣaṣ, Firas. "Qera'a Mukhtalifah le-Methaq al-Sharaf al-Waṭanī le-Jama'at al-'Īkhwān al-Muslimīn fī Suriyya," (A Different Reading of the National Honour Charter of the Muslim Brotherhood in Syria), in www.ahewar.org no. 229, 24, August. 2002.

Rabasa, Angel M; Cheryl Benard; Peter Chalk; C. Christine Fair; Theodore Karasik; Rollie Lal; Ian Lesser and David Thaler, *The Muslim World after 9/11*, Arlington, VA: RAND Corporation, 2004.

Rabil, Robert G. *Religion, National Identity and Confessional Politics in Lebanon: the Challenge of Islamism*, New York: Palgrave Macmillan, 2011.

Raheb, Mitri. "Sailing Through Troubled Waters: Palestinian Christians in the Holy Land," in *Dialog: A Journal of Theology*, 2(41), 2002, pp. 97-102.

I Am A Palestinian Christian, Ruth C.L. Gritsch (trans.), Minneapolis: Fortress Press, 1995.

The Invention of History: A Century of Interplay between Theology and Politics in Palestine, Mitri Raheb (ed.), Bethlehem: Diyar Publisher, 2011.

al-Rahim, Ahmed H. "Whither Political Islam and the 'Arab Spring'?" in *The Hedgehog Review*, Fall 2011, pp. 8-22.

Ramadan, Tariq. *Western Muslims and the Future of Islam*, Oxford and New York: Oxford University Press, 2004.

Rayan, Yasmin. "The Tragic Life of a Street Vendor," in www.aljazeera.net 20, January. 2011.

Reed, Fred A. *Shattered Images: the Rise of Militant Iconoclasm in Syria*, Vancouver: Talonbooks, 2003.

Reynolds, Gabriel Said. *A Muslim Theologian in the Sectarian Milieu: 'Abd al-Jabbār and the Critique of Christian Origins,* Islamic History and Civilization Studies and Texts, Vol. 56, Leiden: Brill, 2004.

Richards, Alan and John Waterbury, *A Political Economy of the Middle East*, Boulder: Westview Press, 1990.

Richmond, Oliver P, and Henry F. Carey (eds.), *Subcontracting Peace: the Challenges of NGO Peacbuilding*, Hampshir, UK/ Burlington, USA: Ashgate, 2005.

Riddell, Peter G. and Peter Cotterell, *Islam in Context: Past, Present and Future*, Grand Rapids, Mich: Baker Academic, 2003.

Robson, Laura C. "Palestinian Liberation Theology, Muslim-Christian Relations and the Arab-Israeli Conflict," in *Islam and Christian-Muslim Relations*, 1(21), 2010, pp. 39-50.

Rosen, Lawrence. *Varieties of Muslim Experience: Encounter with Arab Political and Cultural Life*, Chicago, Ill: University of Chicago Press, 2008.

Roy, Olivier. *Globalized Islam: the Search for a New Ummah*, New York; Columbia University Press, 2004.
Holy Ignorance: When Religion and Culture Part Ways, Ros Schwartz (trans.), London: Hurst & Company, 2010.
The Failure of Political Islam, Carol Volk (trans.), London & New York: I.B. Tauris, 2007.

Rubin, Barry. "Egypt's Revolution: the More they Reassure us, the More We Worry," in www.crethiplethi.com 24, February. 2011.

Rubin, Uri. *Between Bible and Qur'ān: the Children of Israel and the Islamic Self-Image*, Princeton: Princeton University Press, 1999.

Sabbah, Michel. "Sunday Homily to *Pax Christi* International in New Jersey, USA," in www.storage.paxchristi.net 23, May. 2004.

Sabella, Bernard. "Of Pilots, Suicide Bombings and Leadership," at *Theological Reflections* in www.cmep.org 10, October. 2003.

Sabra, George. "al-Kaneesah wal-Syyasah," (The Church and Politics", in *Resalat al-Kaneesah*, 2, 1993, pp. 5-10.
"Two Ways of Being Christian in the Muslim Context of the Middle East," in *Islam and Christian-Muslim Relations*, 1(17), pp. 43-53.
Hiwār al-Haqīqa min Ajl al-Hayāt Ma'ān (Dialogue of Truth for Life Together), Beirut: Near East School of Theology Publications, 2004.

Sachedina, Abdulaziz. *Islam and the Challenge of Human Rights*, Oxford and New York: Oxford University Press, 2009.

Said, Edward. *Orientalism*, London: Penguin Books, 1978.
The Politics of dispossession: the Struggle for Palestinian Self-Determination, New York: Pantheon, 1994.
Ṣowar al-Muthaqqaf (The Images of the Intellectual), Beirut: al-Nahār Publishing House, 1996.

Salame, Ghassan (ed.), *Democracy without Democrats? the Renewal of Politics in the Muslim World*, London & New York: I.B. Tauris, 2001.

Salem, Paul (ed.) *Conflict Resolution in the Arab World*, Syracuse, NY: Syracuse University Press, 1997.

Salibi, Kamal. "The 1860 Upheaval in Damascus Seen by al Sayyid Muhammad abu'l-su'ud al Hasibi, Notable and Naqib al-Ashraf of the City," in *Beginnings of Modernization in the Middle East*, William Polk and Richard Chambers (eds.), Chicago: University of Chicago Press, 1969.

Salt, Jeremy. *Imperialism, Evangelism and the Ottoman Armenian 1878-1896*, London: Routledge/Curzon, 1993.

Samir, Salwa, "The Islamists in Parliament," in http://213.158.162.45/~egyptian/index.php?action=news&id=22881&title=The%20Islamists%20in%20Parliament , 6, January. 2012.

Samir, Samir Khalil. "Lahūt al-Sharq al-'Adna al-Hadīth fī al-Silah byn al-Hawiyyah wal-Ghaīriyyah," (The Theology of Modern Near East on the Link between Identity and Otherness), in *al-Mashreq*, 1(75), 2001, pp. 25-55.

Sarsar, Saliba. "Palestinian Christians: Religion, Conflict and the Struggle for Just Peace," in *Holy Land Studies*, 2(4), 2005, pp. 27-50.

Sayyd Rusas, Muhammad. "Naqdh Ma'ayyer al-Ḥadāthah fī al-Fikr al-'Arabi," (Critiquing the Standards of Modernism in the Arabic Thought) in *al-Adaab Journal*, 1-2, 1999.

Seal, Patrick. *Assad of Syria: the Struggle for the Middle East*, Berkeley: University of California Press, 1989. "The Rise of Political Islam," in www.gulfnews.com 28, October. 2011

Sedra, Paul. "Class Cleavages and Ethnic Conflict: Coptic Christian Communities in Modern Egyptian Politics," in *Islam and Christians-Muslim Relations*, 10(2), 1999, pp. 219-235.

Shafiq, S. *al-Aqbāṭ bayn al-Ḥirmān al-Kanasi wal-Waṭani* (The Copts between Churchly and National Excommunication), Cairo: Dār al-Amin, 1996.

Shahid, W; P.S. van Koningsveld (eds.), *Religious Freedom and the Neutrality of the State; the Position of Islam in the European Union*, Leuven: Peeters, 2002.

Shalaby, Ibrahim M. "Islam and Peace," in *Journal of Religious Thought*, 34(2), 1978, pp. 42-49.

Shehade, Magid. "Internatl Violence: State's Role and Society's Responses," in *Arab Studies Quarterly*, 27(4), 2005, pp. 31-43.

Shenker, Jack; Angelique Chrisafis, Tom Finn, Giles Tremlett and Martin Chulov, "Young Arabs Who Can't Wait to Throw Off Shackles of Tradition," in www.guardian.co.uk 14, February. 2011.

Sherry, V. "The Predicament of Egypt's Christian Minority," in *The Christian Century*, 14, July, 1993.

al-Sibā'ī, Muṣtafa. *'Shtirakiyyat a*-Islam (The Socialism of Islam), Damascus: Damascus University Press, 1959.

Akhlaquna al-Ijtema'īyah (Our Social Morals), Beirut: Islamic Office, 1987.

Hāza Ma 'Allamatni al-Ḥayāt (This is what Life Taught me), Beirut: Islamic Office, 1987.

Siddiqi, A.H. *Non-Muslims under Muslim Rule and Muslims under Non-Muslim Rule*, Karachi: Jamiyatul Falah Publication, 1969.

Sider, Ronald J. *Christ and Violence*, Pennsylvania: Herald press, 1979.

Sivan, Emmanuel. "Illusions of Change," in *Islam and Democracy in the Middle East*, Larry Diamond, Marc F. Plattner and Daniel Brumberg (eds.), Baltimore and London: The Johns Hopkins University Press, 2003, pp. 13-27.

Smit, Dirk. *In Diens Vandie Tale Kona Ans? Q or Sistematiese Theologie*, Stellenbosch: Universiteit Van Stellenbosch, 2000.

Stern, S. "'Abd al-Jabbār's Account of How Christ's Religion Was Falsified by the Adoption of Roman Customs," in *Journal of Theological Studies*, 19, 1968, pp. 128-185.

Stumpf, S.E. *Philosophy: History and Problems*, New York: McGraw-Hill, 1994.

Sulaiman, Yasir. *Arabic, Self and Identity: A Study in Conflict and Displacement*, Oxford and New York: Oxford University Press, 2011.

Talbi, Mohammad. "A Record of Failure," in *Islam and Democracy in the Middle East*, Larry Diamond, Marc F. Plattner and Daniel Brumberg (eds.), Baltimore and London: The Johns Hopkins University Press, 2003, pp. 3-12.

Tamimi, Azzam S. *Rachid Ghannushi: A Democrat within Islamism*, New York: Oxford University Press, 2001.

Ṭarābīshi, George. *Maṣā'er al-Falsafah bayn al-Masiḥiyyah wal-Īslām* (The Destinies of Philosophy between Christianity and Islam), Beirut: Dar al-Saqui, 1998.

Taylor, Charles. *A Secular Age*, Cambridge, Mass: Harvard University Press, 2007.

"Forward: What is Secularism?" in *Secularism, Religion and Multicultural Citizenship*, Geoffrey Brahm Levey and Tariq Modood (eds.), Cambridge & New York: Cambridge University Press, 2009, pp. xi-xxii.

Teroll, Christian. "al-Ta'kīdāt al-Dīniyyah be-'Mtelāk al-Ḥaqīqah wa-'Alaqateha bel-Ta'adudiyyah al-'Jtīma'iyyah wal-Siyasiyyah," (Religious Ascertations about Possessing the Truth and its Relation to Political and Societal Pluralism," in *'Alam Waḥed LlJamī'* (OneWorld for All), Indraows Bachta and 'Adel Teodor al-Khoury (eds.), Jounieh: Paulist Press, 2000, pp. 63-110.

Thomas, David. *Anti-Christian Polemics in Early Islam: Abū 'Īsā al-Warrāq's 'Against the Trinity'*, Cambridge: Cambridge University Press, 1992. no. 45.

Early Muslim Polemics Against Christianity: Abū 'Īsā al-Warrāq's 'Against the Incaranation', (Cambridge: Cambridge University Press, 2002), no. 59.

Tillich, Paul. *Theology of Peace*, Ronald H. Stone (ed.), Louisville, Ken: Westminster/John Knox Press, 1990.

Tlemcani, Rachid. *State and Revolution in Algeria*, Boulder: Westview Press, 1987.

Van Dam, Nikolaos. *The Struggle for Power in Syria: Politics and Society under Assad and the Ba'th Party*, London: I.B. Tauris, 1996.

"Israel and Arab National Integration: Pluralism Versus Arabism," in *Asian Affairs*, 10(2), 1979, pp. 144-150.

Veenhoven, W.A.(ed.). *Rights and Fundamental Freedoms: a World Survey*, The Hague: Martinus Nijhoff, 1976, Vol. 4.

Vidino, Lorenzo. *Al Qaeda in Europe: the New Battleground of International Jihad*, New York: Prometheus Books, 2006.

Von Rohr, Mathieu. "The Fruits of Mohammed: the Small Tunisian Town that Sparked the Arab Revolution," in www.spiegel.de 18, March. 2011.

"The Smiling Islamist: Popular Politician Worries Secular Tunisians," in http://www.spiegel.de/international/world/0,1518,druck-791018,00.html , 10, Nov. 2011.

Wansbrough, John. *The Sectarian Milieu: Content and Composition of Islamic Salvation History,* Oxford: Oxford University Press, 1978.

Ward, Graham. *rue Religion*, Malden, USA/ Oxford, UK: Blackwell Publishers, 2003.

Whithaker, Brian. "How a Man Setting Fire to Himself Sparked an Uprising in Tunisia," in www.guardian.co.uk 28, December. 2010.

Wickeri, Philip L. "The End of *Mission Dei*- Secularization, Religions and the Theology of Mission," in *Mission Revisited: between Mission Theology and Intercultural Theology*, Volker Küster (ed.), Berlin: LIT Verlag, 2010, pp. 27-44.

Wilson, A.N. *God's Funeral: A Biography of Faith and Doubts in Western Civilization*, New York: Ballantine Books, 1999.

Woltering, R. "The Roots of Islamist Popularity," in *Third World Quarterly*, 23, 2002, pp. 1133-1143.

Yoder, John Howard. *The Politics of Jesus*, Grand Rapids: W.B. Eerdmans Publishing Company, 1994.

Christian Attitudes to War, Peace and revolution, TheodoreJ. Koontz and Andy Alexis-Backer (eds.), Grand Rapids, Mich: Brazos Press, 2009.

Younan, Munib A. *Witnessing for Peace in Jerusalem and the World*, Fred Strickert (ed.,), Minneapolis: Fortress Press, 2003.

Zeidan, David. "The Copts-Equal, Protexted or Persecuted? The Impact of Islamization on Muslim-Christian Relations in Modern Egypt," in *Islam and Christian-Muslim Relations*, 1(10), 1999, pp. 53-67.

Zand, Bernhard. "What the Arab World's Past Can Tell Us about Its Future," www.spiegel.de 8, March. 2011.

Zaru, Jean. "A Christian Palestinian Life – Faith and Struggle," in www.globalministries.org 30, October. 2003.

Ziadeh, Radwan. *Power and Policy in Syria: the Intelligence Services, Foreign Relations and Democracy in the Modern Middle East*, (London & New York: I.B. Tauris, 2011.

"Why Syria Will Be Next," in www.all4syria.info 10, April. 2011.

Zisser, Eyal. *Commanding Syria: BasherAl-Asad and the First Years in Power*, London New York: I.B. Tauris, 2007.

Decision Making in Assad's Syria, Washington: Washington Institute for Near Eastern Policy, 1998.

Assad's Legacy: Syria in Transition, London: Hurst & Company, 2001.

Žižek, Slavoj. "Why Fear the Arab revolutionary Spirit?" in www.guardian.co.uk 1, February. 2011.